**Rs. 1600; US$ 54**

ISBN : 978-93-91978-36-5

2024

First Published in India

*Basic Concepts and Ideas in Education*



Published by:

**SHIPRA PUBLICATIONS**

LG 18-19, Pankaj Central Market, I.P. Ext.,
Patparganj, Delhi 110092,
Ph. 22235152, 22236152; 9650028065
info@shiprapublications.com
www.shiprapublications.com

# Preface

We all are aware that in the present times the world is facing many problems like violence, socio-economic imbalances, cruelty, intolerance, unemployment etc. The reason behind it is that the affective and conative dimensions of education are not property attended. With very rich traditions and glorious past, our country is going ahead and it is emerging as a new progressive nation with the effect of implementation of different education politics including NEP 2020.

The present day society is posing a constant threat to our values as democracy, universal brotherhood, peace and harmony etc. Education has to play a significant role in shaping our society in the right direction. Literate citizens know the value of democracy but educated citizens know how to make it effective. Education has to make every citizen conscious of his role in the society. The present book is an endeavour in this direction.

What should an introductory book on basics of education try to do? First and foremost, we believe it should capture the interest of the students and demonstrate both the challenges and process of scientific observation and analysis of human behavior in a readable and interesting way. Second, it should seek to cultivate among the students the habit of scientific analysis of the society. Third, it should present the basic concepts and descriptive material clearly and intelligently. These should be illustrated so vividly that they 'come alive' and become part of the student's thinking. The concepts should not be learned simply in definitions in the form of rote memorization, but as accurate, descriptive names for the ways people act and the things people built.

In this book, the authors tried to do these things. The present book provides clarification about different and renowned educationists as well as philosophers, and impact of their thoughts on the contemporary Indian society, agencies of socialization, bases of aims of education as well as the values enshrined in the Constitution of India. It discusses crucial concepts like nature of education, processes of education, purposes of education, epistemological basis of education, and the role of education in inculcating values among children.

The authors have undertaken the venture to write this book to answer many basic questions of student-teachers as—What is education? what is the primary purpose of education? Which approaches support it? etc. The book has been written in a self-instructional format, which provides the student-teachers with considerable scope for engaging in the processes of inquiry, critical analysis and intellectual discourse.

The authors have taken care that the book should contain the maximum useful material yet it is for our valued readers to judge the true worth of our sincere efforts. We will indeed be grateful to all those students, scholars, in-service teachers, critics, who will point out the shortcomings to us on the mail ID rainugupia31@gmail.com. and we will try our best to improve upon those in the next edition.

We wish to express our heartiest gratitude towards all those scholars; whose books, compositions or thoughts have kept directly or indirectly in the composition of this book. We wish that the book will be a meaningful resource to students, student-teachers, teacher educators, in-service teachers and all stakeholders having interest in this field. Our thanks are also to Shipra Publications for publishing this book with nice get up.

**Rainu Gupta**
**Reena Saroha**

# Contents

# 1

# Meaning and Processes of Education

*"Education is a liberating force, and in our age it is also a democratising force, cutting across the barriers of caste and class, smoothing and inequalities imposed by birth and other circumstances, "*

–Indira Gandhi

## Meaning of Education

Education is absolutely necessary for each and every individual if he or she is to lead successfully the life. Education enables a man to find solutions of the problems of his life easily, The higher the education, the more quickly he solves the difficult problems of his life, This is the reason that importance of education has been realized since the very dawn of history.

Human beings are uniquely endowed with many abilities. The intellectual and cultural aspects of human life make human beings distinct from other animals. Unlike other creatures, human beings are capable of learning and of being educated. Education is able to instill in the child a sense of maturity and responsibility by bringing in him the desired changes according to his needs and demands of ever changing society, of which he is an integral part. Education ensures survival of the human race, maintains its intellectual and cultural conditions and helps in developing enlightened civilizations that history has witnessed through ages.

Education is that conducive process which draws a person from darkness, poverty and misery by developing his personality in all aspects as physical, mental, social, emotional, cultural and spiritual. As a result he becomes a resourceful and enlightened citizen, who contributes all his capacities for the development of his own self, his society and nation. This world would have been enveloped in intellectual darkness, if it had not been illuminated by the light of education.

Education develops the individual like a flower which distributes its fragrance all over the environment. As Locke has aptly remarked, "Plants are developed by cultivation and men by education" Education makes individual fit for their environment—both natural and socio-cultural through the development of their abilities. The process of education which makes human beings successful in their respective environment continues throughout life. In other words, education becomes a life long process. With every experience individual gains understanding of the self as well as of the environment. Thus education is not only preparation for life, it is synonymous with life.

Now the question arises, "What is education ?" Thinkers, philosophers and educationists through different periods of human civilization, have attempted to define education and in doing so, they have left the mark of their own values and philosophics on the definition they have coined. Education is an abstract entity and its concept is dynamic. Society can not remain static as the society changes, the function of education also changes and this is the reason that education is a continuous process. It has passed through many ages and stages in the process of evolution and at every stage it has had a different meaning according to the needs and conditions prevailing in the society. The concept of education is still in the process of evolution because education proceeds according to the goals, values and desires of individuals and society.

## Etymological Meaning of Education

Etymologically, the term 'education' is derived from the Latin word *'educare'* which means to 'bring up' or 'to nourish'. In other words it means that the education is to brought up or to nourish the child physically as well as mentally. The other Latin word is *'educere'* which means 'to bring forth', 'to draw out' or 'a propulsion from the internal to external'. The main purpose of education is to develop the inborn qualities of a child to the full and to provide guidance. There are still others who believe that the word has been derived from the another Latin word *'educatum'* which means 'the act of teaching or training'.

| *Latin word* | *Meaning* |
|---|---|
| Educare | To bring up, to nourish |
| Educere | To bring forth, to draw out |
| Educatum | Act of teaching or training |

The word **'Educo'** is composed of two terms. '*E*' implies a process from inward to outward while *'Duco'* means developing or progressing. Therefore, education means developing or progressing from inside to outside. It should however be noted that nothing can be drawn unless something is 'put in' beforehand. Thus the term education means to provide a nourishing environment that would facilitate or bring out and develop the potentialities of a child.

## Synonyms of Education

In India, there is a rich tradition of education dating back to the dawn of human civilization, where the 'Gurukulas' and 'Guru-Shishya Parampara' developed thousands of years ago. In ancient India, educaton through the

Vedas propounded the doctrine of 'Prajnnam Brahma' *i.e.* knowledge is the embodiment of God.

*Shiksha:* It is derived from the root word 'Shas' means 'to discipline' or 'to control',

*Vidya:* It is derived from the root word 'Vid' meaning 'to know'.

By analyzing the concept of education in English and shiksha in Hindi, it is clear that however they are different in their meaning but there is one similarity in them i.e human development is inhibited in them. Thus discipline and knowledge have always proved to be the foundation stones for the development of superior individuals and of impairer social beings.

*Pedagogy:* Sometimes the word 'pedagogy' is used for education. This word is composed of two words 'Paides' and 'a-gein' which means 'boy' and 'to lead'. It means 'to lead the boy'. Thus it is the science of instruction for the purpose of leading the pupil.

In this way, education is a process of development.

## Indian Concept of Education

Though the definitions of education are rich and varied, often prominently displaying the rich cultural heritage of the human race, no single definition has been found so far that satisfies everyone.

***(a) Old Concept***

1. "Education is something which makes a man self-reliant and selfless." –Rigveda
2. "Education is that whose end product is salvation," –Upnishads
3. "Education is which gives a sterling character to an individual and renders him useful for the world." –Tajnavalkya
4. "Education means training for the country and love for the nation." –Kautilya
5. "Education is the realization of the self." –Shankracharya

***(b) Modern Concept***

1. "Education is the manifestation to divine perfection already existed in man." –Vivekananda
2. "True education—is that which draws out and stimulates the spiritual, the intellectual and physical faculties of the children." –Thandulkar
3. "Man is neither mere intellect, nor the gross animal body, nor the heart or soul alone. A proper and harmonious combination of all the three is required for the -making of the whole man and constitutes the economics of education." –M.K. Gandhi
4. "Education to be complete, must be humane. It must include not only the training of the intellect but also the refinement of the heart and the discipline of the spirit." –S. Radhakrishnan
5. "Education is nothing short of the highest purpose of man—the fullest growth and freedom of soul. To the child, the environment will provide

an ever ready background for its spontaneous activity, to the adolescent, it will be an object of scientific or artistic curiosity; the adult will see in her the soil on which his country and his people grow, the cultural and economic background of human existence." –Tagore

6. "Education is the process of the individual mind getting to its full possible development. It is a long school which lasts life time." –Dr. Zakir Hussain
7. "Education is that by which character is formed, strength of mind is increased, the intellect is expanded and by which one can stand on one's own feet." –Swami Vivekananda
8. Aurobindo Ghosh thinks of education as, "helping the growing soul to draw out that is in itself."
9. "Education 'according to the Indian traditions, is not merely a means of earning a living; nor it is only a nursery of thought or a school for citizenship. It is initiation into the life of spirit, a training of human souls in the pursuit of truth and the practice of virtue. It is a second birth, divityam janma." –University Education Commission Report
10. "Education is to find out that ultimate truth which emancipates one from the bondage of dust and gives wealth not of things but of inner light, not of power but of love making truth its own and giving expression to it." –Tagore

It is clear from the above definitions that Indian thinkers are not in favour of confining the definition of education to teaching and learning alone. It emphasizes thinking, spirituality and research etc, and also includes knowledge of Brahma and knowledge of the thoughts. According to Dr. Radhakrishnan, along with possession of knowledge and efficiency, education should include programmes related to cultural values, community and social responsibilities in order that different scientists and persons getting technical training may be acquainted with their duties and responsibilities. In other words their concept states, that the process of education is to provide opportunities for the flowering of human personality, for manifestation of the qualities that are already present in the child, or for drawing out the best in all aspects of human personality. Human soul is a part of that totality which is manifested in God and education is to realize that divine macrocosm in yourself by working for the welfare of all those others who are part of it.

### Western Concept of Education

#### *(a) Old Concept*

1. "Education is the capacity to feel pleasure and pain at the right moment. It develops in the body and the soul of the pupil all the beauty and all the perfection, which he is capable of." –Plato
2. "Education is the creation of the sound mind in a sound body. It develops man's faculty, especially his mind, so that he may be able to enjoy the

contemplation of supreme truth, goodness and beauty in which perfect happiness essentially lies." –Aristotle

***(b) Modern Concept***

1. "Education" is a natural, harmonious and progressive development of man's innate powers." –Pestalozzi
2. "Education is unfoldment of what is already enfolded in the germ. It is the process through which child makes his internal external." –Froebel
3. "Education is the complete development of individuality of the child so that he can make an original contribution to human life according to the best of his capacity." –T.P. Nunn
4. "The aim of education is the development of valuable personality and spiritual individuality." –Ross
5. "Education is an attempt on the part of adult members of the human society to shape the development of the coming generation in accordance with its own ideas of life." –W. James
6. "Life is education and education is life." –Lodge
7. "The realization of all the possibilities of human growth and development is education." –Francis W. Parker
8. "Education is a process of development from infancy to maturity, the process by which he adapts himself gradually in various ways to his physical, social and spiritual environment." –T. Rayment
9. "Education is the transmission of life, by the living, to the living." –Edward Thring
10. "Education is the deliberate and systematic influence exerted by the mature person upon the immature through instruction, discipline and harmonious development of physical, intellectual, aesthetic, social and spiritual powers of the human beings, according to the individual and social needs and directed towards the union of the educand with his creator at the final end." –Redden
11. "Education is the development of good moral character." –Herbert
12. "Education is the process of living through a common reconstruction of experiences. It is the development of all those capacities in the individual which will enable him to control his environment & fulfill his possibilities." –John Dewey
13. "Education is either from Nature, from man, or from things; the development of our faculties & organs is the education of nature, that of man is the application we learn to make of this very developing, and that of things is the experience we acquire to regard to the different objects by which we are affected. All that we have not at our birth,. and that we stand in need of at the years of maturity, is the gift of education." –Rousseau
14. "It is education that forms the common mind;
Just as the twig is bent, the tree's inclined." –Alexander Pope

It is clear from the above definitions that education is the highest achievement of a human mind and it is the highest form of morality and is based on the appreciation of a direct and easily comprehensible predetermined aim.
These definitions include:

- different facets of human personality —physical, mental, social and spiritual
- that the abilities and powers in all these aspects of human personality are potentially present in every child
- the harmonious or balanced development of the innate powers of an individual is education and
- that such an education would allow the child to grow, constantly removing factors that hinders his growth and providing a nurturent and enriching atmosphere to promote growth.

Thus different educationists, thinkers and philosophers have emphasized different aspects of education according to their own outlook towards life. It is very difficult to give one precise and complete meaning of education. On analyzing Dewey's definition of education, the following characteristics are seen to emerge:

- Education is a life long process, continuous process, because experiences come to an individual throughout his life.
- Behavioural changes lead not only to do development in social skills but also in social morality
- Education brings about changes in our behaviour because it is the process of constructing and reconstructing experiences. Our behaviour changes by an experience.
- Education improves the individual's competence, by virtue of which, not only the individual, but society also benefits.
- The educational process can not be circumscribed or confined to the school or to a particular age level because the process of behavioural changes continues outside and beyond the school going age in consequence of increasing experiences. The family, the peer group, the press, the radio and innumerable other factors brings about changes in the individual's behaviour.

On analyzing Pestalozzi's definition of education, it emerges as:

By *innate powers*—he means those instincts, urges, potentialities, abilities, qualities and capacities in the child which are inborn and not the result of any training or practice. We should take in to account those while providing education to the child.

By *natural development*—he means that development of an individual should take place according to the stages, in which he is passing at a particular time. Psychologically life has been divided in to four stages—infancy, childhood, adolescent and adulthood. Every stage plays an important part in the life of a child.

As playing is an important characteristic of childhood stage, so play-way method should be adopted, Sex is the dominant instinct during the adolescent period, certain activities like dance, music, art and other types of literary and cultural activities should be the medium of education for the sublimation of these instincts. Pestalozzi was of the opinion that no stage in the development of the educand should be bye-passed. The efforts by some parents and teachers to convert the child in to an adult prematurely would be like a 'forward fruit' without sweetness and flavour. So education should be provided to the child in accordance with the stages of development.

The term '*personality*' is very comprehensive in its aspects. It does not mean merely the outer appearance but also includes aesthetic, moral, spiritual, emotional, social and many other aspects. So by *harmonious development*, he means that different aspects of the personality should be developed in harmony taking in to account the situation of life of the individual.

By '*progressive development*' he means that during every stage of development the learner should learn more and more. So far as the level of existence is concerned from animal level based on instincts man should rise higher and higher to the level of moral and spiritual perfection.

On analysing Tagore's definition of education it emerges as:

By '*bondage of dust*' Tagore means pursuit after material possession ignoring spiritual aspects of life which is higher than the material pursuit.

By '*making truth of its own and giving expression to it*' he means to realise this truth and make it a part of one's life.

In nutshell, by education Tagore means to realise the final truth that spiritual existence is superior to the existence at the material level. It is better to pursue life of love and sacrifice for the humanity at large rather than hankering after gain power and prestige motive.

### *Suitable Definition of Education*

If one analyses all the definitions given above, it becomes evident that while some of them confine themselves to the individual, others restrict themselves to society. Some of the definitions consider the individual as well as society. It must be admitted that no definition of education can be offered as universally acceptable, although any liberal definition is likely to be acceptable, to a large number of people, since it would comprehend all the facts and aspects.

Thus we can conclude the meaning of education in the following words as:

*Life is education and education is life. Education is whatever broadens our horizon, deepens our insights, refines our reactions and stimulates our thoughts and feelings.*

**Narrow Concept of Education**

In the narrow sense, education is confined to instruction imparted in educational institutions. The influences are deliberately planned. It has a limited field and it emphasizes, primarily the intellectual development of the child. It usually does not succeed in achieving the development of the child's personality and behaviour. A teacher is a mature person who presents and imparts the experiences of the whole race. Education is mostly limited to classroom teaching of ready-made materials. It refers to the knowledge available to a child at a specific time, at specific place, according to specific curriculum, with specified time-table and by particular set of teachers. According to S.S. Mackenzie, *"In narrow sense, education may be taken to mean any consciously directed effort to develop and cultivate our power."*

For this reason, education is a bi-polar process, the teacher forms one pole in this process; while the child, student or learner constitutes the other pole.

Prof. Drever is of the view, *"Education is a process in which and by which knowledge, character and behaviour of the young are shaped and moulded."*

Thus this type of education is intentional rather then incidental. Education starts when the child enters in an educational institution and ends when he completes his studies or leaves educational institution.

**Broader Concept of Education**

In its wider sense, education is a lifelong process as Lodge describes it: *"Life is education and education is life."*

It is a process of development from cradle to grave. It is the total development of the personality. If we take the broader sense even an illiterate person receives education throughout the life as George R. Geiger elaborated this point and said, *"Education in its broadest sense can be nothing less than the changes made in the human beings by their experiences."*

In this way education becomes the sum total of all the experiences that the child receives inside the institution or outside, through the study of different subjects; through various activities, in the library, in the playground, the workshop; or through other agencies. Hopkins opines, *"Education in its wides sense includes everything that exerts a formative influence, and causes a young person to be, at a given point, what he is"* Thus education is essentially a process of growth and development which goes on throughout the whole life.

The UNESCO Commission of Education in their report entitled 'Learning to be' laid a great stress on education in its wider sense (informal education and non formal education) calling it as the live education in comparison to the circumscribed education given in structured educational institutions.

Education is a mine of well-distilled experience, a laboratory of listed and recorded experiments. The awakening of our best semantics, the cultivation of our best and purest tastes; strengthening the desire to be useful and good and directing youthful ambition to unselfish ends—such are the objects of true education. Life is thus a long process of education and education is synonymous with the art of living.

**Analytical Meaning of Education**

In the above discussion, light has been thrown on the etymological, narrow and wider meaning of education and the definitions of education given by Indian as well as western learners, philosophers and educationists. In the following lines, we are describing analytical meaning of education as:

1. *Education—A Life Long Process;* Education can not be confined to provide knowledge to children in educational institutions. It goes on from birth till death. It includes the effect of everything which influences human personality. In other words everyone learns something or the other throughout life by various experiences and activities. As Madam Paul Richard pointed out, the education of man, "*should begin at his every birth and it is to continue the whole length of his life.*"
2. *Education is Unfolding*—Education is a gradual unfolding. Every child has innate powers, capacities, capabilities and education is to develop these endowments of a child rather than something forced in to the mind from outside. Sri Aurobindo said "*The chief aim of education should be to help the growing soul to draw out that in itself which is best and make it perfect for a noble use.*"
3. *Education—Individual as well as social:* According to the Psychological aspect of the process, the educator must understand the nature, interests, capacities and limitations of the child. Plato brought out a scheme of education according to each individual's capacities to serve the society. William T. Harris said, '*Education is preparation of the individual for the reciprocal union with society, the preparation of the individual so that he can help his fellow men, and in return receive and appropriate their help.*' Contemporary Indian philosophers also exhibits this tendency.
4. *Education—A Bi-polar Process:* The renowned educationist, Adams characterized education as a bi-polar process, in his frame work, 'Evolution of educational theory'. He has analyzed his concept of education in the following manner:
   - Education is a bi-polar process in which one personality influences another so as to bring about desired changes in the behaviour of the later.
   - This process is not merely conscious but also purposeful. It is a process in which the teacher has a definite purpose and he brings about changes in the child's behaviour according to that objective.
   - The means by which the child's behaviour is modified are two–
     (i) the influences of teacher's personality upon the child,
     (ii) the use of various elements of knowledge.

*does not fulfill its objective as long as it does not develop the divine element in the child,"*

3. *Education—Controls, Redirects and Sublimates the Instincts:* Every infant borns with some basic instincts. These instincts direct the activities of every individual. Education is to control, redirect and sublimate these instincts in the proper direction so that they may be conducive to the good of the individual and welfare of the society.
4. *Education—As the Process of Social Adaptation:* One of the most important function of education is to socialize the child. Education being a social process, predominantly has social obligations to discharge. The child is to adjust in the society, so education has to socialize the child. Socialization consists of making the child conscious of the existence and need of persons other than himself to acquire social norms and values to play social roles and to develop a balanced view of rights and obligations.
5. *Preparation for Adult Life:* The child of today is a citizen of tomorrow. Education develops such abilities and capacities in the child that as he grows older, he is able to confront the problem of life courageously and solve them successfully.
6. *Preservation of Culture and Civilization:* Each nation has its own traditions, customs, religion, ideals etc. and wants to preserve it. Education is to transmit the culture from one generation to the other generation.
7. *Education—As an Act of Training:* Education provides training to an individual so that he may be able to find proper place in the society according to his capabilities and potentialities. Each individual needs training for the development of his emotions, behaviour pattern and aspirations into desirable channels. Such type of training will make him a responsible citizen,
8. *Education—As Direction:* Education provides proper direction to the abilities, capacities, tastes, interests, aptitudes, attitudes and potentialities of the child. It can give direction to the ever changing society.
9. *Education—As Growth:* For every individual, education is the process of activating the inherent potentialities, the process of increasing his/her capabilities and the process of growing up. Education seeks to bring out an integrated personality in every child by developing his abilities—physical, mental, emotional, social and spiritual in a harmonious manner.
10. *Education—As Necessity of Life:* Biologically and physiologically humans are neither the strongest nor the biggest or the fastest of all the creatures; nor as they specifically suited to their environment. The human child is full of potentialities. It has possibilities of developing in to a full grown, mature, competent and adult person. The process of education provides the care and simulation necessary for the actualisation of these potentialities. With the help of education, the

human being not only leads his own life, but also facilitates the progress of human civilization as a whole.

11. *Education—Demand of Modern Age:* All of us know that modern age is the age of science. Nobody remains untouched from the progress of science. Education is needed for the development of technology in every field. It is also necessary for fostering national integration and international understanding among the citizens.
12. *Education—As Social Process:* School is regarded as a sub-system of society. The process of education takes place in social settings and society as a whole exercises great control over its process. Education in any society reflects the main features of that society—goals, values, needs and aspirations. Every society uses education as a means for promoting its own interests.
13. *Education—Reconstruction of Experiences:* Education helps us in reconstruction of experiences resulting in the construction of new knowledge. For example at the childhood stage we feel that the earth is flat and sun, moon, and stars are moving around the earth. After going to school and having discussion with teachers as well getting new experiences we know that earth is round not flat and it is moving around the sun not the sun, moon and stars are moving around it. In this way education plays an important role in reconstruction of knowledge in the required direction in order to add new meaning to those experiences. John Dewey had also described, "Education is reconstruction or reorganization of experiences which adds to the meaning of experience and which increases the ability to direct the course of subsequent experiences".

It is well known that human being is a social animal and this belief gives support to the concept of education as a socialization process. The process of education thus takes place in social settings and society as a whole exercises great control over its process. On the other education also influences society by contributing to its goals. Education helps in developing values, ideals, goals, mores, traditions and culture of the society and makes the child an effective member of the society. Thus education as a social process includes initiation into the norms and roles of the society.

We have discussed the process of education in different contests. The meaning that comes out of all these discussion is that through education, the child's innate powers are developed according to needs and values of the individual and the society. Thus, education essentially is a process; the process of developing or bringing out the qualities of the child in accordance with needs and values.

The development of the personality of the child depends upon the process of education. In the process of education, three important elements are prominent. These are 'educand' or the child who is to be educated; the 'educator' or the teacher who provides opportunities and organises learning experience for child's education; and the 'social setting' or socio-cultural influences and forces in which the process of education carried on. The relationship among these three elements can be illustrated as;

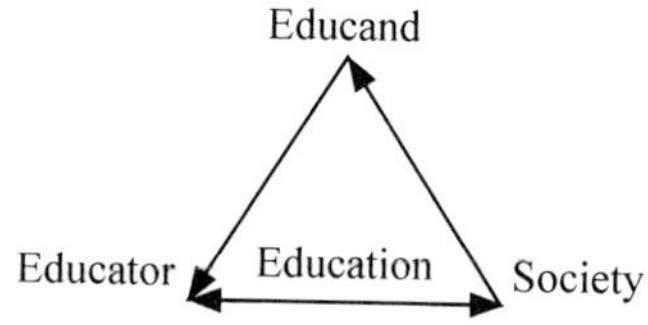


**Fig. 1.4: Process of Education**

Thus education is a triangular process: It is the development of man, as a whole. In the words of Swami Vivekananda, *"Education is man making. Education is that by which character is formed, strength of mind is increased, intellect is expanded and by which one can stand on his own feet."* In real understanding, education is life which includes values, skills, attitudes, interests and morals. Education provides a wide range of activities, experiences and understandings.

## Interdisciplinary Nature of Education

Interdisciplinarity assumes a good knowledge of each other's concepts between the disciplines concerned and is based essentially on a system approach. Its nature can be discussed in the flowing ways:

(i) *Integrated Curriculum:* It involves organisation of the content and the teaching-learning process around theories or activities or problems or processes which require inter-disciplinary learning.

(ii) *Teaching Learning Process:* The pupil must be placed in a situation and required to engage in an activity-relating to one or more objects of that situation. This activity leads to a result which is generally defined in the objective.

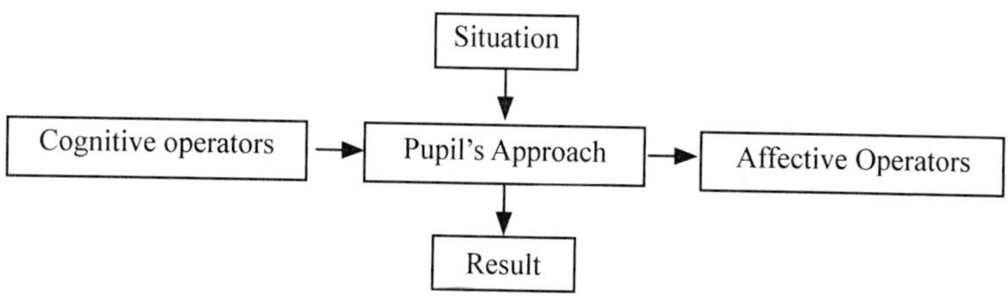


**Fig. 1.5: Teaching Learning Process**

In school education, interdisciplinarity has developed mainly in general education and more particularly at the primary and lower secondary levels. Wallon, Piaget, Dewey, Freinet have helped to make general education, at the lower level; better matched to the psychological realities of the child and the young adolescent to his interests, to his approach to discovery, and to the environment in which he lives. In this way, they have opened the way to an education that is freed from the overriding restrictions of disciplines and slanted on real life situations and the pupil's own approaches.

On the other hand non-formal education is the sector in which interdiscipinarity can easily be introduced. These people are more naturally oriented towards the solution of real life problems than towards the teaching of disciplines for their own sake.

Early instances of indisciplinary education can be traced back to the curriculum integration concept promoted in 1930. But interdisciplinary education really emerged in 1970 with a rich literature. Kockelmans defines interdisciplinary as, "to solve a set of problem whose solution can be achieved only by integrating parts of existing disciplines." Life is interdisciplinary, so education should also be interdisciplinary. With interdisciplinary education students will be able to link ideas and concepts across varied disciplines, promoting a constructive paradigms that will help in deeper understanding. Nissani and Appleby describe the benefits of interdisciplinary education as:

- Demonstrating real life applications
- Meaningful learning experiences
- New opportunities resulting from the crossovers between two disciplines
- Flexibility in problem solving
- Development of critical thinking
- Building confidence
- Greater creativity
- Transferable skills

On the basis of it Brodie and Irving developed a pedagogical triangle as:

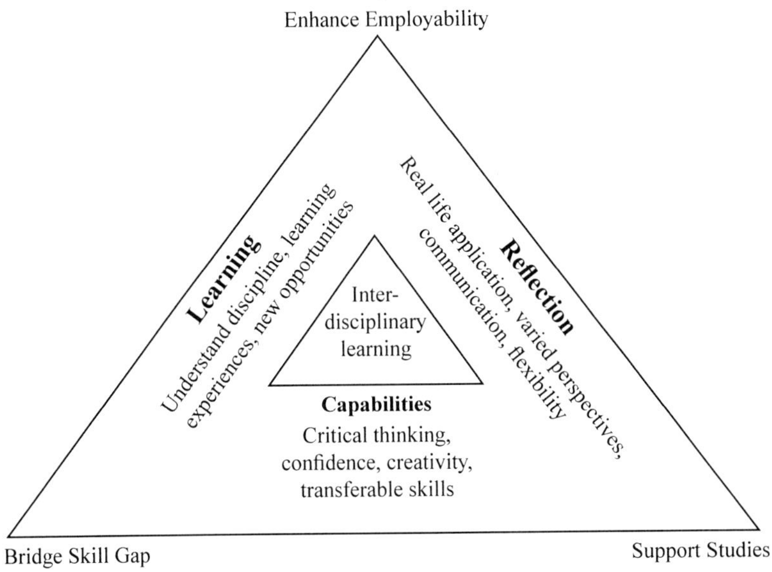


**Fig. 1.6: Benefits of Interdisciplinary Education**

In 21st century government is introducing interdisciplinary approach in education—goals, curriculum, teaching and research. It is a new way of apprehending, acquiring and transmitting knowledge necessary derived the attention of India. There is need to bring educational aims and practice into line with reality and to achieve a harmonious overall development of the individual and the society.

National Education Policy 2020: The NEP 2020 suggests several measures as according to the policy, the existing system of education is fragmented with less emphasis on the development of cognitive skills and learning outcomes and rigid separation of disciplines. Now all the courses at undergraduate, postgraduate and Ph.D. level will be interdisciplinary. The ministry announced that there will be holistic and multidisciplinary education in terms of flexibility of subjects. Major changes have been announced in the pedagogical structure of curriculum with no rigid separation between streams.

It is a reality that education is related with human life. We are to understand the physical, biological and social universe for human survival. Different disciplines of knowledge contribute in the understanding of universe. It is difficult to understand the universe around us and the life processes within by understanding any single branch of knowledge. It has to be looked from a holistic perspective based on several branches of learning as Science, Social Science, Humanities, Languages, Mathematics, Philosophy etc. Hence, education is an inter-disciplinary, multi-disciplinary, meta-disciplinary exercise. Let us examine the interface between the variety of disciplines and education:

### *Philosophy*

Various philosophers defined philosophy in a variety of ways as:

> "Philosophy examines the ultimate principles and laws that regulate the universe." –Brubacker.
>
> "Philosophy is a guide to a way of life." –S. Radhakrishnan.
>
> "Philosophy is concerned with everything as a universal science" –Herbert Spencer.

There are different branches of philosophy as

| *Branch* | *Area of Study* | *Purpose* |
|---|---|---|
| Metaphysics | Study of Existence | What's not there ? |
| Epistemology | Study of knowledge | How do I know about it ? |
| Ethics | Study of Action | What should I do ? |
| Politics | Study of Force | What actions are permissible ? |
| Aesthetics | Study of Art | What can life be like ? |

**Fig. 1.7: Concept Chart of Philosophy**

There is a hierarchical relationship between these branches as can be seen in the concept chart. At the root is Metaphysics, the study of general problems regarding reality, man, nature and God *i.e.* study of existence and nature of existence. Closely related is Epistemology or theory of knowledge, which enquires into the nature of human knowledge, as to how it develops and how far it is able to grasp reality. Dependent on Epistemology is Ethics, which investigates the problems of morality, such as the standards of moral judgement, the highest goal of human life and other cognitive problems; because it is impossible to make choices without knowledge. A subset of Ethics is Politics : the study of how men should interact in a proper society and what constitutes proper. *Aesthetics* deals with beauty, art, enjoyment, sensory-emotional values, Perception and matter of taste and statement is slightly separate, but depends on Metaphysics, Epistemology, and Ethics.

Another recent development of philosophy in the west called *Axiology*, is devoted to the discussion of problem of values. The educational aims given by great philosophers were rooted in their metaphysical views about man, his possibilities and destiny. The function of all philosophies is to answer the fundamental question of education.

***Sociology***

Education is a tri-polar process. While the educand and educator are two poles but the third pole *i.e.* community plays an important role to frame the educational policies, curriculum, methods of teaching, environment in the institutions etc. The school is termed as a sub-social system that serves a social need. The function of education is the transmission, preservation and refinement of the culture.

***History***

If we look into the past, we find that the problems of today are not much different from those faced by our ancestors, across time and space. Many times we found that problems of today had a genesis in the educational policies of the past as there was a recommendation given in the Kothari Education policy to provide skill education to solve the problems of unemployment and to increase productivity. The same recommendation is given in National Education Policy 2020. The limited success of vocational education in India is a historically evolved problem. There is an adage that "If you do not study history and learn lessons from the past then you have to suffer the consequences of the repetitions of mistakes of the past." Thus history plays an important role while framing the educational policies to develop the future.

***Political Science***

National policies of education are defined through political processes. Educational administration and management gets enriched by an understanding of basis of political science. If you have a good theory, supported by a suitable method, you can explain everything that happens in the world. Education within a country gets enriched with an understanding of the policies, practices and methods of education in other countries.

Thus interdisciplinary education promotes a focus on big ideas and thinking beyond the constraints of a single content area through the acquisition of critical thinking, creativity, collaboration and communication skills. As a result, it may be best suited to prepare students for real world challenges as today's problems are not contained with in discrete skills and concepts. Interdisciplinary education will help in developing broad spectrum of skills and integrated competencies.

# 2

# Purposes and Aims of Education

> *"An aim is a foreseen end that gives direction to an activity or motivates behaviour."*
>
> –John Dewey

The educative process has three important aspects, 'Why of education', 'How of education' and 'What of education.'

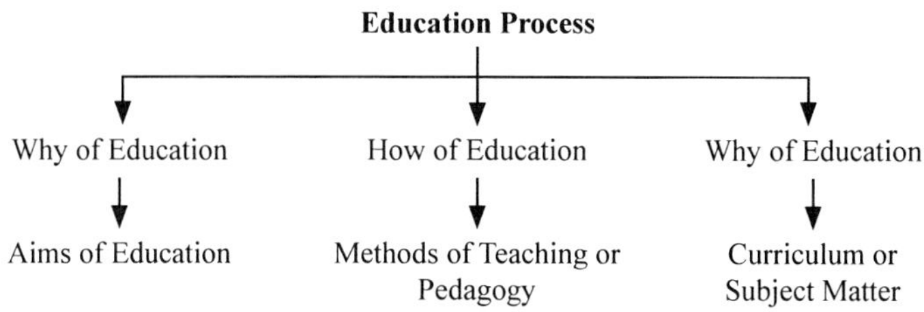


Without considering the purpose/aim of education, the education process will be meaningless. Any activity must end somewhere. The purview of the end of that activity may be termed as the aim of that activity. Education may have several aims. These aims are not static. They go on changing from time to time and from country to country. The basic and fundamental aims may be few and somewhat unchanging but the manifestation of these basic aims changes according to time and place. The success of the educational process can be evaluated in terms of the extent to which the aims of education are realized by both learners and the teachers. Without an end no purposeful activity will have that real force which directs it and makes it meaningful.

Purpose and aims are two terms that are noted as being synonyms. Many people think that these are having same meaning and used interchangeably. Firstly, we are to understand the meaning of aim and purpose.

## Purpose

Purpose defines why the person is doing something, that is the reason behind doing it and what he plans to achieve from it. For example: Anu's purpose behind getting the education is to be a good person. As this statement states, Anu is getting the education but the reason for getting education is to be a good person. That becomes the purpose. Thus the purpose is an intended or desired result; end; goal. It is the determination.

## Aim

Aim is setting a determined course in order to achieve a set target. It requires determination and persistence. It requires that the person stay on a set path and complete the requirements to reach that aim at the end. For example: Rita aims to acquire the required doctorate degree to become a doctor.

### *Difference between Purpose and Aim*

It is very difficult to make differences between these two concepts because these are more or less similar to each. Inspite of the similarly there are some scenarios where the choice of word between aim and purpose can cause a slight difference in meaning.

- Both words mean an object intended to be attained, or in simple words an intention, but purpose carries an additional meaning which is the reason for which something is intended or done.' In other words, we can say that a purpose answers the questions 'why' while an aim answers the question 'what'.
- Purpose is the broader concept, whereas aim involves the result of whole idea.
- Purpose serves as the guiding plan while the aim will be the end result of combined tasks and tactics to achieve the purpose.
- Purpose explains in a broad sense, and it is supported by the aim, which expounds the plan to more specific and highly feasible action points.

## Purposes of Education

> *"The whole purpose of education is to turn mirrors into window."*
>
> – Sydney J. Harris.

A purpose is the fundamental goal of the process, an end to be achieved. It is an expressed goal, more effort is to put in achieving it. It becomes a part of the explicit and official curriculum. The final and real purpose of education is to make every human to be a better person with love for oneself, others and for the nation.

> *"The purpose of education has always been to every one, in essence, the same to give the young, the things they need in order to develop in an orderly, sequential way into members of society."* – John Dewey

The purpose of education is the preservation and enhancement of knowledge and the development of character within our given form of society which will best prepare the individual for the conditions of extreme novelty the near future is bringing. We must understand that 'A child is not a vase to be filled but a fire to be lit'. The main purpose of education is the present scenario are as following:

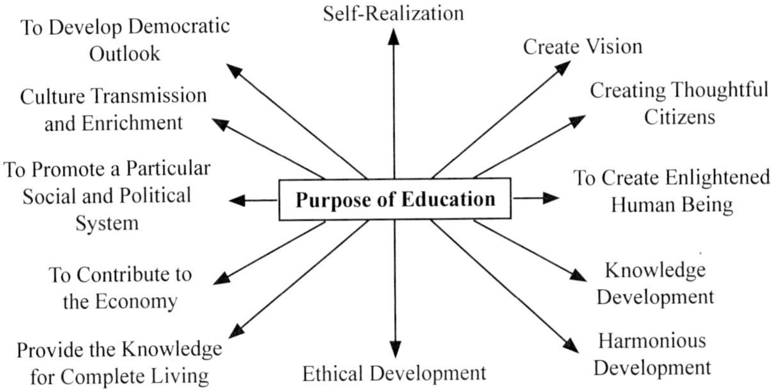


**Fig. 2.1: Purposes of Education**

1. *Enlightenment:* It is one of the main purpose of education. It enables the person with ignorance to awareness of life. It makes the person to reason at every action that he does. It enlightens the person with sound purpose of his life on this earth. As Plato said, *"The purpose of education is to give to the body and to the soul all the beauty and all the perfection of which they are capable."*
2. *Knowledge development:* The purpose of education is to make the person able to take decisions about the life. It will enable the person to wider his knowledge about many things that happen around him and around the world. Malcolm Forbes has rightly said, *"The purpose of education is to replace an empty mind with an open one."* The education imparts both worldly and spiritual knowledge.
3. *Contribution to the economy:* The purpose of education is to provide a foundation for economic development, the ground work on which much of our economic and social well-being is to be built. Education is the key to increase economic efficiency and social consistency. For this purpose, the resources must be exploited and education must be related to productivity to increase national income which, in turn may provide means for a large investment in education in order to create a link between education and productivity. In the words of Malcolm, *"Education is the passport to the future, for tomorrow belongs to those who prepare it for today."*
4. *Provide the knowledge for complete living:* Herbert Spencer said, "Education is preparation to live completely." By the term complete living Spencer understood that education should produce a citizen who, at the same time, is well conducted and is also able to make his way in the

world. He wanted to convey the impression that moral responsibility and self sufficiency are the virtues which education must strive to cultivate in the individual. In order to fulfill this purpose education enables the individual to know the art of self preservation, preparing the pupils to perform well; social and political responsibilities and impart knowledge about bearing and rearing children, who carry the message of previous generation.

5. *Create thoughtful citizens:* The purpose of education is to create thoughtful citizens. The present day pupils will be a part of the community and need the skills to exist within that society as thoughtful citizens. Thoughtful citizens only can run the country in a smoothed manner and can take right decisions at the right moment.
6. *Create vision:* The purpose of education is to inspire every individual to have a vision and to work towards his/her success. It provides guidance to reach the goal and attain the victory in a proper way. James Baldwin has rightly said, *"The purpose of education is to create in a person the ability to look at the world for himself, to make his own decisions."*
7. *Self-realization:* Self-realization means to understand nature, human being and the God. So, many educationists believe that the purpose of education is to develop self of the child, as a result he/she may realize his qualities through the means of society. In the words of Jean Jacques Rousseau, *"The object of education is not to make a soldier, magistrate or priest but to make a man. We should not teach children the sciences, but give them a taste for these."* This purpose contributes to take the individual towards perfection.
8. *Development of democratic outlook:* Democracy is not merely an ethical faith, but a practical creed. No society can claim to be democratic if it does not permit political liberty, freedom of conscience, economic justice, social prosperity, faith in dignity of individual, and opportunity for peaceful and orderly life. Education is a great force to develop democratic outlook. As described by University Education Commission, *"Education is a great instrument of social emanicipation by which a democracy establishes, maintains and protects the spirit of equality among its members."* Education inspires students with a burning passion for social justice; to breakdown barriers of caste, creed and colour; to deeper cultural understanding and sympathy; and broaden their intellectual outlook, to instill a love for honest work and an attachment to national culture.
9. *Ethical development:* Ethical development is the most important purpose of education because education is an ethical art. The purpose of ethical education is to provide people to make decisions by their free wills. You can teach norms easily, but you cannot teach easily to obey these rules unless you teach ethics. The educational institution, of all

institutions, is concerned with the shaping of men, with moulding their characters, their abilities, and their ideas in such ways that they become desired members of society.

10. *Culture: Transmission and Enrichment:* Preservation, transmission and enrichment of culture is regarded as the main purpose of education. Culture relates to the practical side of man's personality, something which gives meaning. Education for culture attempts to cultivate and propagate such knowledge and such habits as the beautified human personality add grace to human life. Culture as a purpose of education will develop men's aesthetic sensibilities to appreciate fine arts. It will broaden his outlook, will enrich interest, and will develop in him 'Social acceptable behaviour.' It is the responsibilities of education to conserve and transmit traditions to the generations in their making. Culture as a purpose of education enables a community to look back and evaluate its present culture; and modify it, if needed as to make it universally acceptable.
11. *Promote a Particular Social and Political System:* J. L. Nehru had rightly remarked, *"Great changes have taken place in the country and the educational system must also be in keeping with them. The entire basis of education must be revolutionised."* It is the main purpose of education to promote a particular social and political system of the country. A national system of education is always inspired by the social and political conditions prevailing in the country. It is a challenging responsibility of education to train every citizen for democratic citizenship. A democratic citizen should have the understanding and the intellectual integrity to distinguish truth from falsehood and facts from propaganda. Education enables them to accept the inflow of new bless that can help in strengthening democratic forces. For making a strong social system, it is important to develop the sense of true patriotism in the citizens. In order to promote a particular social and political system, it is essential to inculcate the qualities of leadership in our youth. Education should train the youth to provide leadership in the social, political, industrial and cultural fields. Leadership calls for a deeper and clearer understanding of social issues and greater technical efficiency.

Thus, the main purposes of education, as such, is to train people to face the future vision, to be broad and tolerant in outlook, to be seeker after peace, and to consider the rights of others.

**Need for Aims of Education**

According to B.D. Bhatia, *"Without the knowledge of aims, the educator is like a sailor who does not know his goal or his destination and the child is like a rudderless vessel which will be drifted alone somewhere ashore"* This means that a system of education without clear aims is bound to fail. All our methods of teaching, curriculum, system of evaluation are shaped and moulded according to the aims of education. So, it is necessary to keep in view the aims of education before undertaking any educational endeavour due to the following reasons—

1. *To provide direction to education:* Aims provide direction to the teacher and student. Education without aims is just like 'riding in a boat without a rudder'. It is only the rudder which helps a sailor to proceed in the right direction otherwise he will be at the mercy of winds. Similarly aims provide a line of action and guidance to the teacher. It does not allow the educational activity to become haphazard, vague and confused.
2. *To evaluate educational process:* With the help of aim we can review the ways and means, we have opted for reaching the desired goals. With its help, we can think of possibilities of further improvement. Aims serve as barometer for evaluation. In fact, the aim is a yard-stick with which we can measure the success and failure of our educational process.
3. *To act in a rational manner:* Aims help us to act in a rational and judicious manner. They help educationist to know the justification of their decisions in the field of education. They help us to act intelligently with a meaning.
4. *To provide efficient school administration:* The efficiency of school administration and organisation depends on aims of education. Various aspects of school administration as selection of teachers, curriculum planning, planning of co-curricular activities are guided by educational aims.
5. *To make education meaningful:* Without aims education has no meaning. Education is a purposeful and organised activity which deliberately endevours to modify the behaviour of the educand, with a specific goal in view.
6. *To motivate learners to realise the aims:* Aims function as motivators and can sustain motivation to the learners for realization of educational aims. The activities done by the learners are influenced by the aims of education. Aims are values. If they are desired, they induce the learner to release his energy to accomplish an aim.
7. *To achieve national goals:* The aims of education process of any country are influenced by national goals. If the efforts are done to achieve educational goal, it means we are achieving national goals. There is change in aims of education due to change in national goals.

**Different Types of Aim**

1. *Individual and Social Aims:* There is a debate regarding what education should aim at—Individual development or social development. The view that provides individual aim stresses that biologically and psychologically individual is unique and every individual is responsible for his/her destiny. T.P. Nunn remarked, *"Nothing good enters in to the human world except*

*in and through the free activities of individual man and woman, and that educational practices must be shaped to accord with that truth".* Spiritualists feel that individual development lies in self-realization, so education should aim at the training and development of the individuals. The view also favours that only such educated and competent individuals can make society good and prosperous.

In contrast, the view that advocates social aim in education argues that a human being is a social animal. Personality development does not take place in a vacuum. It takes place in associating with others, in co-opertative living and in working together for the welfare of the group or society. Individual exists for the sake of society and he should grow up only in accordance with the requirements and desires in the society. Education should aim at inculcation of social values in individuals, preparing individuals for taking up social roles and responsibilities, increasing social efficiency of individuals and creating such human personalities who would contribute substantially for the development of society.

In fact, both individual and social aims of education are complementary. The individuals, whose personalities are fully developed can contribute effectively for the betterment of the society and for the development of personality, man needs a good nourishing society. Rusk has rightly said, *"Individuality is of no value and personality is a meaningless term apart from the social environment in which they are developed and manifested."*

2. *Ultimate and Immediate Aims:* The aims of education relate with philosophy of life and aims of human life itself. Some argue that *'self-realisation'* is the ultimate aim of education. It involves knowing the potentialities and capabilities of individuals and then help the individuals to actualise their capabilities. Some argue that *harmonious development of individual's innate powers* is the ultimate aim. Its aim is to produce a well balanced personality means the harmonious cultivation of the physical, intellectual, aesthetic, moral and spiritual sides of human nature. Rousseau, Pestalozzi and Mahatma Gandhi are among those who favoured this view. Herbert Spencer put forth the idea of *'Education for complete living'*. He writes, *"Education must tells us in what way to treat the body, in what way to manage our affairs, in what way to bring up our family, in what way to behave as a citizen, in what way to utilize those source of happiness which nature supplies. How to use all faculties to great advantage of ourselves and others."* This aim virtually tries to put all the aims of education in to one. The ultimate aims are a sort of final aims towards which the educational processes are oriented. But it is the specific aim which warrants educational programmes. Specific aims must always be in tune with the ultimate aims of education, only then they will be fruitful.

Immediate aims are the stepping stones to achieve ultimate aims of education *'Learning to be'* the report of the international commission on the development of education, lists some specific or immediate aims of education: developing affective qualities, developing aesthetic sense, character building, acquiring the tools of knowledge and promoting physical well-being. Other immediate aims that have exercised considerable impact on the present day educational practices include: equipping individuals with vocational efficiency, spiritual development, building a good morality in the individuals, training in citizenship, development of democratic outlook and making individuals well versed with their culture.

In fact, we can say that education should make individual intellectually enlightened, vocationally self-sufficient, socially and individually efficient, morally strong, culturally polished and spiritually developed. The educational processes following these aims will enable the human being in integrated growth and development. Thus the education system will plan an effective role in making an individual as well as society better and better.

### Aims of Education in a Democratic Setup

Aims of education in a democratic set up cater to promotion of democratic ideals, development of potentialities of all human beings for their own fulfillment and creation of an educated and enlightened citizen for continuance of a democratic society. Democracy is a way of living that stresses the dignity of the individual and the sacredness of human personality in which individuals establish their relationship on the basis of co-operation, tolerance, mutual respect, fellow feeling and for play. Development of individuals, making them grow into autonomous adults, 'Complete human beings' gets high priority among the aims of education in a democratic set up. Education revolves around the child. Education is meant for the child and child is not meant for education. It keeps the individual enjoying a descent standard of living and striving for higher values of life. It is broad based.

It makes every individual capable of earning a livelihood and in the process would contribute to productivity of the society. It is available to all so that every member may participate intelligently in social, economic and political life of the community. Education makes people conscious of their rights and duties. Democracy also needs lenders in various fields of life. Therefore, education should also aim at training children in leadership.

It should be kept in mind that democracy can be achieved through. justice *i.e.* social, economic and political, liberty *i.e.* liberty of thought, expression; equality *i.e.* equality of rights of the individuals and the unity of the nation. The constitution of India in its preamble sets forth these ideals along with the ideals of socialism and secularism. The democratic education should strike a balance between materialism and socialism.

Democracy has a liberal attitude towards change. Education should be useful and effective for evolving a better society. Change is not enforced with force but cause as a result of mutual discussion, persuasion and agreement. To deal with the problems due to change, education must aim at fostering international understanding, national integration and creating national attitudes in citizens toward environment. Democracy achieves peaceful solution to all problem that endanger security of human life and existence. Thus we can say that in a democratic setup education should make individuals intellectually enlightened, vocationally self sufficient, morally strong, culturally polished, rational and spiritually developed.

### Aims of Education in Ancient India

In ancient period, India was predominantly religious in its thinking. Therefore, religions had a great influence on every aspect of life. So education was also related with religion as:

1. *Character Formation:* In those days, Indian Philosophers and educationists believed that education should inculcate normal qualities to form strong character. Hence, it was the sacred duty of the guru to develop a strong character of every child.
2. *To Preserve and Transmit the Culture:* As all of us know that Indian culture is known as the best culture in the world from the ancient times. Education is a powerful instrument to preserve and transmit the culture from generation to generation.
3. *Infusion of Religiousness:* The main aim of education in ancient India was to inculcate a spirit of religiousness in the mind of every child. The child is to live in Brahmcharya Ashram while getting the education. He was to recite regular prayers in the morning and evening and celebrate various religious festivals while living in ashram.

Other then these captained above aims were development of personality, promotion of social efficiency and inculcation of civic responsibilities, The foremost aim was spiritual development because the child was to get education/knowledge regarding Vedas, Shastras etc.

### Aims of Education in Medieval India

The medieval period was known as Mughal period and at that time every person was to believe in Islamic religion. The aims of education were as follows:

1. *Propagation of Islam:* At that time 'Madarsas' were the places of higher learning and in these Islamic history, rituals together with higher knowledge of Islamic religion were taught.
2. *Spread of Education Among Muslims:* The muslim theologists believed that only Mullahs and Maulvies can spread education and it should be provided to muslim children because Islamic ideals and values of life can be inculcated among them.

3. *Propagation of Shariyat:* Shriyat means a code of Islamic laws and rules of conduct to be followed by believers of Islam. These laws were taught to children through education.

The others were identical as in ancient period as character development, development of morality etc. but the main emphasis was to develop the Islamic religion.

**Aims of Education during British Rule**

The Britishers believed in spreading the knowledge of 3R's (Reading, Writing and Arithematic) only. Therefore the main aims of education during that period were:

1. *Spreading English Literature:* The main aim was to spread English culture among Indians, so English was made the compulsory medium of instruction.
2. *Preparing a Class of Interpreters:* The aim to spread English literature was to prepare a class of Indians who could talk in English and understand English. From that period the craze for English was started among Indians and it is still going on till now. The impact of 3 R's education prolonged for a long period even after independence also.

## Aims of Education in India after Independence

India attained freedom on August 15, 1947. There was a great responsibility on the shoulders of educationists, philosophers to shape the future of India according to their plans. Our late Prime Minister Pt. Jawahar Lai Nehru rightly remarked, "Great changes have taken place in the country and the educational system must be in keeping with them. The entire base of education must be revolutionised" Our country was declared as a democratic country and the necessity was to formulate new aims of education in order to base education on Indian culture. The Govt., of India formulated the commissions at different times to recommend suitable aims of education to make democratic society successful.

### *A. Aims of Education according to University Education Commission, 1948*

In 1948, an education commission was established under the Chairmanship of Dr. Radha Krishnan. The aims of education recommended by this commission were as follows:

1. *Development of Leadership:* Success of democracy depends upon able leaders. There was need of efficient leaders for the development of nation. For this training of leadership was necessary. Without this training leaders of high caliber would not be created. A leader must possess virtues like tolerance, wisdom, understanding, discipline and justice. Provision for suitable education is necessary for the development of these qualities.

2. *Preservation of Culture:* With the passage of time many other things which do not belong to the culture, come in to culture. It is the responsibility of education to preserve the culture through books and transmit it through teachers.
3. *Vocational Education:* An individual financially depending on others cannot be called a good citizen of the country. Success of democracy depends upon efficient citizens. Vocational education is necessary for the development of efficient citizens. Agricultural and industrial development of the country is possible only when there is no shortage of skilled workers.
4. *Spiritual Training:* From the ancient period, India always remain a religious country and the ultimate aim of life is to attain Moksha. For its attainment spiritual training is must. Only education can provide this training by creating suitable environment in the school.
5. *Character Development:* Another important aim of education is to develop moral qualities in the child and build his character Education can do it by moulding and sublimating the basic instincts of the child in proper direction.
6. *Social Development:* Man is a social animal. He is integrally related to society. Education should develop a spirit, a social service in the individuals. With the development of feeling of cooperation, brotherhood, tolerance etc. education can fulfill this aim.
7. *Development of Democratic Qualities:* India is a democratic country. Being a citizen of democratic country, there is need of developing democratic qualities among them as sense of responsibility, fellow feeling, love, service, sense of duty and quality of leadership. Imbued with these qualities the citizens promote their own development and bring about national prosperity.
8. *Development of International Understanding:* National development can't take place without the help of other countries. Every human being is not only the citizen of his country only but also of whole world. Every man should feel himself responsible not only for his nation only but for the whole world. For this education should aim at developing the feeling of international understanding.

### *Aims of Education according to Secondary Education Commission (1952-53)*

In 1952, Secondary Education Commission was established under the chairmanship of Dr. Laxman Swami Mudaliar and it is also known as Mudaliar Commission. The following aims of Education were recommended by it:

1. *Development of Democratic Citizenship:* It is necessary for the success of democracy that every citizen should have democracy. Every individual should be trained for citizenship. It involves many intellectual, social

and moral qualities. In order to develop democratic citizenship education should aim at developing the following qualities:

(i) Clear Thinking: For democratic citizenship the capacity for clear thinking is to be developed. A receptivity of new ideas is also to be developed. The citizen has to develop a scientific attitude of mind to think objectively. He should have an open mind and should not think confusedly.

(ii) Clearness in Speech and Writing: Clarity of thought should be accompanied by clearness in speech and in writing. Education should enable every citizen to take decision in important things. Free and clear contemplation is very necessary for free decision. Education should develop intellectual awakening and free thinking in children.

(iii) Training in Art of Living: In a democratic society, every individual is important. So, individual has to be trained in the art of living efficiently in the community. It cannot be learnt without suitable education and experience. Co-operation is a necessary virtue For democracy. Education should develop the virtues like discipline, cooperation, social sensitiveness and tolerance. Progress of society is possible only with the help of these virtues.

(iv) Sense of True Patriotism: The education has to foster the sense of true patriotism in the citizens of a country. The patriotic citizens of a country sacrifice their own interests for the well being of the nation. He should be ready to recognise its weaknesses with the open mind and to work for their eradication. Education should enable them to appreciate the social and cultural achievement of their country, but the feeling of patriotism should not be taken in the narrow sense as Hitler took it.

(v) Sense of World Citizenship: With the help of education, the students ought to be taught that they are not only the citizens of their country but also of the world. Development of one's country cannot take place without the help of others. The students should be prefaced to discharge their responsibilities to the world also. The commission has rightly remarked, *"In a very real sense, therefore, patriotism is not enough and it must he supplemented by a lively realization of the fact that we are all members of one world, and must be prepared mentally and emotionally', to discharge the responsibilities which such membership implies."*

2. *Development of Vocational Efficiency:* Vocational efficiency is necessary for the development of efficient citizenship. Education should aim at providing vocational training to every citizen of the country. Each subject should be given proper place in the curriculum, so that, each child may be able to choose the vocation of his interest and ability which he wants to pursue after finishing his studies. Vocational efficiency is necessary in

order to make everybody efficient in his own field of work. The feeling of dignity of labour will be inculcated among the students. After acquiring efficiency in craft, sculpture, engineering, etc. the tendency of doing white collar jobs would diminish in the individual and thus the foundation of democracy might be strengthened.

3. *Development of Personality:* In a democratic country, every individual has got its own importance. Education should aim at not only the development of one factor of personality but that of the whole personality. For this education should provide such type of environment in which the child will be able to do creative and constructive activities so that he is able to develop his literary, artistic and cultural interests. The development of these interests will enrich the life of the children.
4. *Education for Leadership:* Success of democracy depends upon able leaders. Narrow-minded leaders cannot make progress in the field of politics, science, literature, art etc. A leader must possess virtues like tolerance, wisdom, understanding, discipline and justice. Education should inculcate these values among the citizens of the society.

### *Aims of Education according to Indian Education Commission (1964-66)*

In 1964, Indian Education Commission was established under the chairmanship of Dr. Daulat Ram Kothari and it is also known as Kothari Commission. It presented its report in 1966. The education commission analysed the problem of national development and recommended that education should be related to life, needs and aspiration of the people. It has to become a powerful instrument to bring social, economic and cultural changes, in our country. In order to achieve this the commission had recommended the following aims of education:

1. *To Increase Productivity:* Increase in production is the strong base of economic development, and as long as education and productivity are not linked with each other, and the people are not educated in the use of means of production, it is not possible to fulfill our basic needs. Hence the first task of education is to link itself with productivity. This can be done in the following way:
   (i) Science Education: India was moving from a traditional, hard-bound society to a modern one. A modern society aims to develop technology based upon science. So science education should become a part of all courses at all stages of education. The study of science can help in attaining the following objectives:
      (a) Developing analytical skill suitable to problem solving.
      (b) Weakening the hold of superstitions and irrationality.
      (c) Helping the individual to understand himself and his place in the universe.

(d) Encouraging the tendency to understand fundamental principles with increasing intensity and insight.
(e) Using analytical skills to solve the problems of social life as well as the material environment.
(f) Encouraging curiosity and the tendency to experiment.

(ii) Work Experience: Work experience should be introduced at all stages of education. The education commission recommended that it should be made an inalienable part of any scheme of general education. By work experience, it means participation in any productive activity in the school, at home, on a farm, in a factory or at any other place. The purpose behind it is to relate education with productivity. Its aim is to convert educated manpower in to productive manpower. They will become capable of being used as an instrument of production. It will help to bridge the gap between intellectual and manual work. It was essential to recreate faith in and respect for physical labour by providing training in productive work.

(iii) Application of Science to Productive Process: Work experience should be related to technology and industrialization and science education to productive processes including agriculture. Hence, the highest possible emphasis should be placed upon the research in application of science. It should be used as a tool in practical life.

(iv) Vocationalisation: In fact, India is predominantly an agrarian economy. In any economy of this type, making general education compulsory for a period of seven to eight years is a proposition which can be useful, but at high school level it should be vocationalised, so that youth can be prepared for their potential in vocational and active life. They can be fitted to participate in the efforts to increase national production. At higher education level technical and agricultural education should be non-formational. Industries, farms etc. located in the community should be used as laboratories for developing the vocational skills.

2. *To Achieve Social and National Integration:* Education is the most important instrument for bringing any change in the society. In the conditions prevailing in contemporary Indian society, the commission has taken a note of the growth of local, regional, linguistic and state loyalities. It has suggested several steps to be taken to strengthen social and national unity:

(i) A Common School System: Different types of schools as public schools, convent schools, gurukuls, madrassas etc. are symptoms of inequality. They strengthen the tendency towards a class war. As a result of democracy, it will be necessary to establish a system of education devoid of any distinction based on religion, caste, class or heritage. The education commission has spoken of a common school system in which:

- Unrestricted entry of all children irrespective of any caste, creed, colour, sex, community, religion, economic condition or social status.
- Getting educational opportunities should depend upon talent and not upon wealth or class.
- Common standard must be maintained in all schools.
- No fees will be charged for providing instructional programme.
- The needs of average parent will be fulfilled so that he may not feel compelled to send his children to expensive school outside this system.

(ii) Social and National Service: Literacy is neither the beginning nor the education, hence, we must not confine education to the development of cognitive aspect only. We must lay stress on active and practical education aiming at modification of behaviour. Therefore, education should make social and national service obligatory for all students at all stages. Programmes of different kinds as health service programmes, adult education programme, vocational/industrial development programme, flood/famine relief programmes, presonality development camps can be made effective through National Social Service (NSS), the National Cadet Corps (NCC), Girls Guiding and Scouting and other organisations.

(iii) Development of Language Policy: India is a multi-lingual country. Therefore, the development of an appropriate language policy can assist in social and national integration. The commission has suggested the following policies in this regard:

- Mother tongue should be the medium of instruction in school and colleges.
- With the help of U.G.C., the universities should produce books and literature in regional languages in science and technology.
- The regional languages should also be made the language of administration for the region concerned.
- The study of English should also be continued right from the school stage. For international communication other languages should also be introduced.

(iv) Promotion of National Consciousness: For achieving social and national integration, the major objective of our education system should be to acquaint the people of different regions, sub-cultures, religions and communities as well as languages with the fact of unity in diversity. Education should arouse in them a profound love for their motherhood, only then the citizens of India can become proud of their national culture, tradition, languages etc. In this context, Education Commission suggested the adoption of the following programmes:

(a) Understanding and revaluation of our cultural heritage.
(b) Creation of a strong driving faith in the future.
(c) Strengthening Democracy.

3. *Education for Modernisation:* In this modern age new researches are made by all advanced countries of the world in all fields of human life. Education should help in accelerating the process of modernisation in our country so that we may be able to stand in line with the developed countries of the world. Due to recent explosion of knowledge, education in modern society is no longer concerned with the imparting of knowledge about the preparation of finished product, but with the awakening of curiosity, the development of proper interest, attitudes and values. Education is to develop essential skills as independent study and capacity to think and judge for oneself. Without these skills, the child will not be able to become a responsible member of the democratic India. Education should train an adequate and competent intelligentsia coming from all strata of society whose loyalties and aspirations are deeply rooted in Indian soil. In a traditional society changes were very slow, but in a modern society changes take place very rapidly. This necessitates change in our education system. Education must be oriented to meet the social, economic, political and cultural problems of a new social order. Modernisation is essentially a process, a movement from traditional order to certain desired type of technology, associated form of social structure, value orientation, motivation and norms,
4. *To Cultivate Social, Moral and Spiritual Values:* Only material progress is of no use unless it is supported by the inculcation of appropriate social, moral and spiritual values. It should be remembered that we may become as advanced as possible and develop our economy to the highest level, but we should not give up our cultural foundation which have withstood the ranges of adverse times from time immemorial. Society can continue to exist only if it is based on such values as respect for the individuality of a person, sense of equality, love, sacrifice, self-control etc. and in their absence, it must necessarily fall into decay. For this, active measures should be adopted to give a value orientation to education. In this respect Education Commission has suggested the following ways:
   (i) Some periods should be fixed for giving social, moral and spiritual education in the regular time-table of the school,
   (ii) India is a secular country and as such no religious education should be given in the schools but at least some fundamental moral aspects, common to all the religion can be brought to the notice of the students by the teacher,
   (iii) Special type of literature dealing with moral and spiritual aspects should be prepared,

(iv) In every university, there should be at least one department exclusively set up for the comparative study of different religions and sorting out their common points to be emphasized in education,

(v) Books should be prepared at the national level by competent experts in each religion.

### *Aims of Education according to National Policy on Education, 1986*

Natural Policy on Education in 1986 recommended the following aims of education:

1. *Development of Socialism, Secularism and Democracy:* India is a country in which many communities and religious groups subsist side by side, and hence, we have envisioned a socialistic, secular democracy. The proper use of this is possible only through the medium of education. Education should refine sensitivities and perceptions that contribute to national cohesion, a scientific temper and independence of mind and spirit.
2. *All Round Development:* Education should aim at mental as well as spiritual development of an individual. It can be done with the help of different curricular as well as co-curricular activities. Education is to provide such type of environment which will help in the development of all the aspects as cognitive, conative and affective.
3. *Development of Man Power:* Man-power is an important resource helpful in the economic development of a country. Education should help in developing the man power with the help of vocationalization and it will be the ultimate guarantee for the development of national self-reliance.
4. *Cultivating Moral and Ethical Values:* In Indian culture, the policy has laid stress on education for the development of moral and ethical values. The document says that there has been a steep fall in values and the country is passing through stage of a 'value crisis'. The policy stressed the need of value education. It should be a regular part of the curricular programme of education.
5. *Life-long Education:* Education is a never ending process. A person learns throughout his life. Life-long and continuing education is a cherished goal of educational process. The stress was laid on the opening of open schools and open universities. The future thrust will he in the direction of open and distance learning.
6. *National System of Education:* The policy aims at providing national system of education. This recommendation was also provided by Kothari Commission in 1964-66, but it was not implemented upto 1986. The concept of national system of education implies that all students irrespective of caste, creed, location, colour or sex should have access to education of a comparable quality upto a given level. It envisaged a common educational structure *i.e.* 10+2+3.
7. *Education for Equality:* the main emphasis was laid by the policy on equalising educational opportunities and removal of disparities. All

possible efforts will have to be made for specific needs of different stakeholders. The main recommendations for this include:

(i) Women Education
(ii) Education of the scheduled castes and scheduled tribes
(iii) Education of minorities
(iv) Education of the handicapped
(v) Promotion of adult education

### *Aims of Education as per National Curriculum Framework (NCF)—2000*

In recent times schooling has emerged as an important segment of the total educational system, which is expected to contribute significantly to individual and national development processes. To do this effectively, it needs to be constantly reviewed and updated. The NCF-2000 was the third national curriculum framework in the history of the Indian education system published by the National Council of Education Research and Training (NCERT). It was developed in 2000 according to the 1992 program guidelines. According to NCF-2000, the main aims of education were as follows:

1. *Universalization of Primary Education:* According to the Indian Constitution, the country is committed to provide free and compulsory education to all children up to the age of 14. This commitment has been reiterated in all official documents. Attempts have been made to provide universal access to education, including an emphasis on universal enrolment and universal retention. Thus, proper planning and its effective implementation is the soul of achieving quality education for all, the most cherished goal of universal elementary education (UEE). At the primary level, children need to be equipped with the necessary skills with appropriate behaviour and values to help them to emerge as social human beings, whom will be able to contribute to themselves as well as society and continue to learn throughout life. While this will require concerted efforts in all academic fields.
2. *Education for Equality:* Equality of opportunity means ensuring that every person receives appropriate education at a pace and in ways that fit. Special attention should be paid to children from disadvantaged, and socially discriminatory groups, and those suffering from specific challenges. The provision of equal opportunity for all is a prerequisite for promoting equality, not only in access, but also in conditions for success. The course, it may be reiterated, should create awareness of the inherent equality of all, in order to remove the prejudices and complexes transmitted through the social environment and the factor of birth.
3. *To develop a sense of national unity and preservation of cultural heritage:* Education must promote global world order. It is necessary that the cultural heritage, traditions and history of the various ethnic groups and regions of the country and their contribution are understood

and appreciated in the right perspective. This will help in understanding the nature of the pluralistic society of the country and its overall culture.

4. *Integrating indigenous knowledge and India's contribution to mankind:* Now a days, more than ever, India's indigenous knowledge systems are widely recognized. Education must be related to the social-cultural context of students to be relevant and meaningful. India's indigenous knowledge system must be maintained through active support from societies and groups that are traditional repositories of this knowledge, whether rural or tribe, their way of life, their languages, their social organization, and the environment in which they live. There is a need for innovative ways of preventing the spread of such knowledge, which usually disappear with people, and it is here that education should play an important role. Equally important, we need a parallel analysis of insights between indigenous knowledge systems, on the one hand, and ideas related to some areas of modern science and the origins of life on the other hand.
5. *Development of Life Skills:* Education suffers from differences between, by and large, its content and students' lived experiences. Education should ideally prepare students to meet life's challenges. Some core life skills as problem-solving, critical thinking, communication, self-awareness, coping with stress, decision making, creative thinking and general thinking, interpersonal relationships and empathy, etc. are very important for a successful life. For this, education needs to be intimately connected with different life-skills, adaptive and positive behavior, abilities, which enable people to deal effectively with the demands and challenges of everyday life. Through the development of these skills the students can fight with the challenges of existing situations and problems.
6. *Value Education:* Self-recognition will come to them through fair value education which will facilitate their spiritual march through different mediating stages from the level of sub-consciousness to super-consciousness. Value-based education will help the nation to fight all forms of bigotry, ill will, violence, fatalism, dishonesty, mistrust, corruption, exploitation and drug abuse.
7. *To provide knowledge of socio-cultural context:* India is a multi-cultural and multilingual society. Thus, diversity in social structure is a distinctive feature of Indian society. This process has given an example of India's age unity in diversity and diversity in unity. This long tradition has been transmitted from one generation to the next. Schools should prepare children to participate in socio-economic processes and to do meaningful work with a sense of self-reliance and cooperation, which can improve the society.
8. *Work-related Education:* Work education and vocational education is an integral part of the school education system. Education needs to be implemented more effectively at the primary level as a purposeful,

meaningful manual activity. Work education is a thoughtful strategy to develop an understanding of the facts and principles involved in a variety of tasks and to create a positive attitude towards work.

9. *Interface between cognition, emotion and action:* Education should facilitate the personal development of learners and equip them psychologically to deal with the rapid changes taking place in all walks of life. Thus, the focus of education is moving away from merely developing cognitive skills (traditional 3Rs) to promote individual and inter-personal development. Teachers are realizing that apart from academic shortcomings, there is a distinct and more dangerous deficiency: emotional illiteracy. The components of emotional intelligence or literacy include emotional and social skills, which are related to the education of moral and spiritual development, and also implications for the management and prevention of anger, aggression, stress, alcohol or drug dependence, sexual abuse and redress interpersonal conflicts. Intra-personal intelligence enables us to make sense of the things we do, the thoughts we have, the feelings we get: and the relationship between all these things. Interpersonal intelligence enables us to interact with other people, empathize with them, communicate clearly with them, inspire and motivate them, and understand relationships between individuals. Education should be recognized as an essential element of the educational process in the classroom in order to promote emotions because emotions provide information and direct attention, and facilitate attainment of goals.
10. *Development of Aesthetic Sensibilities:* An aesthetic approach to education seeks to restore an appropriate balance to the learning process by giving equal status to experience, imagination, creativity, and intuition, as it does to know, think, remember, and reason. It will provide a means for activation of the senses for new insights and understanding of the learner.
11. *Education as a Lifelong Process:* Education is a lifelong process that essentially has two major dimensions - temporal and spatial. While this should continue throughout the life span of a person because special developmental tasks have to be done and problems have to be solved, it occurs at the same time, between different life spaces. Education should develop a love for learning and be prepared for the constant and the unknown. Thus, an important objective of education is to empower all students towards knowledge and learning.
12. *Development of Democratic Attitude:* We must build on students with a growing knowledge and understanding of the world based on equality, justice, freedom, respect for human dignity and rights, sensitivity to the well-being and feelings of others.
13. *To develop the scientific tendency and independence of mind and soul:* The discovery of a new academic order is based on scientific

and technical training, one of the essential components of scientific temperament. Therefore, training in scientific sense is required, which is one of the major goals of any contemporary education system. The need for scientific humanism is due to diverse and powerful reasons such as the need for labor, the need to control reality, the need for self-control, the need for scientific method and moral training.

14. *Promotion of social, moral and spiritual values:* NCF-2000 emphasized character building through social, ethical and spiritual values in students at all stages of education. It has recommended that the central and state governments should adopt measures to introduce education in moral, social and spiritual values in all institutions.

Thus NCF-2000 suggested that education liberates man from the clutches of ignorance, privatization and misery, leads to a non-violent and non-exploitative social order, therefore the purpose of the school curriculum is to enable learners to acquire, understand and develop knowledge. Creating skills, positive attitudes, values and habits are conducive to the all-round development of their personality. Young girls and boys should be empowered through education to enhance their potential. In addition, the development of intrinsic values and emotional intelligence of learners is important.

### *Aims of Education as per National Curriculum Framework (NCF)—2005*

The values enshrined in the NCF 2005 constitution reflect its objectives of student learning and development, contemporary concerns to strengthen unity and national identity in a multicultural context and enable the nation to meet future challenges. It reaffirms the belief in the constitutional vision of India as a secular, egalitarian and pluralistic society founded on values of social justice and equality. It addresses the challenge seeks to give the equality of quality in a system, the exclusive triangle of quality and quantity.

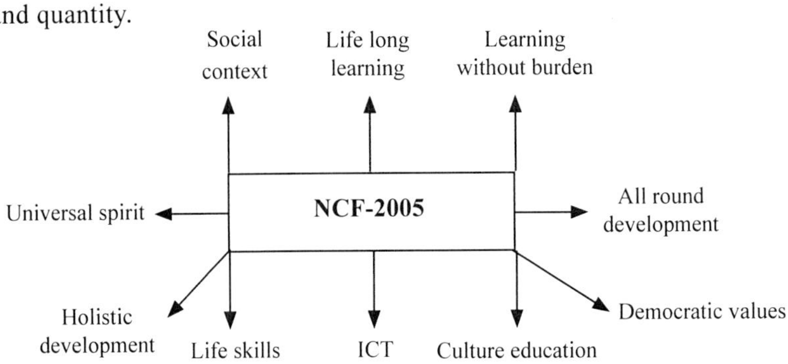


**Fig. 2.2: Aims of Education by NCF-2005**

Confirming the primacy of an active learner requires linking knowledge to life outside school, according to NCF-2005, the basic aims of education should be as follows-

1. *Development of Universal Spirit:* In our cultural and large society, the values to be developed by education should have universal spirit. This will develop a sense of unity among our people. This type of education will remove extremism, religious prejudices, backwardness, superstition, destiny-belief and violence or riots. Furthermore, value education should be based on our rich culture, national and universal ideas and purposes. This aspect should be kept under more stress.
2. *Lifelong Learning:* Education should develop a love for learning and a desire to be continuous and awared. Thus, an important objective of education is to empower all students towards knowledge and learning.
3. *Provide stress-free education:* For a long time there are strong complaints from parents and the community that the school curriculum has become very heavy. The heavy weight of the curriculum is not only physical, but also a lack of understanding of some basic concepts resulting in non-understanding. This is causing a lot of stress and tension in the students and it is a burden to their normal development. In recent times, attempts have been made to look into this problem and find some ways and means of reducing the burden on school students, especially the youth. However, despite several measures being suggested, the school curriculum remains heavy and expectations are high.
4. *Development of Democratic Values:* Being a citizen of a democratic country it is essential that education should help in the development of students' commitment to equality, justice, freedom, respect for human dignity and rights, sensitivity to the well-being and feelings of others, growing knowledge and understanding of the world.
5. *All-round development of personality:* Education frees man from the clutches of ignorance, individualism and plight. This should also give rise to a non-violent and non-exploitative social order. Therefore, the purpose of the school curriculum is to enable learners to acquire knowledge, develop understanding and skills, positive attitudes, values and habits conducive to the all-round development of their personality.
6. *Meaningful work for social change:* Schools should prepare children to participate in socio-economic processes and do meaningful work with a sense of self-reliance and cooperation, which can improve the society.
7. *Development of creativity:* Education should provide means and opportunities to enhance the creative expression of the child. Education should enable learners to respond to new situations in a flexible and constructive manner. Building the learner's knowledge and promoting creativity is essential.
8. *Development of life skills:* Development of life skills such as critical thinking, interpersonal interaction, negotiation skills, problem solving

and self -management is also very important to meet the challenges of everyday life.

9. *Freedom of thought and action:* Another objective of education is the development of freedom of thought and action. It should teach people to think for themselves and take important independent decisions. Education should have enough room for questions in children's thoughts, curiosities and curriculum practices. Linking knowledge across disciplinary boundaries is very important in child development to provide a comprehensive frame work for practical construction of knowledge.
10. *Holistic development of the children:* The school period is a period of rapid development with changes and changes in children's abilities, attitudes and interests. A holistic approach should be taken in the development and learning of learners.
11. *Emphasis on Information and Communication Technology:* The revolution in new technology is a fundamental challenge, transforming the information society into a knowledge society. ICT is bound to influence and change existing educational provisions, by changing existing curricula, bringing in new generation teaching materials and encouraging networking of schools. The integration of ICT in school education will demand that educational planners need to look beyond the current urban classrooms, who are preparing updated plans for education in electronic environments and expanding their design even in remote rural areas, as a result computers become the subject of study. It is not simply integrated into an existing curriculum, instead, becomes an integral part of the schooling process resulting in universal computer literacy, computer assisted learning and, ultimately, computer-based learning across the globe.
12. *To bridge the gap between technology and culture:* There is a need to bridge the gap between formal education system and rich cum diverse cultural traditions of the country. In the love for modern technology, the new generation should not detach its roots from history and culture of India. We need to escape from culturelessness, humanlessness and indifference at every cost. The teaching should work for a synthesis between continuity of changing technologies and cultural traditions of the country and education can do it in an effective way. Education should be enriched through various types of subjects to develop a spirit of beauty, truth and goodness among the students. They should be invited to contribute in the richness of society which include literary and oral traditions of expression. To maintain cultural traditions and for their progress the role of teachers, teaching with traditional methods should be strengthened and it should be recognised.

To summarise, according to NCF-2005, the aim of our education should be to build a commitment to democratic values for equality, justice, freedom, concern for the wellbeing of others and feelings, respect for secularism, human dignity and rights. It should also be aimed at promoting freedom of thought and action, and cultivate the ability to develop a social temperament and work to admire beauty. In addition, it should aim to develop the ability to learn to respond to new situations in a flexible and creative way, participation in the democratic process, and the ability to work and contribute towards the economic progress and social change.

***Aims of Education according to International Commission on Education (1972)***

The UNESCO appointed an International Commission on education, under the chairmanship of Edgar Faure, who submitted its report named as 'Learning to be: The world of education today and tomorrow' in 1972. The major goals of education as spelt out by the commission are:

1. *Development of Scientific Humanism:* Scientific humanism is based on scientific and technological training. Command of scientific thought and language has become indispensable in today's world. Objective knowledge, however, must be directed towards action and primarily in the service of human kind. Here one can speak of science with a conscience, and science at the service of development. Citizens of 21st century must learn to be scientific humanists.
2. *Development of creativity:* Creativity means preserving originality and creative ingenuity of each individual with realism; transmitting culture without shifting the individual; encouraging the use of one's gifts, aptitudes and personal forms of expression without cultivating egoism, and paying attention to the individual's specific traits without overlooking collective activity and welfare. This can be possible only when there is respect for creativity of others and other cultures.
3. *To develop social commitment:* It consists of preparing the individual for life in society, moving him/her in to a coherent moral, intellectual and affective universe compound of set of values. It also consists in the interpretations of the past and conceptions of the future, a fundamental store of ideas and information, a common inheritance. It is necessary for the success of democracy, An individual comes into a full realization of his/her social dimension through active participation in the functioning of social structure and a personal commitment to reform them, when necessary
4. *Development of complete man:* If the individual is to develop for himself/herself as well as for others, the education should respect many sided of his/her personality. It means the development should be in balance among the various intellectual, ethical, emotional, physical and spiritual components of personality.

This philosophy is the guiding principle of learning to be fully human, a complete human person.

**International Commission on Education for the Twenty-first Century Learning: The Treasure Within (1996)**

The Commission, with the major mandate "to study and reflect on the challenges facing education in the coming years and to formulate suggestions and recommendations which can serve as an agenda for renewal and action or policy making and official at the highest levels", initiated its action on March 1993 and adopted the final report in January, 1996. The Commission advocated four types of learning, which are important in a person's life and these four types are popularly called the four pillars of education.

1. *Learning to know:* Education should focus on learning to know. Our traditional approach of learning to know may have to undergo substantial changes specially when access to information is easy. Even if study for its own sake is a dynamic pursuit with so much emphasis now being put on the acquisition of marketable skills, the raising of school learning age and an increase in the leisure time should provide more and more adults with opportunities for private study. The broader our knowledge, the better we can understand many different aspects of our environment.
2. *Learning to do:* It is closely associated with the issue of occupational training. How do we adapt education so that it can equip people to do the type of work needed in the future? According to the commission, its implications go beyond vocational and professional education. Education should focus on learning to do in order to acquire not only an occupational skill but also more broadly the competence to deal with many situations and work in teams.
3. *Learning to live together:* The potential of education for diminishing prejudices and ethnocentrism and for reducing intergroup conflict is powerful. If the people learn to live together in the present scenario, the possible situation will be as provided in the following diagram:
4. *Learning to be:* Education should contribute to every person's complete development-mind and body, intelligence, sensitivity, aesthetic appreciation and spirituality. All people should receive in their childhood and youth an education that equips them to develop their own independent, critical way of thinking and judgement so that they can make up their own minds on the best courses of action in different circumstances in their lives.

These four pillars cannot be anchored solely in one phase in a person's life or at a single place. There is a need to rethink when in pupil's lives education should be provided and the fields that such education should cover. In 21st century, it is required that standardization of individual behaviour must pave the way for the qualities of imagination and creativity, the clearest manifestations of human freedom. The commission emphasizes, *"it is therefore important to provide children and young people with every possible opportunity for discovery and experiment-aesthetic, artistic, sporting,*

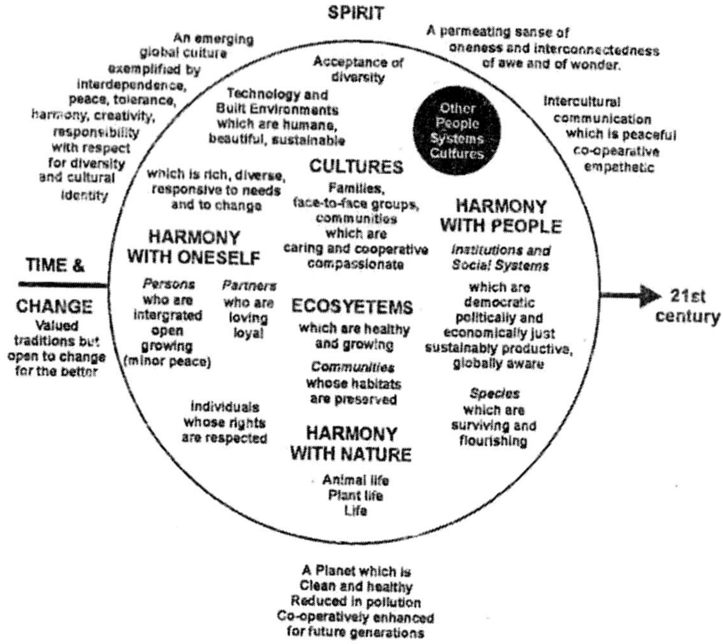


**Fig. 2.3: A Conceptual Framework (Adapted from the work of David)**

*scientific, cultural and social as well as appealing introduction to the creation of their contemporaries or earlier generations".* Thus education must try to foster a fully developed and balanced personality in human beings.

## Aims of Education as per National Education Policy (NEP) 2020

This National Education Policy 2020 aims to address many growing developmental imperatives of our country. This Policy proposes the revision and revamping of all aspects of the education structure, including its regulation and governance, to create a new system that is aligned with the aspirational goals of 21st century education, including SDG4, while building upon India's traditions and value system. It is based on the pillars of-

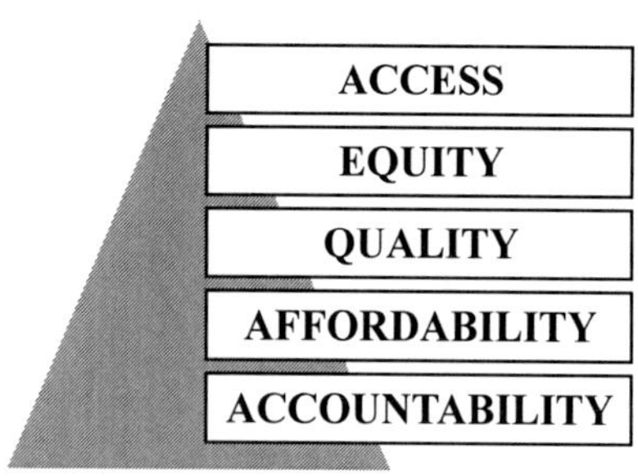


**Fig. 2.4: Pillars of NEP 2020**

The vision of the Policy is to instill among the learners a deep-rooted pride in being Indian, not only in thought; but also in spirit, intellect, and deeds, as well as to develop knowledge, skills, values, and dispositions that support responsible commitment to human rights, sustainable development and living, and global well-being, thereby reflecting a truly global citizen. According to NEP-2020, the main aims of education should be as follows:

1. *Early Childhood Care and Education:* Over 85% of a child's cumulative brain development occurs prior to the age of 6, indicating the critical importance of appropriate care and stimulation of the brain in the early years in order to ensure healthy brain development and growth. Presently, quality ECCE is not available to crores of young children, particularly children from socio-economically disadvantaged backgrounds. Strong investment in ECCE has the potential to give all young children such access, enabling them to participate and flourish in the educational system throughout their lives. The overall aim of ECCE will be to attain optimal outcomes in the domains of: physical and motor development, cognitive development, socio-emotional-ethical development, cultural/ artistic development, and the development of communication and early language, literacy, and numeracy.
2. *Emphasis on the development of the creative potential of each individual*—Education Policy lays emphasis particulary on the development of the creative potential of each individual. It is based on the principle that education must develop not only cognitive capacities - both the 'foundational capacities 'of literacy and numeracy and 'higher-order' cognitive capacities, such as critical thinking and problem solving — but also social, ethical, and emotional capacities and dispositions.
3. *Holistic development:* The aim of education will not only be cognitive development, but also building character and creating holistic and well-rounded individuals equipped with the key 21st century skills. Ultimately, knowledge is a deep-seated treasure and education helps in its manifestation as the perfection which is already within an individual. All aspects of curriculum and pedagogy will be reoriented and revamped to attain these critical goals. Specific sets of skills and values across domains will be identified for integration and incorporation at each stage of learning, from pre-school to higher education. The main aim of NEP-2020 is recognizing, identifying, and fostering the unique capabilities of each student, by sensitizing teachers as well as parents to promote each student's holistic development in both academic and non-academic spheres.
4. *Multidisciplinary knowledge:* Multidisciplinary education would aim to develop all capacities of human beings -intellectual, aesthetic, social, physical, emotional, and moral in an integrated manner. Such education

will help in developing well-rounded individuals that will possess critical 21st century capacities in fields across the arts, humanities, languages, sciences, social sciences, and professional, technical, and vocational fields; an ethics of social engagement; soft skills, such as communication, discussion and debate; and rigorous specialization in a chosen field or fields. Multidisciplinary knowledge and a holistic education across the sciences, social sciences, arts, humanities, and sports for a multidisciplinary world is essential in order to ensure the unity and integrity of all knowledge.

5. *Conceptual understanding:* Education should lay emphasis on conceptual understanding rather than rote learning because rote learning closed all the doors of creativity. Creativity and critical thinking encourage logical decision-making and innovation.
6. *Development of ethics, human and Constitutional values:* Development of ethics, human and Constitutional values like empathy, respect for others, cleanliness, courtesy, democratic spirit, spirit of service, respect for public property, scientific temper, liberty, responsibility, pluralism, equality, and justice through education will help in making the people useful not only for individual development but for the development of society also.
7. *Development of life skills:* Life skills play an important role in the development of a human being. Education should focus on the development of life skills such as communication, cooperation, teamwork, and resilience.
8. *Extensive use of ICT:* Use and integration of technology to improve multiple aspects of education will be supported and adopted, provided these interventions are rigorously and transparently evaluated in relevant contexts before they are scaled up. An autonomous body, the National Educational Technology Forum (NETF), will be created to provide a platform for the free exchange of ideas on the use of technology to enhance learning, assessment, planning, administration, and so on, both for school and higher education. Education system will focus on extensive use of technology in teaching and learning, removing language barriers, increasing access for Divyang students, and educational planning and management.
9. *Provide full equity and inclusion:* Education system will provide full equity and inclusion as the cornerstone of all educational decisions to ensure that all students are able to thrive in it. Respect for diversity and respect for the local context in all curriculum, pedagogy, and policy, are to be given keeping in mind that education is a concurrent subject.
10. *Development of Indigenous knowledge:* Indian knowledge system, including tribal knowledge and indigenous and traditional ways of learning, will be covered in school system.

11. *Awareness about culture, art and languages:* The promotion of Indian arts and culture is important not only for the nation but also for the individual. Cultural awareness and expression are among the major competencies considered important to develop in children, with a sense of identity, belongingness, as well as an appreciation of other cultures and identities. It is through the development of a strong sense and knowledge of their own cultural history, arts, languages, and traditions that children can build a positive cultural identity and self-esteem. Thus, cultural awareness and expression are important contributors both to individual as well as societal well-being. All languages in India, and their associated arts and culture will be documented through a web-based platform/portal/wiki, in order to preserve endangered and all Indian languages and their associated rich local arts and culture.

**Fig. 2.5: Means for Development of Culture**

12. *Development of Skills:* To develop the important skills in student, contemporary subjects will be introduced at all levels like artificial intelligence, environment education, organic living, design thinking, holistic health, global citizenship education, computer coding etc.

The purpose of NEP 2020 is to develop good human beings capable of rational thought and action, possessing compassion and empathy, courage and resilience, scientific temper and creative imagination, with sound ethical moorings and values. It aims at producing engaged, productive, and contributing citizens for building an equitable, inclusive, and plural society as envisaged by our Constitution. This National Education Policy envisions an education system rooted in Indian ethos that contributes directly to transforming India, that is Bharat, sustainably into an equitable and vibrant knowledge society, by providing high-quality education to all, and thereby making India a global knowledge superpower. The Policy envisages that the curriculum and pedagogy of our institutions must develop among the students a deep sense of respect towards the Fundamental Duties and Constitutional values, bonding with one's country, and a conscious awareness of one's roles and responsibilities in a changing world. The vision of the Policy is to instill among the learners a deep-rooted pride in being Indian, not only in thought, but also in spirit, intellect, and deeds, as well as to develop knowledge, skills, values, and dispositions that support responsible commitment to human rights, sustainable development and living, and global well-being, thereby reflecting a truly global citizen.

Thus it will be noted that the aims of education recommended by different commissions made a valuable contribution in modern India. If we sincerely implement the recommendations of the commissions, we shall surely lead the Indian masses towards their mental, moral, social, economic, intellectual and political advancement. Thus the purposes and aims of education are bound to vary from time to time according to the prevailing conditions in the society. Whatever these are at a particular time and age, they must be related to the life, needs and aspirations of the people.

# 3

# Analysis of Concepts of Education

*"Education is the process of the individual mind getting to its full possible development. It is a long school which lasts a life time."*

– Dr. Zakir Hussain

Education, at times is confused with some other identical terms *i.e.* teaching, instruction, learning, schooling, training, indoctrination etc. which have something in common, something identical and something different than education as a discipline. Every person should understand these concepts clearly so that he may not be confused while defining them as education, while these may have some common ground with it.

Education may be called the 'mother' which has given birth to different concepts, It is like an ocean and so broad in its dimensions that ail other concepts may be considered as rivers and streams of this vast ocean.

## I. EDUCATION

*For 'Analysis of Education', please read chapter 1.*

## II. TEACHING

Traditionally teaching is the act of imparting instructions to the pupils in the classroom situations. It is a bi-polar process, in which teacher provides information to the pupils and the students are to follow it. But this concept is changing in modem times. Now a days teaching is not teacher centered, but it is learner or child centered i e. the teacher is to keep in mind the psychology of the learner while teaching as well as the orderly presentation of subject matter which will be helpful in attaining the pre-determined goals. In this way the process of teaching establishes the relationship between teacher. student and curriculum.

### Definition

- H.C. Morrison, *"Teaching is an intimate contact between a more mature personality and a less mature one which is designed to further the education of the latter."*
- N.L. Gage, *"Teaching is a form of interpersonal influence aimed at changing the behaviour potential of another person."*
- B.O. Smith, *"Teaching is a system of actions intended to produce learning".*

- Thomas Green, *"Teaching is the task of teacher which is performed for the development of a child."*
- Burton, *"Teaching is the stimulation, guidance, direction and encouragement of learning."*
- Yoakam and Simpson, *"Teaching is the means whereby the experienced member. of the group guide the immature and infant members in their adjustment of life."*

The educationists define the concept of teaching in both ways. *i.e.* narrow and broader. Some say that it is the interaction between teacher and student, A teacher by his knowledge and experiences influences the behaviour of the student. Some believe that a book, nature, teaching machine, tape recorder, etc, may play a role of a teacher. If the activities done by these instruments results in one or some other type of learning it may be termed as teaching. Thus by analysing the above definitions of teaching, we can say that teaching is a triadic relation, tri polar process, involving the source of teaching (human or material), student and a set of activities designed and manipulated primarily to bring changes in the behaviour of the child.

**Analysis of Teaching**

- *Teaching—a Tri-polar Process:* 'As, education is described as a tri-polar process, teaching is also a tri-polar process. The three poles are (i) the teacher, (ii) the pupil and (iii) the subject matter. The teacher and the pupil interact with the help of subject matter to attain some pre-determined goals.
- *Teaching—Means of Preparation:* The teacher prepares the students for the future life with the help of teaching. So teaching is means of preparation. Physical mental, emotional, intellectual, spiritual, development take place with the help of teaching.
- *Teaching—Development of Communication Skill:* Teaching is an interaction between teacher and students. It is a communication process by which student and teacher influence each other by their ideas and learn something. The communication shall dominates the process of teaching. Teaching will be effective if the communication ability of the students, with it improves.
- *Teaching—Motivation to Learn:* As we can take the horse to the water tank but can't compel it to drink, in the same way, we can bring the child to the classroom but if he is not ready to learn, we can't force him. The teaching does not mean only to provide information but it means to motivate the students to learn. As it is a fact that

  *'A poor teacher tells,*
  *An average teacher explains,*
  *A good teacher demonstrates*
  *and a great teacher inspires.*

Burton considers teaching as the stimulation, guidance, direction and encouragement to learning. In this way teaching is only a means and its purpose is to provide guidance. It helps in the development of the child in a selected environment to adjust himself in the world in which he lives.

- *Teaching—Various Forms and Styles:* As education is of various types, in the same way, teaching may have various forms as formal or informal, functional or informational, training, conditioning, indoctrination, directional, institutional, descriptive or remedial etc. It depends on the teacher that in what type of circumstances he uses which type of teaching in a different style.
- *Teaching—Related to Time and Place:* The process of teaching is flexible. It depends on the capability, knowledge., efficiency of the teacher and the social environment. As the time passes, there is change in society, its ideals and its values. This is the reason that teaching is different in the different states of India as well as in different countries.
- *Teaching—Concerned with Observation and Analysis:* Teaching can be observed, analysed and assessed through teacher behaviour, pupil-teacher interaction and the changes brought in the behaviour of the pupils. This will help in bringing desirable changes in the process of teaching, way of learning and teaching-learning situations.
- *Teaching—An Interactive Process:* Teaching is a two way traffic. It is an interactive process carried out between the teacher and the child for the attainment of some specified objectives and goals.
- *Teaching—A Linguistic Process:* As teacher communicates ideas to the students in the process of teaching, so it is not possible without the use of language. The teacher is to explain the concepts, to motivate the students to describe the fact with the help of different languages.
- *Teaching—Multiple Levels:* Teaching relates with multiple levels—memory level, understanding level and reflective level. Each level is a complicated process in itself.
- *Teaching—As Continuum:* Teaching is a continuum for developing behaviour to the formation of beliefs. It has four modes of operations or behaviour *i.e.* conditioning, training, instruction and indoctrination. Thus teaching starts from conditioning and reaches upto indoctrination. It is concerned with shaping behaviour and habits; conduct and skills, communication of knowledge and formation of beliefs.
- *Teaching—An Art:* According to Douglas it has become increasingly evident that the teacher acts as director of learning activities in the classroom. Every minute and every situation in a classroom is to some extent is a novel one. Teaching is considered to be an art because use of different skills is involved in it as to disseminate knowledge, to maintain the interest and attention of the learner; to modify the behaviour of the students by handling their problem etc.

- *Teaching—As Science:* The scientific approach to teaching advocated by Davis points out that teaching is a process of managing human behaviour for learning. Teaching is a scientific process and its major components are content, communication and feedback. There is a close relationship between teaching and learning. The terminal behaviour of the student in terms of learning structures can be established by appropriate teaching environment. Teaching skills can be developed and strengthened by means of feedback devices with or without sophisticated techniques. The systematic order of providing knowledge, applying skills directly indicate that teaching is a science applied in nature. Teaching is an applied science because it incorporates systematic and methodical approach.
- *Teaching—A Profession:* Teaching is a profession which demands of its practitioners occupational qualities and sincere devotion to human betterment. Teaching involves intellectual operations. It qualifies the criteria of possessing an educationally communicable technique because of the reason that it emphasizes the involvement of intellectual competence, the ability to perform all those skilled services upon which the continued functioning of modern society depends. In this way teaching is a profession.

Thus teaching, as a whole, is aimed to bring changes in the behaviour of pupils. It helps in developing the personality of the child and prepares him to participate creatively in the activities of society.

**Characteristics of Teaching**

1. Teaching is a matter of drawing out rather than a matter of putting in any thing from outside.
2. It is encouragement and stimulation to the child,
3. It is imparting information.
4. It is formal as well as informal.
5. It is a linguistic process *i.e.* communication by the use of language.
6. It means helping the pupil to learn and to do things himself.
7. It is helping the child to adjust himself to his environment in an effective manner.
8. It is training of emotions of the child.
9. It prepares the children for life.
10. It is an interactive process or face to face contact between the teacher and the taught.
11. It is a professional activity.
12. It is an art as well as science.
13. It is modifiable by the mechanism of feedback devices.
14. It is both a conscious and unconscious process.
15. It is organisation of learning.

16. It is a tri-polar process.
17. It satisfies social needs.
18. It is a source of creativeness and recreation.
19. It is both diagnostic and remedial.
20. It inspires the pupils for independent study, self-development and self-advancement.

**Difference between Education and Teaching**

| | *Education* | *Teaching* |
|---|---|---|
| 1. Meaning | Education means to draw out the best of the child and man. | Teaching means to give knowledge and informations. |
| 2. Scope | The scope of education is very wide. It is a life-long process from birth to death *i.e.* it starts from the child's birth and continues up to death. | The scope of teaching is narrow and limited. It is confined to that period only for which the child remains in contact with the teacher. |
| 3. Period | Education is a life long process. | Period of teaching is confined to that period only when teacher teaches the child. |
| 4. Aspects | There are formal, informal and non-formal aspects of education. | Teaching is concerned with formal and non-formal aspects. |
| 5. Environment | Natural and artificial, both types of environment are provided in education. | The atmosphere in teaching is artificial. |
| 6. Importance | In education, the important place is given to the child. | The important place is given to the teacher. |
| 7. Methods of Teaching | The range of methods of imparting education is very wide. | Some fixed methods of teaching like lecture, demonstration, project and discussion methods are used. |
| 8. Teacher | Every members of the society can play the role of the teacher. | Teaching relates with qualified teachers. |
| 9. Discipline | Education believes in self-discipline. | In teaching emphasis is on strict discipline. |
| 10. Agencies | The agencies of education are radio, television, peer group, school, community, home, state, press etc. | Educational institutions are the agencies of teaching. |
| 11. Agents | The agents of education are parents and other family members, friends, colleagues, neighbours, community etc. | Teachers are the agents of teaching. |

| | | *Education* | *Teaching* |
|---|---|---|---|
| 12. | Process | Education is a continuous dynamic process. | Teaching is a static process. |
| 13. | Evaluation | The evaluation in education continues throughout the life. It may be direct as well as indirect. | In teaching evaluation is direct and by fixed methods to know the effectiveness of teaching and to test the understanding of pupils. |
| 14. | Relationship | Education relates with life. | Teaching relates with that knowledge which helps in passing the examination only. |
| 15. | Place | The place of education is the whole society. | The place of teaching is confined to educational institutions. |
| 16. | Planning | It may be planned as well as incidental. | It is always planned and methodological. |
| 17. | Area of Development | Education aims at the multi sided development of the child | Teaching primarily aims at cognitive development. |
| 18. | Approach | Approach is flexible | Approach is rather rigid. |
| 19. | Co-curricular Activities | A variety of activities are organised. | Activities related to cognitive development are given more prominence. |

Thus it can be said that teaching is only a part of education, not the whole education. The process of education goes on from sun rise to sun set and the teaching activities are in operation only when teacher is involved in teaching and students are in learning.

## III. TRAINING

Training is to provide perfection in any skill. It implies identification, development and perfection of skill and competence of the learner, It consists of drilling and practice as practice makes a man perfect. It is primarily concerned with developing professional competencies, and psychomotor dimensions of man's personality. It aims at operating efficiency in manual and technical skills. It aims at practising professional, vocationally useful techniques and skills. It prepares skilled workers. Education primarily involves preparation of theoreticians while training trains technicians who might become specialists where both theory and practice are mastered in an integrated way leading to higher professional education.

It is concerned with the use of new labour saving services and problem solving techniques practised by technicians whereas education is concerned with understanding their importance. It also perceives in different meanings as formal training under the traditional concept of faculty, psychology;

training to cultivate, control and generalise instincts, emotions and desires; which means to bring out the best in man to raise him to the desired state of standard of efficiency by constant practice. Bringing out the best is the end of education and training as such is an important tool of education.

The concept of training includes:

Education has a conscious purpose to train the children for fulfilling responsibilities of adult life. Animals are also trained by initiating the actions of adults but in their training the purpose is neither conscious nor well designed. Since the children have to enter in complicated society when they grow adults, so education provides them training for adult life. An individual needs training to use his own resources so that thereby he may learn to live orderly life or a normal life.

Education is the training of the eyes and the mind, so that the individual should make correct responses to the problems and the opportunities of life. Responses are of two kinds: physical and mental. If a child bows automatically while he is in the company of others, he may be called a trained child and his response is physical response. If the child bows out of respect, then he may be called an educated child and this is his mental response. Thus true education means training of the individual to discriminate between good and evil both at the level of physical as well as mental response. The body and the brain are to be trained so that they do the right thing in the right manner at the right time. In short, education is the training of the intellect, body and spirit.

**Analysis of Training**

1. *Emphasis:* More stress on psycho-motor development,
2. *Part of education:* It is a part of education not the whole.
3. *Scope:* Its scope is limited.
4. *Practical:* More emphasis is on practical aspect.
5. *Emotions:* It is far away from emotions.
6. *Skills:* It helps in developing and attaining perfection of skills.
7. *Competencies:* It helps in developing professional of competencies.
8. *Activities:* It lays stress on desired outer activities.
9. *Period:* It is time bound.
10. *Belief:* It believes in physical responses.
11. *Teacher:* The teacher works as the trainer.
12. *Discipline:* It implies strict rules and regulations for students.
13. *Process:* It is imparted by an instructor to a trainee in a formal and systematic manner.
14. *Institutions:* It is almost always provided in specific institutes.
15. *Area:* It is confined to training only.

**Difference between Education and Training**

| | | *Education* | *Training* |
|---|---|---|---|
| 1. | Mode | Education is imparted formally, informally and non-formally. | Training is imparted by a trainer in a formal, planned and systematic way. |
| 2. | Scope | It has a wider scope. | It has a limited scope. |
| 3. | Aim | The aim of education is all round development of the personality | The aim is to develop a particular skill in the trainee. |
| 4. | Process | Education is a life long process. It starts from the day of conception and continues till death. | It is imparted in the fixed duration by trained persons to untrained. |
| 5. | Benefits | Material and non-material benefits are derived from it. | It leads only to material benefits. |
| 6. | Teacher | In informal education all the members of society helps in modifying the behaviour of the child whereas specialist teachers teach in formal education. | Specially trained teachers in different areas provide skilled training. |
| 7. | Agencies | Formal, informal and non-formal agencies are involved in the process of educating the child. | Only formal agencies provide training to the trainee. |
| 8. | Curriculum | There is definite curriculum, in formal and to some extent in non-formal education of theoretical as well as of practical nature. | Definite curriculum with the dominance of practical aspect. |
| 9. | Approach | Education as a discipline does not always be in rigid approach. | It has always a rigid approach. |
| 10. | Evaluation | Evaluation is done in formal education as well as non-formal education but not in informal education. | Evaluation is always done on the completion of the training. |
| 11, | Certificate | Certificates are provided in formal education not in informal education. | Certificates are provided to the trainees after the completion of their training. |
| 12. | Programme | Education does not have a specific programme to follow. | Training has a specified programme to be followed. |
| 13. | Importance | It helps the child to become a useful member of the society. | A trained man may or may not be a social one. |
| 14. | Sources of Inspiration | There are many sources of inspiration in education. | Economic aspect is the main source of inspiration in training. |

Thus all training is education but all education is not training. It is the reason that training colleges have re-named as colleges of education. Education has a broader area or surface to cover training.

## IV. INDOCTRINATION

Some believe that indoctrination is a part of educational process and in fact some have equated it with education. Indoctrination is a word derived from 'doctrine' which means a 'principle' or 'thought' or 'point of view'. So, it has come to mean as efforts to make a person or a group of persons blind followers of a principle. The aim of it is to bring about changes in beliefs, ideas and thinking of the child. It is also called a brain washing process.

The term is employed only when there is the direct objective of changing the faith or connection of a person or a group. It aims at advocating and imposing a doctrine or notion through the dictates of authority. It involves strict discipline, control and obedience to the rule. Being dictatorial in nature, its force is inevitable. It is a powerful tool of direct teaching and regiment instructions and an important instrument for affecting behaviour modification along a set pattern.

In indoctrination, on the one hand there is very limited quality of knowledge to be believed to the child, while on the other hand, the method employed for this purpose is also quite different from the methods used either in education or in instruction. It touches the cognitive aspect literally; since it focusses primarily on the conative or sentimental part of the personality.

Authoritarianism is the hall mark of indoctrination. As such authoritarian schools treat indoctrination as the only method of imparting education. They make instructions teacher dominated and curriculum or content authority directed. These schools are so structured that they make the learner totally dependent on the teacher. There is little freedom for the child to learn by himself or to direct the process of learning as per needs, aspiration and interest. Everything including aims and objectives, content and subject matter, activities and programmes for the education are selected and settled by the authorities. The learner is simply a passive recipient of the learning experiences which kill his initiative and curiosity. It makes learning dull.

It is uni-directional or one sided, with the whole purpose of forcing information, ideas, practices from outside as a part of education. It follows the techniques of rote learning and repeated drilling to make learning mechanical as well as monotonous. It treats the learner as mere empty picture to be filled by what the teacher chooses to fill. It regards the learner as an object and the teacher as the subject of the learning process.

### Analysis of Indoctrination

1. *Discipline:* It involves strict discipline.
2. *Direction:* It is unidirectional.
3. *Effect:* It brings change in ideas end beliefs.
4. *Belief:* It believes in education by imposition.
5. *Approach:* It is teacher dominated,

6. *Logic:* It suppresses logical thinking.
7. *Aim:* It is goal directed.
8. *Age:* Childhood is generally believed to be the best period for indoctrination,
9. *Aspect:* It bypasses the individual's cognitive faculty and impinges purely upon his conative faculty.
10. *Use:* It is employed primarily in religion and politics.
11. *Direction:* It directs itself towards neither the student nor the teacher, but to the doctrines which are sought to be inculcated in the learner's mind.
12. *Objective:* Its objectives is to bring change in the behaviour pattern of the learner.
13. *Curriculum:* Its curriculum is authoritative.
14. *Technique:* The techniques of rote learning are followed.
15. *Dominance:* It depends mainly upon the predominance of sentiments, not upon that of reason.

*Difference between Education and Indoctrination*

| | *Education* | *Indoctrination* |
|---|---|---|
| 1. Aim | Its aim is the all round development of the personality. | Its aim is to bring about change in behaviour, attitudes, values and beliefs in a particular direction. |
| 2. Scops | The scope is very wide. | The scope is limited and narrow. |
| 3. Importance | It is child centered. | It is belief centered *i.e.* ideas, beliefs, values are given prime importance than child. |
| 4. Process | It is a life long process. | The childhood is the best period because at this stage his mind is not developed for the arguments. |
| 5. Type of students | Modification of behaviour is more pronounced in intelligent students. | It is successful on the persons with lower level of intelligence. |
| 6. Development | It develops the power of reasoning, independent thinking and rational judgement among the students. | Students are induced to have blind faith. 'Do and die' and never ask 'why'. |
| 7. Type | It is both formal and informal. | It is predominantly formal. |
| 8. Environment | The natural as well as artificial environment is provided. | Only artificial environment is provided dominated by authority. |
| 9. Curriculum | Curriculum is provided related to whole life. | Curriculum is confined only to beliefs, ideas, and values related to political, social and moral aspects. |
| 10. Methods of Teaching | Various methods are used to provide education. | Only lecture method is emphasised. Poem recitation, music etc. also play their important role. |
| 11. Discipline | Society plays an important role in the discipline. | Strict discipline is provided. |

| | *Education* | *Indoctrination* |
|---|---|---|
| 12. Approach | It is individual oriented. The interest of an individual child kept in mind while providing education. | It is knowledge centered. Teacher centers only the ideas and beliefs. |
| 13. Influence | Education influences all the aspects of life. | It influences only the political and religious aspects. |
| 14. Freedom | It provides freedom to the child to learn. | There is no freedom to the child to learn by himself. |
| 15. Evaluation | Evaluation may be done by-watching social adjustment of the person. | The beliefs and ideas play important role and evaluation of the person is done on the basis of these criteria only. |

Thus education is the process of learning and teaching, in which the educand and educator interact with each other, exchange thoughts, argue etc. but indoctrination does not allow any argument. It directs itself only to the doctrines which are sought to be inculcated in the mind of the learner.

## V. LEARNING

Learning is a key process in human behaviour. All the skills, knowledge, habits, attitude, interests and other personality characteristics are the result of learning. It involves new ways of doing things and attempts to adjust to new situations. It is a continuous process which starts right from the time of birth of an individual and continues till the death. We all are engaged in the learning and endeavours in order to develop adaptive capabilities as per the requirements of the changing environment.

*Gates and others, "Learning is the modification in behaviour to meet environmental requirements."*

*Freemen, "Learning is the process of acquiring the ability to respond adequately to a situation which may or may not have been previously encountered."*

*Colvin, "Learning is the modification of the reactions of an organism through experiences."*

*Skinner, "Learning is a process of progressive behaviour adaptation."*

*Kolb, "Learning is the process whereby knowledge is created through the transformation of experience."*

*Munn, "Learning is the process of being modified, more or less permanently, by what happens in the world around us, by what we do, and by what we observe."*

*Heidgerken, "Learning is not an addition of new experiences, 'per se', nor it is old experiences summed up, rather it is synthesis of old and the new experiences which result in completely new organisation or pattern of experience."*

*Harriman, "Learning is the improvement in efficiency of adjustment as a result of practice, insight, observation, imitation and conditioning".*

Thus the psychologists and educationists define the concept of learning in their own way. Learning has no universally agreed definition. The way, one defines it emanates from as well as influences, the way one theorize learning. Thus there are as many definitions as there are theories of learning.

**Analysis of Learning**

1. *Learning—is growth:* Learning is growth through experiences, because the learner grows mentally through his/her daily activities. Although it is latent, yet we can perceive the growth.
2. *Learning—is intelligent:* When a child learns something unintelligently, he is likely to forget it very soon. Meaningless efforts do not produce permanent learning. Only those efforts, which done intelligently, have lasting effects.
3. *Learning—an active process:* While learning, the learner uses sensory inputs and constructs meaning out of it. Learner needs to do something. Learning is not the passive acceptance of knowledge which exists. It does not take place without a purpose and self activity.
4. *Learning—an organizing experience:* Learning is not mere acquisition of facts and skills through skill and repetition. It is not mere an addition to the previous knowledge. It is the reorganization of experiences through constructivism.
5. *Learning—is contexual:* We do not learn isolated facts and theories. We learn in relationship to what else we know, what we believe, our prejudices and our fears. We cannot separate our learning from our life.
6. *Learning—both individual and social:* Learning is both individual as well as social activity. Individual is always influenced by friends, relatives, peers, teachers, parents etc. and learns their ideas, feelings and notions. Social agencies like home, school, community etc. have tremendous influence on the child. Thus an individual learns at his own as well as through society also.
7. *Learning—time consuming process:* Learning is not spontaneous. We need to revisit the ideas before applying them. Learning takes place with the help of experiences gained time to time. If we reflect on anything that we have learned, we soon realize that it is the product of repeated exposures and thoughts.
8. *Learning—product of the environment:* Environment plays an important role in the growth and development of an individual. If the environment will be healthy in the educative process, the learning will be enhanced.
9. *Learning—affects the conduct of learner:* After every experience, there is a change in the mental structure of the learner. It also affects the conduct of the learner.

10. *Learning—goal oriented:* Learning takes place as a result of response in some situations. No learning will take place, unless the individual has some unsatisfied need or drive. It is caused by that need and oriented towards a goal.

In this way learning includes:

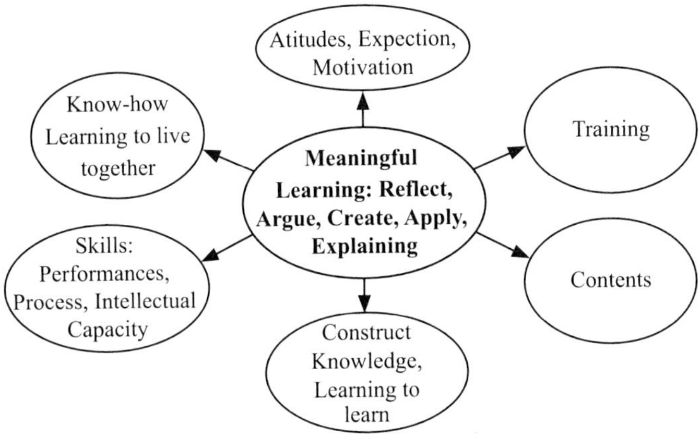


**Fig. 3.1: Aspects of Learning**

Thus learning is the process of acquiring knowledge, skills, values etc. As we grow up, we acquire new experiences and exposed to various situations. Learning usually creates a change in the individual. The world around the child fascinates him, making him eager to learn new things.

## Characteristics of Learning

1. Learning is a process and a product.
2. Learning prepares an individual for adjustment and adaptation that may be necessary.
3. It is an addition to his previous experiences.
4. It is purposeful.
5. Its scope is too wide covers nearly all fields—conative, cognitive and affective.
6. It is universal and continuous.
7. It leads to change in behaviour.
8. It is intelligent comprehension.
9. It is a synthesis and integration of old and new experiences.
10. It results in change in behaviour.
11. It is relatively a permanental change.
12. It is not directly observable.

13. It is vertical and horizontal.
14. It is intentional or incidental.
15. It is transferable.

### *Difference between Education and Learning*

Mark Twain once said, *"The only thing that enterprises with my learning is my education."* Both education and learning are two words that are related with the acquisition of knowledge. Education is the process of receiving or getting or giving systematic instructions, especially at an institution where as learning is the acquisition of knowledge or skill through study or experience. It is important to notice that not only humans have the ability to learn, but animals, plants, and even some machines also have the ability to learn. The difference between these two is as follows:

1. Education is a process through which a society passes on the knowledge, values and skills from one generation to the other.
   Learning is a process of acquiring new skills, knowledge and values.
2. Education is imparting of knowledge, values, skills, attitudes, etc. that can be beneficial for an individual. Learning is the process of adopting knowledge, skills, values, attitudes etc.
3. An individual gets education from an outside source *i.e.*, from any school, college, university or from informal agencies like community, mass-media etc.
   Learning evolves in the inner-self. An individual learns from his surroundings.
4. Education has set standards where as there are no set standard of learning.
5. Education is acquired by an individual.
   Learning is the basic instinct possessed by the individuals.
6. Education is knowledge gained through teaching, instruction, indoctrination etc.
   Learning is knowledge gained through experiences.
7. Education is well organised.
   Learning is something that is related to an individual's perception.
8. Education is something that one gets at some point in his/her life.
   Learning is an ongoing process.
9. Education is formal, informal and non-formal process.
   Learning is an informal process.
10. Education is a basic human right.
    Learning is not the human right, depends upon individual's instinct.
11. Multiple students can get education under a certified, trained teacher in one classroom.
    Learning is individualistic.
12. Education has extrinsic value because the term education cannot be used to measure the knowledge or the content of individual's learning.

13. Education can be limited to a number of years.
    Learning occurs throughout the life span of an individual.
14. Education can work as a mechanism for conformity, but learning does not.
15. Education is a push model, an attempt to extend some one's knowledge or skills.
    Learning is a pull model, an act of absorbing and extending knowledge or skills.
16. Education is for livelihood, learning is for life.

Thus education employs learning is a process to bring about change. However, since learning would happen due to a planned act or due to chance, it could be seen as the bigger umbrella.

**Fig. 3.2: Relationship between Education and Learning**

Education is the prerequisite but cannot ensure learning. The student can memorise the content to pass the examination and get the certificate but it does not mean he has learning also. The learning pull can occur with or without the education push, and the education push may or may not result in learning.

## VI. SCHOOLING

Education and schooling go hand in hand, so, many people think that these two terms have the same meaning, but, education and schooling are not the same concepts. The concept of schooling is extremely important in education. Its principle premise in that schooling is instrumental to success in life. It helps the child to be able to function effectively in the world. School is the initial stage of formal education in most countries. Webster's Dictionary defines schooling as 'the process of being taught, such as in school'.

It is often thought to occur in the lower grades, where children are taught the basics which enable them to continue learning at the higher educational institution.

Schooling is also thought to be accomplished in a particular vocational skill or trade as a 'mechanics' or 'beauty' school.

The historical evidence of education institutions similar to school in the present day runs back to the days of ancient Greek, Rome and Indian civilizations. In all these ancient contexts attendance to formal education institutions was considered a privilege and depended on social classes. Since the child begins in ignorance, he needs instructions, training and schooling to grow from infancy to maturity. It implies identification and cultivation of individual strength for a meaningful life.

In the words of John Dewey, *"School is a special environment where certain qualities of life and certain type of activities and occupations are provided with the object of child's development along desirable lines."*

It means preparation for life is an end of schooling. It refers to the activities and curricula of general as well as of technical kind at school level, which is useful and relevant for success. As such it is the process of systematic organisation of education at different levels of schooling as primary, secondary and senior secondary level.

The concept of schooling was begin with 3R's (Reading, Writing and Arithmetic) to provide the knowledge of basic literatures, humanities and science essential for intellectual growth of the child. The knowledge was not only treated to be useful for general success in life but also as the strength of the foundation for higher education in different subjects and disciplines including the technical, vocational and professionals.

The concept of modern schooling though in the liberal spirit includes also a bit of preliminary vocational skills to make schooling a little broad based, yet the fundamental concern of schooling remains primarily on intellectual development which is the cornerstone of success in life and in different streams of education available for further studies.

Schooling is a formal form of education where students are taught in a classroom about different subjects based on the prescribed curriculum including different activities. Teachers direct their lesson plans around the core of the curriculum for the students to be successful according to the society. One can be educated without schooling also.

No one actually knows when formal schooling began. Could it have been with the cavemen training their children with the survival skills to continue their lives, and pass their skills on to countless generations of descendents? Prior to written language, learning processes existed solely as oral traditions. Societies were developed based on communicating this knowledge or 'schooling' the next generation. One of the earlier examples of schooling found, was in Egypt, around 3000 BC.

There are different varieties of schooling that have been popular and unpopular over the last several centuries. Grouping students together at common places has existed and continued since the ancient Greek times. Another method of schooling is called 'self-paced'. It is when the students learn at their own pace and they are not forced to follow a fixed curriculum. Home schooling is also another type of schooling.

Thus in schooling teachers try to drill learning in to the people according to some plan often drawn up by others. Pasulo Freire famously called this banking making deposits of knowledge.

### Analysis of Schooling

- Process: It is the process of systematic organisation of education.
- Importance: It is an important instruments of education.
- Base: It provides the foundation for higher education.
- Aim: The hall mark of schooling is a disciplined way of life.
- Purpose: It caters to transmit the knowledge from one generation to other.
- Logic: Its aim is to provide conditions and resources favourable for systematic education.
- Curriculum: It has specific curricula intended for each age group or grades.
- Student: The students are educated in classroom sitting with teachers acting as resources persons.
- Teaching Process: The teaching process is pre-scheduled.
- Approach: A rigid structure involved in everything including student categorization, administration and promotion to higher levels.

### Difference between Education and Schooling

| | *Education* | *Schooling* |
|---|---|---|
| 1. | Education is imparted formally, informally and non-formally. | Schooling is the first stage of formal education in most of the countries. |
| 2. | It has a wider scope. | It has a limited scope. |
| 3. | Education is a life long process. | Its duration is fixed. |
| 4. | Education influences all aspects of life. | It lays emphasis on the development of certain capabilities and skills. |
| 5. | Education is acquired by a child naturally. | The education got by schooling is artificial |
| 6. | Education has no specified curriculum, duration, time, methods or programmes. | It has specified curriculum, duration, time, method and programmes. |
| 7. | Evaluation is a life long process in education. | Evaluation takes place after a certain period of time and certificates are awarded after passing the examination. |
| 8. | It starts from the day of conception and continues till death. | It starts from the day the child enters in the school and ends when the child leaves the school after the completion of his/her studies. |
| 9. | In informal education all the measures of the society helps in modifying the behaviour of the child whereas specialist educators teach in formal and non-formal education. | In schooling only the trained and specialist educators teach the child. |
| 10. | Formal, informal and non-informal agencies are involved in the process of education. | Only private and public schools are involved in the schooling. |
| 11. | Education as a discipline does not always fit in rigid approach. | It has always a rigid approach. |
| 12. | The range of methods of education is very wide. | It is usually confined to discussion, question-answer, experiment and test book methods. |

| | *Education* | *Schooling* |
|---|---|---|
| 13. | Social disruptive and social control are involved in education. | It is associated with structures. |
| 14. | There are many sources of inspiration in education. | Mental development is the main source of inspiration. |
| 15. | It prepares the child to face life situations and to workout the solutions of problems. | Schooling prepares the child for higher education. |

Thus schooling stands for the formal education system and take place in school while the term education include a number of different sources of knowledge *i.e.* formal, informal and non-formal. Schooling is only a part of education. It is only a means, neither the beginning nor the end of education.

The aim of education is all round development of personality. Teaching helps in achieving the aim of education. Training helps in developing skills. Indoctrination helps m bringing changes in affective aspect of behaviour, thoughts, beliefs and values. Teaching, schooling, instruction, indoctrination and learning play important roles in fulfilling aims of education.

# 4

# Epistemological Basis of Education

*"Epistemology is the theory of knowledge, especially with regard to its methods, validity and scope and the distinction between justified belief and opinion."*

The term epistemology comes from the Greek word 'episteme' which means 'knowledge' or 'to know', The concern of this branch of philosophy is mainly with the theory of knowledge. It deals with knowledge as a universal matter and aims to discover what is involved in the process of knowing. It is the study of nature of knowledge, justification and the rationality of belief. The main concern of epistemology is the philosophical analysis of the nature of knowledge and how. It relates to such concepts as truth, belief and justification. It addresses the questions as:

- What makes justified beliefs justified?
- Is knowing a special sort of mental act?
- What does it mean to say that we know something?
- How do we know that we know?
- Does knowing make any difference to the object known?
- Can we know something beyond the objects with which our senses acquaint us?

The idea of epistemological predates the word. John Locke describes it as an inquiry "into the original, certainty and extent of human knowledge, together with the grounds and degrees of belief, opinion and assent."

## KNOWLEDGE

One of the basic question of epistemology concerns the nature of knowledge.

*"Knowledge is power."* – Hobbes

Philosophy, according to Locke, is the true knowledge of things, including the nature of things (physics), that which man ought to do as a rational voluntary agent (ethics or practice), and the ways and means of attaining and communicating such knowledge (logic).

All our knowledge is founded on, and ultimately derived from experience. The two sources of all our ideas are sensation, through which the mind is furnished with sensible qualities and reflection, or internal sense, which supplies the mind with ideas of its own operations, such as perception, thinking, doubting, believing, reasoning, knowing, willing etc.

They know enough who know how to learn.

All knowledge is but remembrance.

All the knowledge that we mortals can acquire is not knowledge positive, but knowledge comparative and subject to the errors and passions of humanity.

There are four sorts of men:

*He who knows not and not knows he knows not:*
*he is a fool—shun him;*
*He who knows not and knows he knows not:*
*he is simple—teach him.*
*He who knows and knows not he knows:*
*he is asleep—wake him.*
*He who knows and knows he knows:*
*he is wise—follow him.*

## Meaning of Knowledge

Every man has a desire to know but the first half is for interest, the other for show. A man of the best parts and greatest learning, if he does not know the world by his own experience and observation, will be very absurd, and consequently very unwelcome in company. He may say very good things, but they will be probably so ill-timed, misplaced or improperly addressed, that he had much better hold his tongue.

There are three classes of people in the world. The first learn from their own experiences—these are wise, the second learn from the experiences of others—these are the happy; the third neither learn from their own experiences nor from the experiences of others—these are fools.

> *"Knowledge without common sense," says Lee, "is folly; without method, it is waste; without kindness, it is fanaticism; without religion, it is death". But with common sense, it is wisdom; with method, it is power; with charity, it is beneficence; with religion, it is virtue, life and peace".*
>
> –Farrar

Spencer believes that knowledge is a complete unified system of thought. The knowledge of the ordinary man is ununified, disconnected, inconsistent means the various parts do not hang together. Science furnishes us with partially unified knowledge. Philosophy, however is completely a unified knowledge, an organic system. Its problem is to discover the highest truth from which the principles of mechanics, physics, biology, sociology and ethics can be deduced.

Every addition to true knowledge is an addition to human power. Generally the word knowledge is used in three meanings.

1. *Acquaintance:* When we are acquainted with some person then we think that we have knowledge about that person. But the whole knowledge is not related with mere acquaintance. If we want to know about a person, we can get the knowledge about him with the other sources also.

2. *Ability to do something:* Sometimes the word knowledge is used in terms of ability to do some thing as a teacher teaches, a swan swims. The term ability means the efficiency to do some work.
3. *Propositional knowledge:* This type of meaning is important in the area of philosophy. When we say that we know it means we know something, as I know teaching, our mother tongue is Hindi, is propositional knowledge.

> *Half knowledge is worse than ignorance.*
> *Knowledge advances by steps, and not by leaps.*

Thus knowledge is of much importance to the man. In modern period, there is much explosion of knowledge. There is no limit or boundaries of knowledge. It is in itself a complete whole. A man living on this earth can't say that he knows everything. It is not so important to know everything as to know the exact value of everything, to appreciate what we learn, and to arrange what we know. Today the real scientist feels that the ocean of knowledge is a vast and boundless one, and though he seeks to sail on it, he is humbler and more hesitating than his predecessors.

It is well for us to realize that the great increase in knowledge in this world does not necessarily make us better or wiser. We must know how to use that knowledge properly before we can fully profit by it. We must know whether to go before we rush ahead in our powerful car. We must, that is, have some idea of what the aim and object of life should be. Vast number of people today have no such notion and never worry about it. This present period, is the period of science. Everything is changing and relates to reasoning. But the ideas that govern the man and their actions belong to ages long past. It is natural that problems and difficulties should arise. A clever monkey may learn to drive a car, but he is hardly a safe chauffeur.

Modern knowledge is amazingly intricate and widespread. The field of knowledge is so vast that each worker has to be a specialist in his own field. Often a man is unaware of other departments of knowledge, and as a result, though he is very learned in some branches of knowledge, he is unlearned about many others. It becomes difficult for him to take a wise view of the whole field of human activity.

The wise man realizes how little he knows: it is the foolish person who imagines that he knows everything.

In India, as in China, learning and erudition have always stood high in public esteem, for learning was supposed to imply both superior knowledge and virtue. Before the learned man, the ruler and the warrior have always bowed.

## Forms of Knowledge

There are three things, which are interrelated and interdependent—Information, Knowing and Wisdom.

1. *Information:* A person can have the information about other person, thing, place, happening or about any other aspects of human life. This is low level of knowledge. The reason behind it is that an uneducated person can collect the information from different sources and provides it to the other person. It is not related with the process of mental development. It can be in the form of qualitative as well as quantitative or both.
2. *Knowing:* Knowing is that form of knowledge, through which we provide meaningful status to the knowledge of abstract and concrete. We provide meaning to different terms. It presents the truth and reality. It includes mental change. Mind is developed in this process. It is medium level of knowledge.
3. *Wisdom:* Wisdom is related with the experiences of reality which is related-with life, world and inter connection between them. It is based on information and knowing.

> *"It is wise to get knowledge and learning from every source—from a sot, a pot, a fool, a winter—mitten or an old slipper."* –Rabelais
>
> *"Knowledge describes, wisdom applies"* –Quarles

The human mind is not only the idea of the body, but is at the same time conscious of own actions or self conscious. This is the highest level of knowledge.

Knowledge comes, but wisdom lingers.

Spinoza distinguishes three principal levels of cognition:

1. Obscure and inadequate ideas have their source in sensation and the imagination; they depend on sense perception, which has, as its objects, the modification of the body. Uncritical experience and mere opinion do not yield genuine knowledge.
2. We also have adequate knowledge, clear and distinct ideas and rational knowledge. Reason contemplates things as they are, knows their necessary connections, conceives them under the form of eternity. It comprehends the universal essence of things and understands these in relation to God's being: such knowledge is self evident.
3. It advances from an adequate ideas of the objective essence of certain attributes of God to the adequate essence of things. By it everything is conceived as necessary grounded in God's being and following from it. This is the highest kind of knowledge. It enables us to distinguish between truth and error.

## Characteristics of Knowledge

1. Knowledge is like money; the more a man gets, the more he craves.
2. Knowledge, is truth, is the great sun in the firmament.
3. Knowledge, like religion must be experienced in order to be known.

4. Knowledge is the only fountain: both of love and the principle of human liberty.
5. Knowledge once gained casts a light beyond its own immediate boundaries.
6. Facts and values are the basis of the structure of knowledge.
7. Knowledge advances by steps, not by leaps.
8. Knowledge never decays.
9. Information is the source to knowledge.
10. Knowledge is power.
11. Knowledge exists to be imparted.
12. Knowledge is the consequence of time.
13. Knowledge is boundless.
14. The word knowledge implies three things viz, truth, proof and conviction.

Thus the desire of knowledge is like the thirst of riches, which increases even with the acquisition of it. In this life, nothing is more estimable after health and virtue than knowledge. The seeds of knowledge may be planted in solitude, but must be cultivated in public,

## Types of Knowledge

Knowledge always appears in the form of judgements in which something is affirmed or denied, but not every judgement is knowledge. In broader sense knowledge is of two types:

1. *A Priori Knowledge:* There are such judgements never doubted for a moment. We find them in the basic principles of physics and in mathematics. The existence of such knowledge is in metaphysics. There is no causal judgement without a mind, thinking in terms of cause and effect. To be knowledge, a synthetic judgement must be necessary and it must be universal *i.e.* admit of no exception. Universality and necessity have their source not in sensation or perception, but in reason. We know without experience and in the sense prior to it—that the sum of the angles of a triangle must be equal to two right angles and that it will always be so, Thus analytical judgements are always a priori. We know without going to experience that all extended things are extended. Such judgements are based upon the principle of contradiction alone.
2. *Empirical or a Posteriori Knowledge:* Empirical knowledge is derived from experiences. It informs us, for example, that an object has such and such properties or behaves thus or so but not that it must have these qualities. In other words, such judgements, are lacking in necessity. Reason does not compel their acceptance, as it compels the acceptance of a mathematical proposition. They are lacking in universality. We cannot say, because some objects of a class have certain qualities, that all have these.

This type of knowledge is not scientific. A posteriori judgements add to the knowledge. But the knowledge yielded is uncertain and problematic. This type of knowledge is gained through observation, perception, supervision and experiences.

In view of Indian philosophers, knowledge is of two types:

1. *Para Vidya:* The knowledge which we get with the help of our sense organ and reasoning is known as para vidya. It is related with the outer material world. Our knowledge is the amassed thoughts and experience of innumerable minds.
2. *Apara Vidya:* The end of learning is to know God, and out of that knowledge to love Him, and to initiate Him, as we may be nearest, by possessing our souls of true virtue. Apara vidya is related with the knowledge about the other world *i.e.* spirituality. This is the highest knowledge of human nature. It is well to say "Know thyself."

## Other Types of Knowledge

1. *Intuitive Knowledge:* All knowledge is gained by means of ideas and our most certain knowledge is nothing but the perception of the connection or agreement and disagreement of any of our ideas. We perceive that white is not black, that the idea of black and idea of white do not agree. This is intuitive knowledge. The mind perceives at once that white is not black, that a circle is not a triangle, that three is greater than two. This is the clearest and most certain knowledge. It need not be proved and cannot be proved. It is irresistible, self evident. On the certainty of direct intuition depends whatever certainty and evidence our knowledge possesses.
2. *Demonstrative Knowledge:* Sometimes our mind, though it is unable to perceive the agreement or disagreement between two ideas immediately, can establish it indirectly by comparing them with one or more other ideas. This knowledge by intervening ideas is called mediate, rational or demonstrative knowledge. Its proof is certain, yet its evidence is not quite so clear and bright, nor the assent so ready as in intuitive knowledge. Such demonstration is employed in mathematics and wherever the mind can perceive the agreement or disagreement of ideas with the help of intermediate ideas.
3. *Sensitive Knowledge:* Ordinary perception, when we are awake, affords a kind of evidence which is beyond any reasonable doubt. This knowledge of the particular existence of external things goes beyond bare possibility. Locke calls it sensitive knowledge. The apprehension we have by our senses of the existence of things outside us, though not so certain as intuitive knowledge or the deduction of the reason, yet has an assurance that entities it to the name of knowledge.
4. *Authoritative Knowledge:* Most of our knowledge is neither based on reasoning *i.e.* demonstrative knowledge and nor gained by perception.

We have knowledge about some principles that are permanent, irresistible and universal as earth revolves around the sun. These facts are proved by scientists. We read them from the books and some knowledge is provided by our teachers. This type of knowledge is given by some authorities and this is the reason that it is known as authoritative knowledge.

5. *Pragmatic Knowledge:* Sometimes we base our conclusions on experiences. This type of knowledge is based on philosophy of pragmatism *i.e.* based on the idea of John Dewey. The evidence of matter of fact which lies beyond the testimony of sense or memory is derived entirely from the relation of cause and effect. This type of knowledge is based on experiences, experiments and observations. This is individualised knowledge and helps the individual to adjust according to the environment.
6. *Revealed Knowledge:* Besides the two substances, body and mind, there is another spiritual substance, God. We have no innate idea of God, but we may, by the right use of our innate abilities, attain a knowledge of him. It is as certain that there is a God as that the opposite angles formed by the intersection of two straight lines are equal. This is revealed that the knowledge provided in Vedas is revealed by some great persons and then they were written in their own words. Quran by Muslims, Bible by Christians, Guru Granth Sahib by Sikhs and Vedas by Hindu are said to be revealed. This type of knowledge is gained in religious books. This knowledge is universal and traditional. Man knows with certainty that he himself exists. He also knows that bare nothing cannot produce real things.

Thus we have an empirical knowledge of right and wrong, a demonstrative knowledge and a revealed knowledge. God has so arranged it that, given a desire for happiness in human nature, man will evolve a moral code to promote the happiness. God has also endowed him with reason which will enable him to acquire knowledge and moral truths by demonstration. Finally, he has revealed in the scriptures the same laws which can be reached by experience and reason.

## BELIEF

Epistemology has a second, justificatory or normative function. Philosophers concerned with that function ask themselves, what kind of belief (if any) can be rationally justified. The normative approach quickly takes one into the central domain of epistemology raising questions as:

- Is knowledge identical with justified true belief?
- Is the difference between knowledge and belief merely matter of probability?
- What is justification?

In epistemology, philosophies use the term 'belief' to refer to personal attitude associated with true or false ideas and concepts. However, belief does not require active introspection and circumspection. In common speech, a 'statement of belief' is typically an expression of faith or trust in a person, power or other entity—while it includes such traditional views, epistemology is also concerned with what we believe. This includes 'the truth' and everything else we accept as 'true' for ourselves from cognitive point of view.

It is a conviction that we generally accept to be true, especially without evidence. They are the assumptions, we have about the world and our values, attitudes and behaviour are generally influenced by these beliefs. They grow from different sources; they can stem from what we see, hear, read and experience.

For example if a person believes that a bridge is safe enough to support him, and attempts to cross it, but the bridge then collapses under his weight, it could be said that he believed that the bridge was safe but that his belief was mistaken.. it would not be accurate to say that he knew that the bridge was safe, because plainly it was not. By contrast, if the bridge actually supported his weight, then the person might say that he had believed the bridge was safe, whereas now, after proving it to himself (by crossing it) he knows it was safe.

On the other hand, *beliefs can also stem from what is taught.* For example, religious beliefs do not naturally, usually taught from childhood. It is usually a generalisation as a person may believe that killing is bad, consuming alcohol is bad, but every religion will not support these beliefs.

*The beliefs are difficult to change.* Any person can continue to hold any belief if they would really like to. Beliefs are everything we hold in our field as truth. These beliefs are our programming that creates our reality. The universe is a mirror reflecting back to you what you hold as belief, both consciously and subconsciously.

*Belief is often contrasted with knowledge.* For example, I do not know where he lives, but I believe he lives in India. Knowledge is what we aim at in all our enquiries and investigations. But often we cannot get it. Belief is a second book. It is not what we wanted, but it is better than nothing. The differences between knowledge and belief is just a difference of degree. There are many different degrees of belief, ranging all the way from merely suspecting or surmising at the one end, to complete conviction at the other. Knowledge is the name we give to the highest degree of belief-believing a proposition with complete conviction, being absolutely sure about it.

In the word of Plato, "Something that is a justified true belief is knowledge."

Let us discuss the terms used in this quotation to understand it.:

'Justified' means something that is rational and reasonable.
'Truth' means something that is in accordance with fact.
'Belief' means something one holds to be true.

So, if you have a belief, you have a reason enough to believe in, and if your belief is in accordance with the truth, it becomes your knowledge.

*Belief is a psychological state.* A belief is not something that can be seen, heard, smelled, tasted or touched. It is all in the mind; something that we all feel but cannot prove by the scientific method.

Thus knowledge and belief are inter related and inter dependent. Culture, religious teachings, upbringing, experiences etc. contribute to the formation of beliefs. For example, we all have inadequate information about 'God', but we all don't have the same beliefs about 'God'. As soon as your knowledge increases, there will be change in your belief, but your beliefs would not change your knowledge. Inspite of this, the act of believing in itself is indispensable, as to need to believe in what you know, to realize that it is knowledge.

To conclude, belief is what keeps us going. Knowledge was, is and will always be incomplete. All that we can hold on to and depend on, are our beliefs.

## INQUIRY

Inquiry, the search for truth, is a rational process of setting doubts. It is the process of advancing the knowledge. It implies a need to know, where the individuals seek answers and want to find resolutions. Individuals carry on the process of inquiry from the time they are born until they die. This is true even though they might not reflect upon the process. Infants begin to make sense of the world by inquiring. The process of inquiring begins with gathering information and date through applying the human senses as seeing, hearing, touching, tasting, and smelling. Individuals construct much of their understanding of the natural and human designed world through the process of inquiry.

John Dewey defined inquiry as *"The controlled or directed transformation of an intermediate situation with one that is so determinate with constituent distinctions and relations as to convert the element of the original situation into a unified whole."*

Knowledge has no end. No one can ever learn everything, but everyone can better develop their skills and nurture the inquiring attitudes necessary to continue the generation and examination of knowledge throughout their lives. While questioning and searching for answers are extremely important parts of inquiry but the outcome should be in the form of generating effective knowledge. Just as the individuals should not be focused only on content as the ultimate outcomes of learning, but they should accumulate knowledge. Inquiry in education should be about a greater understanding of the world in which they live, learn, communicate and work.

## REASON

Epistemologists are philosophers who seek to understand what knowledge is, whether we have any of it, and whether, perhaps we can improve our ability to gain more of it. Reasoning is also a process of advancing the knowledge. One essential thing to think is that in addition to being true or useful, knowledge requires having good grounds, reason or evidence for what is known. It is reasonable to believe that 6 + 4 = 10 or in fact we may even know it or because the answer is determined by the rules of arithmetic with in a fixed notation system. But this does not provide a general answer to the question of good reasons because most areas of thought do not have tightly or defined rules and fixed meanings of mathematical sort. Still the mathematical case might be illuminating. What is promising about it is that there is an acceptable starting point for good mathematical reason—the axioms—and an acceptable procedure for drawing conclusion the rules. If there is something like that in the non-mathematical domain, then we might be in a better position to understand good reasons both in ordinary life and in science.

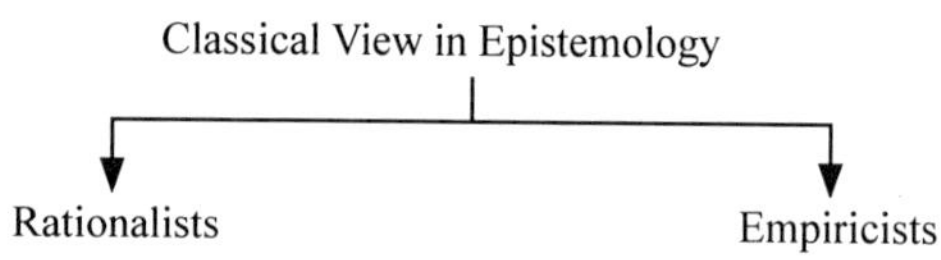


Rationalism is the epistemological view that reason is the chief source of knowledge and the main determinant of what constitutes knowledge. More broadly, it can refer to any view which appeals to reason as a source of knowledge or justification. Rationalism is one of the two classical views in epistemology, the other being empiricism. Rationalists claim that the mind, through the use of reason; can directly grasp certain truths in various domain including logic, mathematics, ethics and metaphysics

Historically and intuitively perceptions has seemed a good starting point for forming rational beliefs. Perception, as we shall see comprises of sensation and reasons. If someone sees, or hears or otherwise perceives something, we think that generally that is an acceptable basis for him/her to form beliefs about that thing, and for those beliefs consequently to be rational. To be sure, there are instances where we could not think that. If someone has reason to suspect that her perceptional experience is distorted or otherwise unreliable, then we would not think that his/her beliefs formed on the basis of that perception are reasonable.

Rationalists are of the view that empiricists fail to justify the knowledge about the truths of logic and mathematics. For them, the highest kind of knowledge consists in universally valid and necessary judgements. In other words, it is a prior knowledge which is found in concepts, principles and laws, not just in physical sensations. Plato was the father of this school of thought in philosophy. He believed that reason is the best source of knowledge and sense organs provide raw material, whereas reason gives shape to this raw material. The raw data of sensation must be organised by mind into meaningful pattern before anything worthy of the name knowledge appears.

Both rationalism and empiricism are one sided and extreme theories. None of them give us a satisfactory theory of origin of knowledge. Rationalism is partly right, when it emphasizes the necessary character, and universality of knowledge as found in science and mathematics. Universal knowledge cannot be derived from sense experience. But rationalism was wrong in accepting innate ideas. If knowledge is nothing, but analytical deduction from innate principles, then there cannot be any progress in knowledge. True knowledge must be universally valid knowledge and at the same time it must contain an element of novelty.

Thus we can conclude that much recent work in formal epistemology is an attempt to understand how our degrees of confidence are rationally constrained by our evidence and much recent work in feminist epistemology is an attempt to understand the ways in which interests affect our evidence, as well as our rational constraints. No school of epistemological theory is sufficient or complete or perfect so far knowledge formation is concerned. As a teacher, it is our responsibility to help students to attain the maximum of knowledge level. Hence, we can make it clear that none of the knowledge system can be redundant. One is complementary to other.

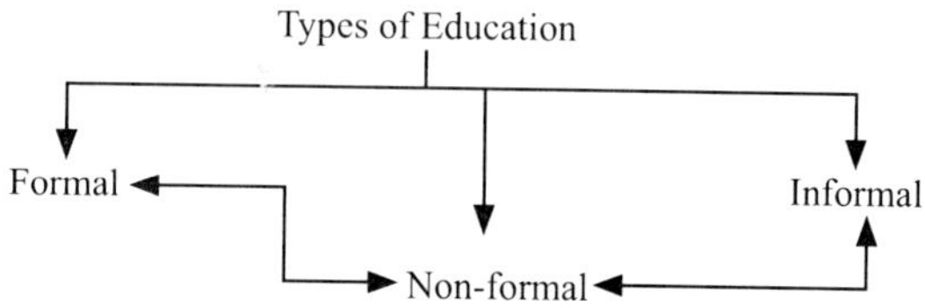


**Fig. 5.1: Types of Education**

## I. Formal Education

Formal education is that education which is organised around some pre-determined aims and ideals. It is provided to the child in a formal way with a prefixed curriculum at a particular time with specified duration. The job of providing education *i.e.* entrusted to specialists in their particular areas. In this field general, specific and direct education is provided to the child. It is equivalent to instructions that an individual receives through formal agencies of education in educational institutions. The education is systematic, conscious and deliberate. This type of education is provided to meet the needs of the individuals and society. With the growth of civilization and advancements in the field of science and technology, the accumulated fund of knowledge have become more and more complex and as a result the need for formal education has also became more pressing and widespread. It inculcates appropriate knowledge and skills among the students and also leads to their character formation so that the students of today may become useful productive citizens of tomorrow It is not confined to so called 'schooling' only. It also includes different types of vocational education imparted by teacher. Specialised in different vocations are prepared by this type of education. It is also provided to meet the political, economic, social needs and the philosophical ideology of the place. Educator establishes rapport with the educand with the help of direct interaction.

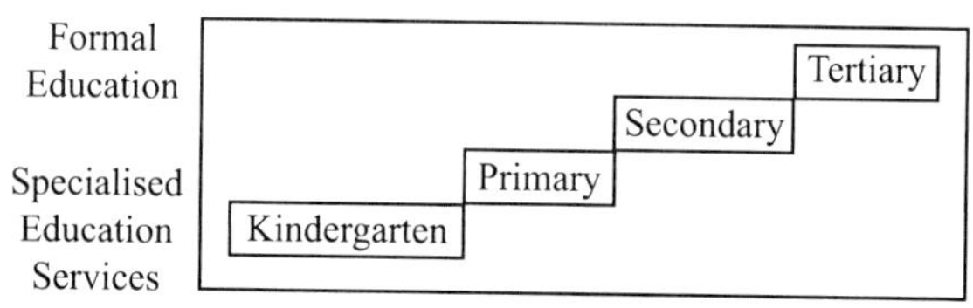


**Fig. 5.2: Levels of Education**

Pre-school education at the kindergarten level must aim to develop children in all aspects *i.e.*, physical, social, emotional and cognitive, so that, they will be better prepared to adjust and cope with life situations and the demands of formal schooling. Elementary education is concerned with providing basic education and usually corresponding to 8th grade. Its main objectives are to provide knowledge and develop the skills, attitudes and values essential to the children's personal development; to provide learning experiences that prepare them for constructive and effective involvement and to promote work experiences that prepare them to engage in honest and gainful work. The objective of secondary education is to equip the students with skills for productive endeavour or for higher education. Tertiary education is to train the nation's manpower in the skills required for national development; to develop the professionals for leadership of the nation and to advance knowledge through research work for improving quality of human life.

It can be scientifically and consistently provided to a large number of children simultaneously but the main drawback behind it is, it often fails to touch certain aspects of one's personality and leaves it completely undeveloped. At times, it can also become so detached from reality that it hinders rather than helps the educand in satisfying his needs. In some countries, we can observe that the child receives formal education only to pass the examination and have a degree but with it he is not able to face the problems of real life. Our formal education is more theoretical rather than practical. It is far-far away from the real life. The main purpose of formal education is to bring about development of child's theoretical knowledge. Commonly it starts from the age of four to five and continues to age of twenty-five. Individual and collective education is provided under the head of formal education. It is provided on a pattern determined by syllabus which is itself framed with a view to achieve certain fixed targets. Financial resources are required to provide such type of education. It is not merely confined to class-room activities but it also includes those activities outside the class-room which are consciously and deliberately planned. In this way curricular and co-curricular activities fall under the domain of formal education.

***Characteristics***

1. It is provided by formal agencies of education.
2. It has fixed time of entry and exit.
3. It is pre-planned and deliberate.
4. Its time schedule is fixed.
5. It involves both teacher and students.
6. The atmosphere provided under this education is artificial.
7. It is imparted by trained and qualified teachers.
8. Examinations are held at proper time.
9. Certificates are given after passing the examination.
10. The age at entry level is fixed.
11. It planned in accordance with definite aims.
12. Formal methods are used for teaching process.
13. Generally strict discipline is followed which is based on certain rules and regulations.
14. It does not utilize all human resources.
15. Curriculum is fixed.

16. Organisation is done by government or some organised bodies.
17. The place of giving education is fixed *i.e.* four walls of educational institutions,
18. Financial resources are arranged by government or different organised bodies.
19. There is direct interaction between educator and educands.
20. It not only provides general education but vocational education also.
21. It leads to mental strain because importance is given to cognitive aspect only.
22. It is imposed by the teacher.
23. Its scope is narrow and limited.
24. Both educator and educand remain conscious about the process.
25. It is structured hierarchically.
26. It has a chronological grading system.

***Advantages***

- It is organized and scheduled.
- It has up to date course content.
- Easy access at school level.
- Institutions are managerially and physically organized.
- It is certified.
- It is the most basic knowledge that is to be acquired by every individual to learn various other things.
- It is intermediate, and final assessments are ensured to advance students to the next learning phase.
- Students acquire knowledge from trained and professional educators.

***Disadvantages***

- It is rigid.
- Sometimes bad habits may develop due to presence of some bad students in the class.
- Sometimes brilliant students may feel bored due to the long wait for the other students to finish the task to promote to the next stage.
- An unprofessional and non-standard education system may also cause wastage of time and money.
- Exams and grades sometimes lead to stress and anxiety.

### II. Informal Education

It is complementary to formal education, without which formal education remains incomplete. It is natural and incidental. It brings modification in the behaviour which comes about necessarily and spontaneously, without any conscious efforts for it. It is a life long process. All are eligible to receive informal education irrespective of their age. It has no specific time or place.

This type of education has no pre-planning, no prefixed curriculum and aims. The child learns through experiences, so the knowledge gained by the child is more lasting in comparison to formal education. Informal education is more pre-dominant in the early period of the life as the mind is more elastic during this period. Such education is not provided by any organised agency. It does not require any financial resources to proceed. It is needed to lead a more successful family and community life because informal education aims at the comprehensive and practical development of the child. There is no standard of measure. It also does not provide a certificate or degree to the recipient. Informal education is a gradual process and it provides general education.

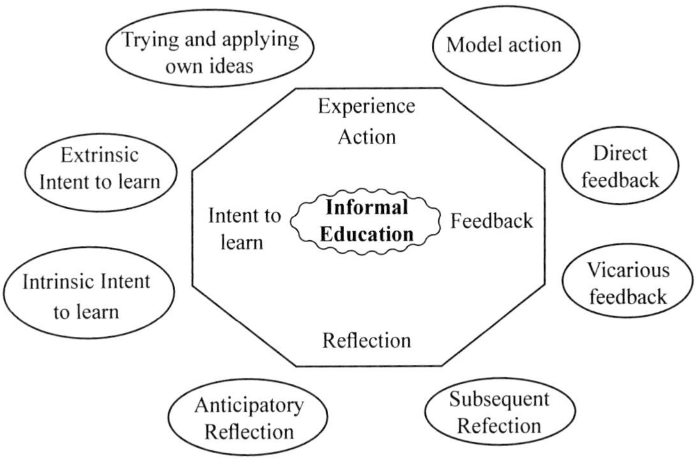


**Fig. 5.3: Aspects of Informal Education**

Thus informal education may be a parent teaching a child how to ride a bicycle. The children can get informal education by reading many books from a library or online. The child can get a spontaneous type of learning with it as if a child standing in a bank learns about opening and maintaining the account at the bank from someone.

***Characteristics***

1. It is complementary to formal education.
2. It is natural and incidental.
3. It begins from birth and continues till death.
4. It has no formal end.
5. It has no definite aims.
6. It is provided through informal agencies as family, playground, mass-media, society etc.
7. It has no formal means.
8. It has no specific place.
9. It has no specific time.

10. It does not require any financial resources to proceed.
11. There is no examination system.
12. No provision of providing certificate.
13. Its scope is very wide.
14. Nobody is teacher, nor learner. Everybody plays the role at a time as a teacher, the other time as a learner.
15. No fixed methods of teaching.
16. It has no definite curriculum.
17. It needs self discipline according to the society.
18. It utilizes available resources for education.
19. It is not imposed.
21. It is a gradual process and provides general education.
21. There is no question of entry or exit.
22. There is no organising body for it.
22. It utilizes available human resources.
23. There is no mental strain on the learner.

***Advantages***

- It does not have a specific time span.
- Variety of techniques can be used to learn.
- No need to hire experts or professionals.
- Money saving.
- The child can learn anywhere from his/her daily experiences.
- The learning process is time-efficient.
- It requires regular practice.
- It involves natural learning process.

***Disadvantages***

- The results are not predictable.
- Absence of discipline among the learners.
- The child may get plenty of misinformation available on various social media platform.
- The techniques used in this may not be appropriate.
- It is not scheduled.
- Sometimes lack of confidence may be developed in the learner.

## III. Non-formal Education

Both formal and informal education have their own limitations. On the one hand formal education is rigoristic and rigid, on the other hand informal education is flexible and unorganized. In recent times, it is felt that whatever shortcomings are there in formal and informal type of education should be met by non-formal education or continuing education. It is such type of education which is neither confined to schools. colleges or educational institutions like formal education nor too incidental and natural like informal education. It is a midway between formal and informal education. Its major intrust is on the out of school population in matters like mass literacy, functional literacy, improving skills, techniques and life systems. Due to explosion of knowledge consequent upon scientific and technological development this concept has developed after the publication of the report of the International Commission on the development of education entitled 'Learning to Be'. This commission felt that inspite of the vast financial resources being spent on education, vast majority of people do not get the desired education. Due to their involvement in earning, they may find it difficult to join formal educational institutions during prescribed time. The commission, therefore, suggests that alternative arrangements should be made for those people who have desire to study, should have an opportunity to study in their leisure time.

In our country, the need for this kind of education was clearly perceived, and as a consequence, many programmes as adult literacy, correspondence courses, postal courses, open universities, non-formal education for drop-out etc. have been taken up. Their objectives are social and economic development of every section of society. It is life-oriented and environment-based and prepares the individuals to change for the future.

In the words of McCall, *"Non-formal education is the entire range of learning experiences outside of the regular graded school system."*

In the words of Combs, *"Non-formal education is a residual category. It could conceivably include all socialisation and skills learned in the process taking place outside the formal education."*

In the words of Paulson, *"Non-formal education includes any structured, systematic, non-school education and training activities of relatively short duration in which sponsoring agencies seek concrete behavioural changes in fairly distinct target population."*

In the words of La Bella, *"Non-formal education refers to organised out of school education programme designed to provide specific learning experiences for specific target population."*

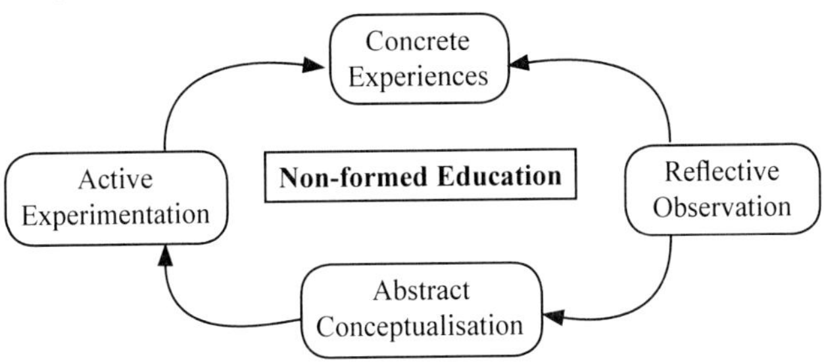


**Fig. 5.4: Aspects of Non-formal Education**

Non-formal education provides concrete experiences. It includes adult basic education, adult literacy education or school equivalency preparation.

***Specific Features of Non-formal Education***

1. *Comprehensive:* In this form of education, the learner obtains new opportunities for learning, and these opportunities are granted in every sphere, for instance–literacy, agriculture, industry, trade, health, social services, technology etc.
2. *Flexibility:* It is characterised by the quality of flexibility to a great extent, because timing in it are fixed taking in to account the convenience of the educand. It has flexible entry and exit, re-entry and re-exit and so on throughout the life span of the individual.
3. *Different Agencies:* The facility and opportunity of non-formal education can be made available to the learner by almost any agency irrespective of its being a governmental or non-governmental as computer centres, big industries, open schools, open universities, clubs, workshops etc.
4. *Adaptable Curriculum and Methodology:* in this mode of education. curriculum and methodology is adopted according to the need of the time, place and learner. It enjoys comprehensive curriculum and different types of methodology.
5. *Life-long Education:* Non-formal education is available to children, adolescents, adults and even aged persons. It is flexible from every point of view. It is a life-long process integrated with life and work. It constantly enriches life with new experiences.
6. *Community Based:* It is a process to understand social goals. It is related to the social, economic and cultural needs of the community, Its curriculum is community centred.
7. *Maximum Motivation:* Non-formal education is motivated by individual growth, self renewal and maximise human abilities, interest and potentialities. It helps in developing an open end, critical and self-reliant awareness.
8. *Increase in Knowledge and Skills:* Like other types of education, non-formal education aims at increasing the learner's knowledge and skills but the method employed for this is different.
9. *Positive Attitude:* The learners learning through non-formal education have positive attitude towards life. It develops self-reliance in them. It is an attitude of ever-marching forward.
10. *Self Dependence:* The learners become self dependent because there is interaction between the learned and learners for a short span of time and the learner is to learn himself on the basis of his activities and experiences.

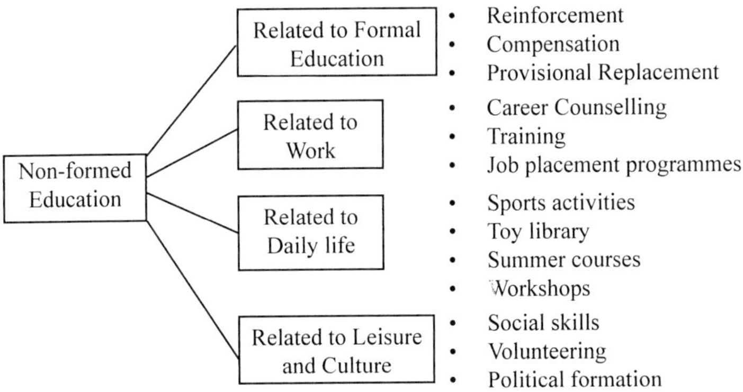


**Fig. 5.5: Features of Non-formal Education**

Thus non-formal education is a multifaceted process. It is designed not only for the children and youth but also for the adults who, at any age, may have a desire to learn. It prepares learners for active life and effective work. It educates them to adopt or adapt themselves to a variety of life opportunities and jobs. It facilitates optimum mobility in the field of education as well as employment. It helps for the upliftment of the underprivileged,

***Objectives of Non-Formal Education***

1. To motivate the dropouts to come back in to the field of education.
2. To develop expertise with regard to work-experiences and occupation.
3. To develop mastery in linguistic skills.
4. To develop proper habits and attitude for healthful living.
5. To make children able to understand and appreciate the scientific phenomenon of their environment.
6. To provide functional literacy, numeracy and technocracy.
7. To provide part time instructions to the non-enrolled children and to those who can not follow full time programmes.
8. To link educational programmes to the needs, interests, abilities and aptitudes of the learners.
9. To encourage a positive set of attitude towards themselves, their fellow men and their society.
10. To provide them the introductory occupational vocational skill programmes to prepare them for employment and self-employment.
11. To provide them the basic knowledge for understanding various social, economic, scientific and technical changes in the midst of which youth have to live and work.
12. To undertake remedial instructional programmes for the dropouts.

13. To make educational process to lead learners to problem-solving initiative and participation.
14. To motivate the unprivileged learners to start learning and to continue to do so.
15. To facilitate multiple entry in to general stream of education.

***Advantages***

- It has flexibility in age, curriculum and time.
- It involves practical application of the theoretical knowledge obtained.
- Ease of entry and exit.
- It involves literacy with skillfulness growth in which self-learning is appreciated.
- It includes practice and vocational training.
- Sometimes examinations are not needed because diploma, certificates and degrees are not essential to be awarded.

***Disadvantages***

- Sometimes it is just wastage of time because some students don't take it seriously in the absence of examination.
- Some institutions provide fake certificates through online courses for the sake of earning.
- It is difficult to learn basic reading and writing skills.
- Lack of accreditation.

In this way the realisation of need of non-formal education is of recent growth. The history of respected status achieved by this is no more than a couple of decades old This is a form of education which has taken the world by storm, since the philosophy underlying it and its impact have been discussed in every part of the world. The entire ancient educational system in the world actually had its inception in non-formal education. It is rooted in the learner's willingness to learn. It is based on the objectives of low costs and high profits.

## Difference between Formal, Informal and Non-formal Education

Formal, informal and non-formal education can better be understood with the help of following task showing comparison:

| *Aspects* | *Formal Education* | *Informal Education* | *Non-formal Education* |
|---|---|---|---|
| 1. Meaning | Formal education implies modification of behaviour through an organised system of education. | It is that modification of behaviour which comes about necessarily and spontaneously without any conscious effort for it. | It is a method of taking education to the door steps of those learners who can not get education in formal institutions. |

| *Aspects* | *Formal Education* | *Informal Education* | *Non-formal Education* |
|---|---|---|---|
| 2. Aim | It has definite aims. | It has no definite aims. | It has clear cut aims. |
| 3. Scope | Its scope is narrow and limited. | Its scope is much wide. | Its scope is very wide. |
| 4. Duration | It begins from school and goes upto university. | It is a life long process. | It is a continuous process. |
| 5. Entry | The entry and exit age is fixed. | There is no age to enter and exit. | It has flexibility in entry and exit. |
| 6. Place | It is confined to four walls of educational institutions. | Its place is whole society. | Its place is outside the four walls of formal education. |
| 7. Agencies | It is provided in schools, colleges, universities etc. | It is provided through peer group, community, family, religions etc. | It is arranged through national open universities, national institution of open school, distance education departments non-govt. organisation etc. |
| 8. Teacher | The teacher should be a qualified person. | Anyone from the society can play the role as teacher. | It is also given by qualified and experienced teachers. |
| 9. Organisation | It is an organised effort by state or voluntary organisations. | There is no organised body behind it. | It is also provided by some organising bodies. |
| 10. Curriculum | The curriculum is fixed and narrow. | It has no definite curriculum. | Variety and flexibility are in this curriculum. It has sometimes fixed and sometimes adapt able curriculum. |
| 11. Methods of Teaching | Fixed and formal methods of teaching are adopted like lecture, narration, discussion etc. | The learners learn by experience and interaction with others. | The methods of teaching are generally learner-centred. |
| 12. Conscio-usness | Both the students and teachers remain conscious about the education process. | Neither the educator nor the learner is conscious about the process. | There is partial consciousness among the teachers and students |
| 13. Atmosphere | The atmosphere is artificial. | The atmosphere is natural. | The atmosphere is combination of natural and artificial. |
| 14. Planning | It is well planned. | There is no planning. It is incidental. | It is also well planned like formal education. |

| *Aspects* | *Formal Education* | *Informal Education* | *Non-formal Education* |
|---|---|---|---|
| 15. Time schedule | Its time schedule is fixed, The student is to reach in time at the school. | There is no fixed timing. | It has flexible time schedule. |
| 16. Discipline | It involves strict discipline based on some rules and regulations. | It needs no discipline. The child is to work only according to the society. | There is primarly self-discipline, inner discipline and social discipline. |
| 17. Evaluation. | After a fixed time period the system of evaluation is fixed | There is no fixed evaluation system. The society members play the role as evaluator. | There is also the provision of evaluation but it is more comprehensive because evaluation is concerned with the learner as well as non-formal programme. |
| 18. Certification | Certificate is provided after the examinations. | No provision of providing certificate. | Certificates are provided on the basis of evaluation. |
| 19. Mental strain | It lays mental strain because serious efforts are made. | It lays no strain on the learner because it is natural. | It involves a limited mental strain. |
| 20. Motivation | It is motivated because teaching-learning process is so arranged that it involves both teachers as well as students. | It is self motivated. | It is motivated for receiving education or skill or training. |
| 21. Imposition | It is imposed by the teacher on the learner. | It is not imposed. | It is a process of sharing, exploring, analysing and judging together with maximum participation. |
| 22. Confidence | It helps in development of self confidence among the students on acquiring knowledge. | It develops much confidence, | It also helps in development of confidence. |
| 23. Dependency | The pupils become dependent on his teacher to acquire knowledge. | The learners become self dependent. | The pupils become self dependent. |

| *Aspects* | *Formal Education* | *Informal Education* | *Non-formal Education* |
|---|---|---|---|
| 24. Supervision | It is supervised. | There is no provision of supervision. | Supervision is there to some extent. |
| 25. Interaction | There is face to face interaction. | Interaction is incidental. | Interaction depends upon the situation. |
| 26. Resources | Relatively higher resources are needed. | Resources are not needed. | Comparatively less resources are required. |

## Importance of Different forms of Education

Education involves different subjects and disciplines. It is a life long process in the modern setup, it is to continue at all the stages of life. It is to expedite the social change acquire all the knowledge, training and self reliance. All the different types of education has a strong role to play. Society/community plays an important role. All types of education are inter-dependent and inter-related. They are needed for the complete development of the individual and the society. Efforts should be made to integrate all in to one comprehensive educational system for the enrichment and transmission of culture, knowledge and experiences, development of skills and harmonious development of the individual. None of them is lesser important. All of them will continue to have their own importance in the modification of behaviour and as such developed in their own ways.

# 6

# Ethics, Values and Ideals

*'Peace of mind produces right values, right values produce right thoughts and right thoughts produce right action.* –Robert M. Possig

The idea of ethics, values and ideals is present in every act, choice and decision of a person. When we pick two functions as course of action, we are to decide which of them is better, then our decision will be in favour of that which we count as better in all dimensions. In this process of choice and action, the notion of ethics, values and ideas is involved. Throughout the civilization, the ethical concepts of right and wrong, good and bad, virtue and vice has always been acted upon the everyday's action of mankind. Each culture places values and importance on certain qualities and characteristics. Culture passes these values, as work ethics or honesty, down from generation to generation and they are inscribed in the institutions of that culture. Every civilization has certain distinctive peculiarities and ideals. For example, the Indian civilization compounded ethical, social, emotional and spiritual values. In India, all human efforts are linked to the central aim of life *i.e.* to get moksha or to achieve salvation.

Cultures also hold certain deals, or expectations for an ideal type of person. Sometimes these ideal are specific to a type of person as an ideal mother; is thought of as warm, supportive and nurturing. Sometimes these ideals are more general. An ideal Indian citizen is always loyal to his country, making thoughtful, informed decision on its governance. Often, unattainable ideals set a standard for people to strive forward.

Ethics are guidelines or rules that are set for an organization or society rather than for an individual. These are mainly based on virtues, rights and obligations. For example, the obligations to refrain from crime, killing, and rape is an ethical aspect. A society's values and ideals inform the principles or directives on how a person should act or behave, that the society operates under. These principles are often informal and unwritten, dictate appropriate behaviour by the members of the society. One classic example; the Golden Rule, treat others in the way that they would want to be treated.

## ETHICS

Ancient Greek word 'Ethios' means 'relating to one's character' which itself comes from the root word 'ethos' meaning 'character, moral nature'. This word was transferred to Latin as 'ethica' then into French as 'ethique' from which it was transferred to English.

It is a branch of philosophy that is concerned with human conduct. It consists in a code of conduct of human beings living in a society. Ethics examines the rational justification for our moral judgements. It studies what is morally right or wrong, just or unjust. In philosophy ethics defines what is good for the individual, for society and establishes the nature of rules that people own to themselves and to one another. It aims at individual good as well as social good, the good of mankind.

Ethics is an attempt to guide human conduct and it is also an attempt to help man in leading good life by applying moral principles. They refer to well based standards of right and wrong that prescribe what humans ought to do, usually in terms of rights, obligation, benefits to society, fairness or specific virtues. Ethics is related to issue of propriety, rightness and wrongness. What is right is ethical and what is wrong is unethical. Ethics is a matter of practical concern. It tries to determine the good and right thing to do, choices regarding right and wrong, good and evil; question of obligation and value. Ethics is to consider the practice of doing right actions or what we may call the act of living good life.

It is also defined as the science of highest good. In the words of Meckanzie, *"Ethics is the study of what is right or good in human conduct"* The science of an ideal involved in human life.

Applied ethics is the practice that aims to guide the moral judgement governing in decision we make in all areas of our lives. In the content of ethics, values are our standards of right and wrong.

Rushworth Kidder states that *"standard definition of ethics have typically includes such phrases as the science of the ideal human character or the science of moral duty."*

Richard William Paul & Linda Elder, *"Ethics is a set of concepts and principles that guide us in determining what behaviour helps or harms sentient creatures."*

Cambridge Dictionary of Philosophy states that the word 'ethics is commonly used interchangeably with 'morality' and sometime it is used more narrowly to mean the moral principles of a particular tradition, group or individual.

Paul and Elder further state that most people confuse ethics with behaving in accordance with social conventions, religious beliefs, the law and don't treat ethics as stand-alive concept.

As bioethicist Larry Churchill has written, "Ethics, understood as the capacity to think critically about moral values and direct our actions in terms of such values, is a general human capacity'.

The ideas of right and wrong, good and bad are meaningless without any reference to the idea of ultimate end or highest good. Activities are right if they are contributing to the highest good, differently they are faulty. Consequently, ethics may also be specified as an inquiry into the nature of the ultimate end of human activity, the highest sound of mankind and also the way of making it.

## Ethics in Indian Tradition

Indian ethics are one of the greatest traditions of moral thoughts in world philosophy. These have sources in spiritual and philosophical thinking. From time immemorial, various religious faiths have flourished here. Every religious and philosophical system of India has a prominent ethical component. In every religious tradition, good moral conduct is essential for a happy and contented life. Without following the truth of righteousness, no one can attain supreme goal (moksha) of life.

What are the qualities of good character? What type of human behaviour is good or bad? How should one act in life? These are sources of the fundamental questions of ethics.

India has a very ancient history of thinking about 'ethics'. Its central concepts are represented in Rigveda, one of the oldest knowledge texts not only of India but of the entire world. In it, we come across the idea of an all-pervading cosmic order which stands for harmony and balance in nature and in human society. In Indian tradition, the concept of cosmic order gave rise to the idea of dharma. Here, dharma does not mean mere religion, but it stands for duty, obligation and righteousness. It is a whole way of life in which ethical values are considered supreme and everyone is expected to performs his/her duty according is his/her social position and status in life.

In Indian traditions, the concept of four ends of life (purusharthas) is also very important. These are righteousness (dharma), worldly gain (artha), fulfillment of desire (Kama) and liberalism (moksha). Dharma and moksha are most important from ethical point of view. They give right direction and purpose to human life.

Ethics is a branch of philosophy that involves systematizing, defending and recommending concepts of right and wrong behaviour. The field of ethics, alongwith aesthetics, concerns matters of value and this comprises the branch of philosophy called axiology.

## Characteristics

- It is connected intrinsically with questions of correct conduct within society.
- It indicates a concern of virtuous people, reliable character and proper conduct.
- It indicates what we should do in some circumstances or what we should do as participants in some form of activity or profession.
- It is not limited to the acts of a single persons.

- It is also interested in the correct practices of Govt. corporates, professionals and many other groups.
- It is sometime identified into an inflexible set of rules as self-righteous moralizing. Rules say an action is either right or wrong.
- It is not static. It consists of dynamic framework of principles and values.
- Our ethical values reflect our deepest convictions and attachments.
- They define who we are, and give us an ethical identity.
- It is the process of inventing new and better ethical responses to problems and conflicts.
- It is applied to human beings only as they have freedom of choice and means of free will.

**Nature of Ethics**

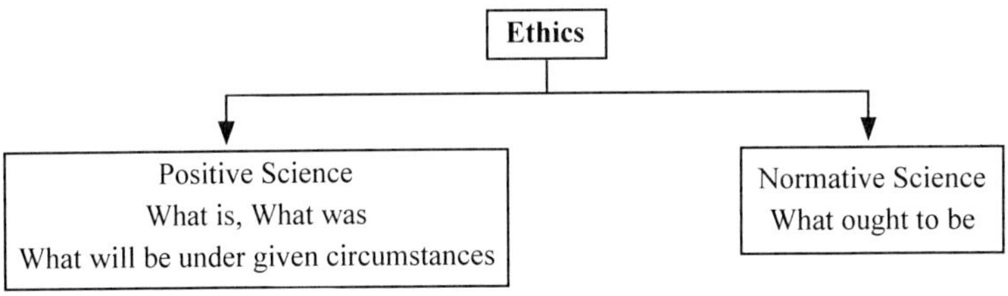


**Fig. 6.1: Ethics as Science**

***Ethics as Positive Science***

Every science is concerned with a particular sphere of nature. As a science ethics has its own particular sphere; deal with certain judgements, that we made about human conduct. It deals with systematic explanation of references or wrongness in the light of highest good of man.

A positive science deals with things as they are. It explains their cause and effect. But it remains strictly neutral as regards ends; it refuses to pass moral judgements. It includes those statements which disclose factual information. Ethics deals with ethical facts. These describe what is, what was and what would be under the given set of circumstances. All these statements are capable of empirical verification. On the basis of empirical verifications, we can ascertain the degree of truth in such statements. These statements are not based on individual opinion, that without following a path of righteousness, no one can attain supreme goal of life *i.e.* moksha.

***Ethics as Normative Science***

It is concerned with what ought to be done rather than what is the case. It differs from positive science. It does not deal with facts, but with values.

A normative science deals with things as they ought to be. It has no objection to discuss the moral rightness or wrongness of things. It pronounces value judgements. What constitutes tolerance? An enquiry into this shall immediately become a normative enquiry, because here we are required to discuss things as they ought to be. A normative enquiry is linked indissolubly with ethical considerations. A positive enquiry, on the otherhand, cuts itself apart from ethical motives.

### Types/Theories of Ethics

The field of ethics or moral philosophy involves concepts of right or wrong behaviour. Ethical theories are usually divided in the following areas of study:

What does righteousness mean?

- Meta-ethics

How should people act?

- Normative-ethics
  - Teleological ethics
  - Deontological ethics
  - Virtue ethics

How we take moral knowledge and put it into practice?

- Applied-ethics

**Fig. 6.2: Theories of Ethics**

- ***Mata-ethics***

The term 'meta' means after or beyond. Meta-ethics is the study of origin and meaning of ethical concepts. It tries to see the nature of ethical properties, statements, attitudes and opinions. It investigates from where our ethical principles come and what they mean. It is the branch of philosophical ethics that asks how we understand, know about what we mean when we talk about what is right and what is wrong. An ethical question pertaining to a particular situation as 'should I eat this particular piece of cake?', cannot be a meta-ethical question (rather it is an applied ethical question). A meta-ethical question is abstract and relates to a wide range of more specific practical questions as 'Is it even possible to have secured knowledge of what is just or unjust?' Meta-ethics answers to those questions focus on the issue of universal truths, the will of God, the role of reason in ethical judgements, and the meaning of ethical terms. Thus, meta-ethics are about the theoretical meaning and references of moral propositions and how their truth values (if any) may be determined. It considers questions as 'what is goodness?' and in this way, seems to understand the nature of ethical properties and evaluation.

- ***Normative Ethics***

It is the study of ethical actions. It is the branch of ethics that investigates the set of questions that arise when considering how we ought to act, morally speaking. It involves calculating the good habits that we should acquire, the duties that we should follow, or the consequences of our behaviour towards others. The key assumption in it is that there is only one ultimate criterion of moral conduct, whether it is a single rule or a set of principles. It differs from meta-ethics because it examines standards for the rightness and wrongness of actions while meta-ethics studies the meaning of moral language and metaphysics of moral facts. It also differs from descriptive ethics as descriptive ethics would concerned with determining what proportion of people believe that killing is always wrong *i.e.* an experimental inquiry of man's moral beliefs, while normative ethics is concerned with whether it is correct to hold such a belief. There are three different approaches taken by normative ethical theories:

(i) *Teleological Ethics:* According to this, a morally right action is that which will create good outcomes or effect. This theory conceives duty or moral responsibility in terms of what is good or worthy as an end to achieve. Although it has been largely replaced by the more straight forward term 'consequentialism'. It holds that the consequences of one's conduct are the ultimate basis for any judgement about the rightness or wrongness of that conduct.

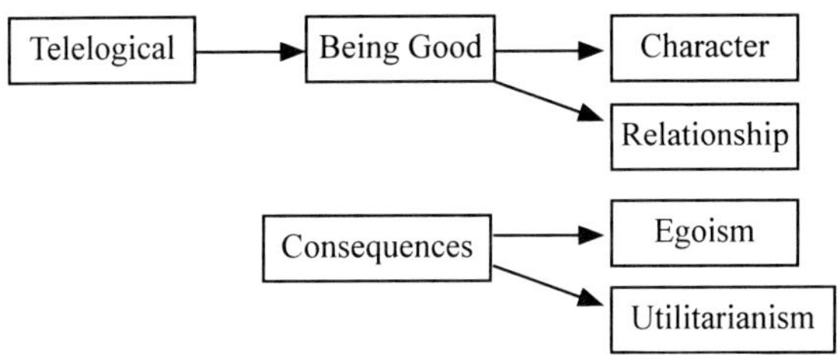


**Fig. 6.3: Consequences of Teleological Ethics**

(ii) *Deontological Ethics:* Deontological means a duty based morality as it is concerned with what people do, not with the results of their activities. These theories stress the concepts of obligation, ought, duty and right and wrong. These set forth formal or relational criteria as equality or impartiality. This approach calls for doing certain things on principle or because they are inherently right.

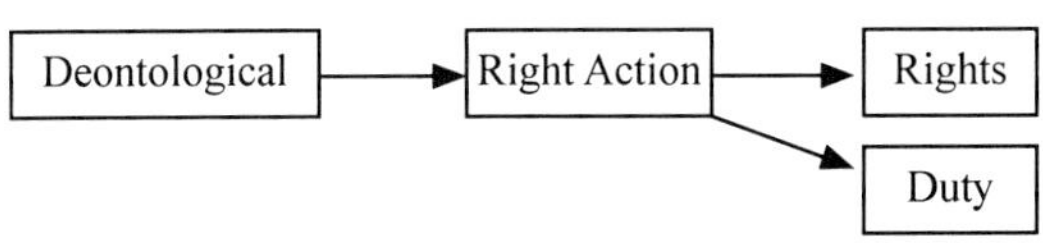


**Fig. 6.4: Principles of Deontological Ethics**

(iii) *Virtue Ethics:* Virtue ethics emphasize virtue of mind, character and sense of honesty. It may initially be identified as the one that emphasizes the virtues, or moral character, in contrast to the approach that emphasizes duties or rules (deontology) or that emphasizes the consequences of action (consequentialism). Virtue ethics describe the character of a moral agent as a driving force for ethical behaviour. This theory assumes that once a virtuous disposition is achieved, one will know what to do for the best. Aristotle assessed that soul of man had three natures–body (physical/metabolism), animal (emotional/appetite) and rational (mental/conceptual). Physical nature can be arranged through activities and care, emotional nature through indulgence of instincts and urges, and mental nature through human reason and developed potential. Man should not simply live, but live well with conduct governed by nature. Virtue denotes doing the right thing, in the right way, at the right time, for the right reason. According to Aristotle, by having virtuous habits, people will likely make the right choice when faced with ethical challenges. So, virtue ethics helps us to understand what it means to be a virtuous human being and it gives us a guide for living life without giving us specific rules for resolving ethical dilemmas.

• ***Applied Ethics***

Applied ethics is the most practical philosophical ethics. It is real application of ethical theory in order to select an ethical action in a given subject. It deals with difficult moral questions and controversial issues as abortion, war, use of animals for food etc. This discipline has many specialised fields as:

1. *Bio-ethics:* It is study of controversial ethics brought about by advancement in biology and medicine. Bio-ethicists are concerned with the ethical questions that arise in the relationship among life sciences, bio-technology, medicine, politics, law, and philosophy.
2. *Business Ethics:* Business ethics is a form of applied ethics or professional ethics that examines ethical principles and moral or ethical problems that arise in a business environment including fields like medical ethics. It represents the practices that any individual or group exhibits with in an organisation that can negatively or positively affect the business core values. It applies to all aspects of business and is relevant to the conduct of the individual and entire organisation.
3. *Military Ethics:* Military ethics are concerned with questions, regarding the application of force and the ethics of the soldier and are offen understood as applied professional ethics. It involves as decisions about who may be targeted in warfare, standards for handling military prisoners etc.
4. *Political Ethics:* It is that practice of making moral judgements about political actions and political agents. It is also known as public ethics or political morality.
5. *Public Sector Ethics:* It is a set of principles that guide public officials in their services to their constituencies including their decision making on behalf of their constituents.
6. *Publication Ethics:* It is the set of principles that guide the writing and publishing process for all professional publications.

7. *Relational Ethics:* These are related to ethics of care. They are used in qualitative research especially ethnography, and auto ethnography.
8. *Animal Ethics:* It is a term used in academics to describe human-animal relationships and how animals might to be treated.

Thus applied ethics involves more or less all the fields of society. Everybody while doing any work should take care of applied ethics. The main objective of this ethics is well being of human beings. Although it is not theoretical completely, it needs help from normative theories or principles to solve concrete problems in different areas.

## Importance of Ethics

Ethics significantly effect all the aspects of man's practical life whether social, political, economic, religious, legal, educational or cultural. The proper solution of the vital problems of these areas depends completely upon the correct knowledge of what is right and what is wrong. As the backbone to the society, ethics play an important role because it arises from the morality. The importance is as follows:

- Ethics is a belief and standard that helps to make harmonious and conforming environment.
- Through the interaction with human, ethics can help the people to build trust and intimate relationship in society.
- Alignment of ethics with values, moral and attitude strengthens mutual trust and reduce social conflicts.
- It promotes self-discipline among people to behave in a manner commensurable to standards otherwise attract social isolation.
- It lends to society's organic growth in to more mature and balanced group which caters to the needs of each and every member irrespective of his status, gender, race etc.
- It helps in promoting peace among the diverse society and helps in avoiding useless violence and compassion helps the people to help others in need.
- Ethical rules and principles enable us to take a cooler view of moral problems.
- High sense of ethics and values makes a man trustworthy and representable.
- At national and global level, respect for national symbol and emblems, contribution in nation's growth by advancing our capabilities and skills and adopting scientific and humanistic temper and recognition to the feet of shared development may make world a better place to live.

## How to Develop Ethics

The teachers often grapple with the question of how—and how often–to develop ethics. They try to do it across the curriculum, but sometime they struggle to fit ethics into their content-rich classes. Teachers' and students' experiences of school as a site for ethical practice imply the value of: striving for ethical awareness, building ethical relationships, and encouraging ethical actions. It is becoming important for the institutions to develop ethics among their students because these are deteriorating day by day in the present times. The questions we are facing now a days are not how can we live within our group, but how can our group live well with other groups in the work. According to Weinstein, children today are looking to the culture at large for ethical guidance and many adults are not setting examples. He says children are looking even at the conduct of athletes, as some beef themselves with steroids. A majority of teenagers value happiness and personal success more than concern for others. The schools can be viewed as a site for ethical practice where relationships and behaviour play a central role in teaching and learning. There is a need to turn the invisible into something tangible. Some methods suggested by different educationists are as follows:

*Make room for ethics:* If the teachers want to develop an ethical decision making ability, it requires students to spend valuable time exploring and discussing ethical dilemmas. It is the responsibility of the teacher to discuss various situations in the class.

*Use real world examples:* The examples from real life can make ethics more concrete to students, as they reveal the implications of unethical behaviour.

*Connect ethics to students' own lives:* The teacher should place their students in specific ethical dilemmas they might have encountered or might encounter. It will provide them the opportunity to explore possible actions and outcomes.

*Practice, practice and practice:* The teacher should try that their students are to do practice more and more in taking ethical decisions. As a result they will be prepared to make ethical decisions at their own.

*Highlight reason and impacts:* The teacher should expand the ethical conversations beyond right or wrong and delve deeper into how specific ethical decisions or actions impact all the persons involved.

*Make the students courageous:* The teacher should give the students courage to ask the right questions regarding ethical decisions. For this he/she is to provide proper educational environment.

*Generalize the Ethics:* The teacher should help students to understand that ethics is not just about an individual person. Allow them to realise how they can shape the fullness as leaders, managers, good teachers, etc. by nurturing an environment that enables ethical decisions.

The other things which can be done are as follows:

- Create a code of behaviour for teachers as well as for students.
- Help students to see that the 'good' in others is more than academic success.
- Be vigilant to prevent and stop scape grating of one student by others.
- Promote a project for each class that contributes positively to the school or neighbourhood community environment.

- Regularly weave any character into your discussion of any discipline as language, social science, mathematics, science etc. asking 'what is the right thing to do?' and follow up with a discussion.
- Treat ethical issues like other intellectual issues—get the facts, gather evidence, weight consequences and option, make a decision and follow through.
- Share stories of ethical conflicts from literature, current subjects, in the news or movies etc.
- Teach students to analyse the media critically on ethical grounds.
- Teach justice and compassion by helping students separate the doer from the dead.

However, ethics does not develop itself without moral philosophy, sociology, and psychology. It primarily exists in interaction of individual and society. Not a days ethics had been polluted and erosion of ethics had been dramatically increased due to people have different views in judging different situations. Globalization also plays a strong role in affecting the ethical behaviour of the masses. The rape has shown, what is the need of sex education in the society? But it is still under debate in our society. The need of ethics is felt more than ever in present scenario when the case of terrorism, crime, violent against women, girl foeticide etc. are rampant. The issue of corruption can be dealt with ethics. Thus sensitizing our teachers, doctors, public servants, managers etc. towards ethics is the need of the hour.

The problems of the present world can be dealt with if ethical values are enshrined in the heart and minds of people. The purpose of NEP 2020 is to develop good human beings capable of rational thought and action, possessing compassion and empathy, courage and resilience, scientific temper and creative imagination, with sound ethical mooring and values. It aims at producing engaged, productive and contributing citizens for building an equitable, inclusive and plural society as envisaged by our constitution.

## VALUES

Values are conscious and unconscious preferences, accepted by the majority of members of the society and are socially regulated. One important characteristic of value is that they are not absolute, They are relative to the society in which they prevail. If there is change in economic, social, political, religious and other circumstances of the society, it will lead to change in values. On the other hand many people are of the view that values can never change.

Man acts to satisfy his needs or wants. Anything which satisfies human needs becomes thereby a thing of value. In psychology the term value is generally employed to designate a dominant interest, motive or broad evaluative attitude.

3. *Moral Values:* Moral values are important for the life of an individual. This value is defined in terms of honesty, truthfulness, good character, kindness, self-discipline, God fearing personality and simple living and high thinking. Self control, reliability persistence in action, industriousness, sense of responsibility and justice are significant moral values which form part and parcel of character.
4. *Democratic Values:* This value is characterized by respect for individuality, absence of discrimination among persons on the basis of caste, colour, sex, religion, race and family status, ensuring equal social, political and religious rights to all. It also includes impartiality and social justice and respect for the democratic institutions.
5. *Economic Values:* This value relates with money. It stands for desire for money and material gains. A man who has high economic value is guided by consideration of money and material gain in the choice of his job. His attitude towards rich persons and the industrialists is favourable and he considers them helpful for the progress of the country.
6. *Aesthetic Values:* It is characterised by beauty of nature and work of art. It also includes love for literature, music, dance, sculpture, poetry and architecture, love for decoration of the home and the surroundings. It considers neatness and system in the arrangement of the things.
7. *Hedonistic Values:* It is defined here as the conception of desirability of loving pleasure and avoiding pain. For a hedonistic person the present is more important that the future. A person with hedonistic value indulges in pleasure of senses and avoids pain.
8. *Knowledge Values:* It stands for love of knowledge and love of discovery of truth. A person with it considers a knowledge of theoretical principles underlying a work essential for success in it. He remains aspire to get more and more knowledge known as the seeker of knowledge.
9. *Bodily Values:* It relates to the health efficiency and beauty of the physical life. It also implies the consideration for self preservation. The person having bodily values considers good physical health, essential for the development and use of his abilities.
10. *Power Values:* The power value is defined as the conceptional of desirability of ruling over others and also of reading others. The characteristics of a person of high power values are that he prefers job where he gets opportunity to exercise authority over others.
11. *Recreation Value:* It refers to the values of play and leisure enriching the life.
12. *Internal or Subjective Values:* Some believe that values are internal. They are biological and psychological in origin. They satisfy the wants and desires. They do not have any intrinsic or inherent worth of their own. They are according to the needs and emotions.

13. *External and Objective Values:* Some believe that values are inherent in objects and activities in accordance with their qualities and attributes. Social environment influences the quality or value of an object.
14. *Instrumental Values:* It is dependent on the outcome or consequence. In the words of Brubacher, "Instrumental values are those what are judged good, because they are good for something." It is temporary and extrinsic. It is subjective and change according to the change in the circumstances.
15. *Intrinsic Values:* It is an end in itself. It is permanent and ultimate. It is not applied by outside agency. It is judged good not for something also, but is good in and of itself. It is not accidental. It is self-contained. Generally truth, beauty and goodness are intrinsic values.

Thus values are of various kinds according to their specification. They have formed integral parts of social life everywhere and at all stages of human history.

**Need and Importance**

At present, when social, moral, cultural and spiritual values are deteriorating day by day, religion is loosing its hold, power and knowledge are misused for vested interests, when countries do not trust one another, black marketing, corruption, indiscipline, violence are fast spreading, it is essential that education for values should be imparted. It is the task of the education to develop, preach and practice social, political, moral and spiritual values for the following reasons:

1. *To Make Democracy a Success:* In democratic society, there is a great need that all the members of the society should respect and love each other. They should live with 'we' feeling instead of 'I' The democracy stresses the dignity of the individual and the sacredness of human personality. These values should be imparted to make democracy a success.
2. *Change in the Life Style of the People:* In the present age, there is tremendous advancement in science and technology. As a result the life style of the people has completely changed. Today man believes in dynamism. It is very necessary to develop moral consciousness among the youth.
3. *Basis of Humanitarianism:* At present, there is exploitation, corruption, disaster, selfishness, aggression and hate in the world, People are becoming soulless and Godless creatures. There is chaos and disorder. The education for values will eradicate the present ills of the world. It will encourage the policy of live and let live and provide the basis of true humanitarianism.
4. *To Maintain and Develop Traditional Values:* There is degradation of moral values in our country like rest of the world. In modern age, religion is finding itself incapable for the development of morality. Therefore there is a dire need to identify appropriate values and to inculcate them with the help of education.

5. *To Make Life Easy and Enjoyable:* With the passage of time life is becoming faster as well as more complex. The family, society and political environment is continuously becoming more and more complex day by day. The students of today may have to face a situation where instead of depending upon others they may have to make a decision for themselves. To make life easy and enjoyable values should be developed among the people.
6. *Development of Wider Attitude:* Now a days every man is becoming selfish. He believes in 'I' feeling. It shows that narrow attitude is developing. There is need to develop wider attitude for the development of human beings, society as well as nation, Education for values makes a man dynamic and enlightened. He becomes courageous enough to face the problem of life boldly and solve them in the best of his efforts and intelligence.
7. *Moral Development:* In the modern age, morality is degrading day by day. All the education commissions laid stress on moral development with the help of education. It inculcates in children truthfulness, humility, tolerance, honesty, sincerity, courtesy, fellow feeling, affection and sacrifice which form a noble character of child and develops his personality.

It must be kept in mind that values of life are ornaments which shine like stars in the personality of the individual who possesses these values. In the words of Shri Radha Krishnan, *"The troubles of the whole world including India are due to the fact that education has become a mere intellectual exercise and not the acquisition of values."* The political tension at the present times is mainly due to the fact that knowledge has increased but values have lagged behind. It is education for values which should impel man to utilize atomic energy for the betterment of humanity rather than for its destruction.

**How to Develop Values?**

Educational institutes are meeting places of values and also full of values. Teachers do important work together with students, to encourage them to manage their own learning and personal development. Students are valued through being the future of society. These meetings are also full of values due to human beings' different backgrounds and expectations. Human actions are governed unconsciously or consciously by fundamental values. Students learn important values like respect, honesty and tolerance in meeting with other people in the institutions.

We are not born with values, so how do people develop their values? There are three periods during which values can be developed. Sociologist Morris Massey has described three stage during which values can be developed:

| *Imprint Stage* | *Modelling Stage* | *Socialization Stage* |
|---|---|---|
| Upto the age of seven, we are like sponge, absorbing everything around us and accepting much of it as true especially when it comes from our parents. | Between the age of 8 and 13, we copy people, mostly parents but also others. | between 13 and 21, we are largely influenced by our peer group. |

| *Imprint Stage* | *Modelling Stage* | *Socialization Stage* |
|---|---|---|
| Much of the confusions are created. The blind belief of this period can lead to the early formation of trauma and other deep problems. | Rather than blind acceptance, we are trying the values as wearing a dress, to see how they feel. | As we develop as individuals and look for ways to get away from the early programming. |
| The critical thing in this period is to learn a sense of right and wrong, good and bad. | We may be much impressed by our teachers, peer group. | We turn to those people who seems more like us. |
| Everything is imprinted in this stage. | You may remember the influence of junior school teachers. | Media also influences at this stage, especially those part which seem to resonate with the values of our peer group. |

Human behaviour is determined by the consolidated values. These provide predictability of human behaviour and indeed the very foundation of the personality that has been described as the style of man/woman.

According to Marmar Mukhopadhyay, value development takes place in the following stages.

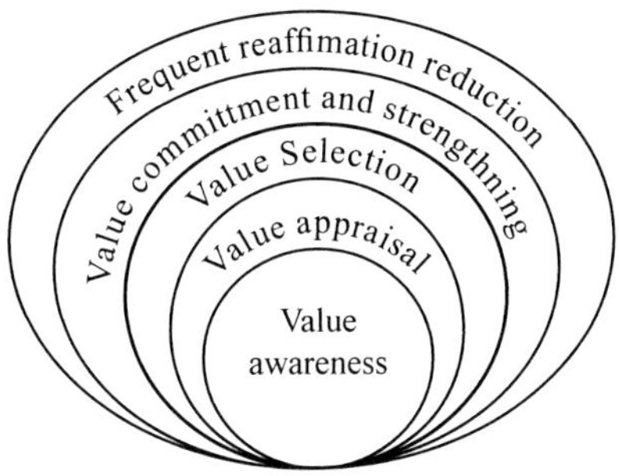


**Fig. 6.5: Stages of Value Development**

Education in India puts due emphasis on physical, intellectual, emotional, social, moral and spiritual values. The traditional approach to education has been to see its utility and purpose in terms of social and moral awareness, to impart beauty and dignity to life and also to provide with a code of conduct for a good social and moral order. 'Character Building' was the key phrase in the Gandhian philosophy. We trace in the writings of our philosophers is that education provides us with a family for positive discrimination between right and wrong, between virtue and vice.

The power of modern education can be realised by achieving a happy integration of utility and value, integration of body and mind, emotions and ideas, individual and society, society and the world. In the wake of phenomenal and dimensional development on the educational front, reorientation of values in the post-modernist education assumes special significance.

Now the question arises how to inculcate values among the children with the help of education. Education is a process of bringing about desirable changes in the way one thinks, feels and acts in accordance with one's concept of the good life. Our aims of education—*development of personality, pursuit of knowledge, preservation of culture, training of character*—are no more than statements of one value preferences. Towards realizing them we design a curriculum; a planned collection of desirable knowledge, skills, attitudes, values which we wish to pass on to the younger generation. And this we do in ways that do not violate the freedom and autonomy of the learner. In other words, education, curriculum and methods, are inseparably linked with values. Each one of these elements is briefly described below:

1. *Changing the Way We Teach:* Adopting more learner-centred methods in all subjects, using co-operative learning techniques and similar methods which foster group work and help in developing individual creativity are in themselves steps towards creating a more conscious and socially responsible citizen and help in developing his hidden capacities and potentialities. While teaching science, the teacher can give opportunities to the students to discover and apply scientific principles. He can provide them with the observation, analysis, inference, generalization and application skill which are necessary for systematic learning. Experiential, participatory, cooperative and integrated methodologies of education are in themselves value laden. They with help in developing the capabilities related to value of scientific enquiry, of questioning, of independent search for truth, or systematic learning, of cooperation, of good governance, of expression of hidden talents etc. Introducing such changes in teaching methodologies is therefore in itself an important step in the inculcation of values through education.
2. *Direct Value Education Sessions:* While much can be done with the help of regular curriculum and methodologies of teaching yet some time must still be made in the school schedule to allow for periods specifically dedicated to the inculcation of values. Such classes can introduce the relation between spiritual and material, of the oneness of mankind, of prejudice and removal of prejudice, the process of personal and collective development and the importance and nature of service. These classes should be designed in such a way as to load students to discover each of these principles and the implications by themselves.
3. *Indirect Education for Values in Subject Matter:* All subjects can become partners in the process of inculcation of values. For example, mathematics helps to increase the capacity to think systematically and solve problems. In every science subject, spiritual insights can be derived from the physical principles. Language classes can become means to express this learning

and to use these metaphors effectively. In doing so, the teacher should be able to reinforce explicitly the values that are intrinsic to the topic at hand (for example, accuracy and logical reasoning, beauty and order in mathematics, objectivity and inference in science; beauty, clarity depth of thinking in language classes etc.). They can also bring in values through analogies and metaphors, for example, respect for God's creation can be introduced in science classes, rectitude at conduct can be discussed in social studies or civics classes etc.

4. *Personal and Collective Growth Processes:* Inspiring students with the attitudes of service and developing in them the capacity for moral behaviour cannot be done through improved teaching and through theoretical classes and the conveying of concepts alone. For sustained behavioural change to occur, student must be given an opportunity to grow and help others to grow by participating in systematic and structured processes of collective action. The curriculum must, therefore, include both, individual growth processes focussing on acquiring virtues and developing individual potential, and collective growth processes, focusing on learning the skills and attitudes of working together in a path of service.

   This can be done with the help of some individual and collective activities organised in the school as:

   (i) Collective service activities in and out of school
   (ii) Planning and implementation of morning assemblies
   (iii) Exhibition
   (iv) Cultural and artistic activities
   (v) Skits and dramas
   (vi) Declamation contests
   (vii) Celebration of birthdays of great persons
   (viii) Celebration of national and international days
   (ix) Value-oriented projects
   (x) Girl guiding, scouting and National Service
   (xi) National Cadet Corps

   The set of activities described above exist in many institutions and is often referred as 'co-curricular' activities. The activities in themselves do not matter so much. It is what is learnt from them systematically in terms of personal and collective growth that matters.

5. *School Involvement in the Community:* The learning process described above cannot be confined to the walls of the school. The learning experiences we provide must, therefore, be extended beyond the walls of the school to the community that surrounds it. A true learning partnership must be established between the school and the community. This is necessary to provide real life experiences to the students.

6. *Role Modelling by teaching Staff:* The teachers can prove very useful in inculcating values among the students. A teacher who has acquired a new

Max Weber argued that ideal types are imperative in the functioning and stability of societies because individual members of society can associate their own views and experiences with these ideals, as a point of reference. For example, ideal types can help us to appreciate and comprehend the roles of schools and teachers, which are constructed and developed over time through lived experiences and reflection, as well as on the basis of some ideas, expectations and anticipations about their roles and responsibilities.

For instance, knowledge of an ideal body temperature, amount of sleep, weight or blood pressure allows us to compare with an agreed, accepted or popular standard. These ideals provide a transparent benchmark, which can be challenged and revised, if necessary. Although these examples of ideals are in quantitative form, but the construction of ideal can also be qualitative with richer descriptions. For example, an ideal candidate for a job, an ideal teacher for a school, an ideal doctor for a hospital, even though the selection process may include consideration of implicit or hidden factors that reject internal priorities.

In the broader context of philosophy, the terms 'ethics and ideal' have been inherently tied.

According to Rushworth Kidder, *"Standard definitions of ethics have typically included such phrases 'as the science of the ideal human character'."*

In the worlds of Plato, *"Ideals exist in a kind of independence from humanity such that reason discovers the principles rather than simply creates them."*

Nicholas Rescher in 'Ethical Idealism; An Enquiry into the Nature and Function of Ideals' states that the metaphysical nature of ideals gives them a particular status as 'useful fiction' in terms of their special existence. According to him, *"The reality of an ideal lies not in its substantive realization in some separate domain but in its formative impetus upon human thought and action in this imperfect world."*

In the words of De Raytor, *"Ideals are vision, visualisation, and imaginations of a perfect state of affairs in which excellent values have some realities; they express a kind of transcendence. Ideals consider as a special kind of values, that are not realised or very hard to realise or never fully realisable."*

Many thinkers have emphasized that ideals as such constitute things that must be said to live in the real universe, retaining a substance partly to the same extent as flesh and blood in people and similar physical bodies.

Ideals are beliefs that drive a character. These can include ideas such as generosity or greed, respect or might, or tradition or freedom. These ideals help to define the character's alignment which defines how others view the character. Developing ideals help define what a character deeply believes in and shapes their history as well as how they will play the role in situations which threatens various beliefs.

Ideals might answer any of these questions.

- What are the principles that you will never betray?
- What would prompt you to make sacrifices?
- What drives you to act and guides your goals and ambitions?
- What is the single most important thing you strive for?

You can choose any ideals you like, but your character's alignment is a good place to start defining them. In everyday language, the word 'ideal' is often used to describe dreams and aspirations, as ideal house, holiday, job, car, etc. Most people will have some ideal of imaginations about such ideals. These ideals, riddles with expectations, can also be applied to social roles and positions, as the ideal citizen, man, woman, teacher, student etc.

**How to Develop Ideals**

School can play an important role in the development of ideals. Values and ideals are interconnected. Honesty is more valuable than arithmetic. Industry is more valuable than geography. Information is only a means towards an end, and this end is the proper development of fundamental ideals.

It is extremely difficult to develop high ideals in individual child. Most of the teachers are constantly facing the problems as how to make dishonest children willing to be honest, untidy children desire to be neat, naughty children eager to remain disciplined, and lazy children anxious to be industrious. The most baffling problem that the teacher meets is the development of character and personality.

The teacher can develop ideals through the following techniques.

- *Create the desire:* It is easy to create desire for ideals in youths and in adults. When he/she begins to face the future, or is already engaged in a vocation, he/she is sensitive to the development of those ideals which will make him/her a successful person in the chosen field. A teacher should try to develop the traits from the very childhood, so that the child may get success in later life.
- *Diagnose the Situation:* Whenever a person possesses a weak personality trait, some causes may be responsible for it. The teacher should not only diagnose the weaknesses, but it is also necessary to diagnose the individual child to see what incentive will create the desire when we search for the hidden springs of ideals, we are led back into a most complex field. Ideals are the visible tops of the submerged continents of instincts, emotions, and habits which run down into early childhood and ancestry.
- *Use Problem finding:* Instead of problem solving, teachers can help students look at the world by finding gaps to fill using problem finding. It requires an intellectual and imaginative vision to seek out what might be missing or should be added to something important.

- *Develop a plan of action:* Sometimes the teacher thinks that when the desire is created, plan for developing ideals may safely be left to individual child. While thinking so, he/she is not correct. They must do more than inspire a child to be neat or ambitious or industrious. The desire can be created by organising inspirational talks, but these must be followed with advice about how to apply the ideals to the ordinary events of life. Unless application are made to concrete situations and a plan of action worked out, the ideals will seldom be applied to the practical life of the pupil.
- *Mindset:* A change in mindset, mood, and overall classroom vibe begins with the teacher. If the educators are excited about their subject matter, students will tend to follow, because he/she may be ideal for the students. Educators must have passion for the subjects they are teaching. However, a teacher's mindset regarding how to design and deliver content will be helpful in developing the idea about ideal teacher among students.
- *Practice:* Frequently it happens that the student may have the desire to follow an ideal and may know what to do and yet fails to perform the action which the present situation requires. What we seek in the full development of ideals is a sustained desire which does not greatly fluctuate. It will not be possible without consistent practice.
- *Reward:* It is fact that no one will practice an ideal, unless it gives him satisfaction. We want to be honest because honesty is the best policy. If honesty does not yield satisfaction, we will and must inevitably cease to be honest. In real life it happens many times that people earn money by means of dishonesty. At the school or college level, the reward should come from outside for good efforts. The teacher must praise the effects. When an individual becomes mature enough, the reward may be internal. When a person has felt the actual glow of satisfaction which comes from being honest, courteous, we need not usually worry greatly about the permanence of these traits as ideals.
- *Generalise Ideals:* Sometimes it happens that we follow the ideal in some specific situation not in the other. For example when we have cleanliness drive as announced by the government, we started keeping our house clean but not the area outside our house. The answer is simple, we had not generalized the ideal of cleanliness. This failure to generalize an ideal and make it apply to all types of situations is an extremely common spectable. Another example may be a student who is classed as obedient when the regular teacher incharge teaching, becomes wildly disobedient when a trainee teacher arrives. Therefore, an ideal may have its widest influence in the life of an individual, it is necessary that he/she not only to know how to apply the ideal to specific situation but that also to generalize the ideal that he/she will apply it to all situation.

  Now a days everyone is saying that there are no ideals among the youth, but there are some factors in education responsible for it. The information is over emphasized. More attention is paid on the development of cognitive aspect only and it is more tangible than ideals. The task of transforming information is entirely definite, whereas ideals possess no such erectness. When we inquire what honesty is in real sense. No portion of course of study is devoted to a consideration of ideals. We teach ideals only as an occasion arise. We teach honesty in cases of stealing, lying and we teach obedience when disobedience appears. If we know that ideals are important for individual development as well as for the development of society, these have to be developed with the help of education. The teacher is to administer his/her instructions in such a way that by the time the child has completed the work of the class, he/she will have instructions on these points.

- *Art and Ideals:* Art is especially important in conveying ideals. An ideal is a high point on some dimensions of evaluation. It is the heroic act, the perfect day, the man of your dreams, the person of unimpeachable character. Life is a constant pursuit of goals, a constant striving for what we conceive as good for us. There are as many ideals as there are virtues of character, realm of achievement, and modes of experiences. The creative and talented artists can represent them in many ways. But regardless of the content or medium of the ideal, the function of art is to embody the abstract standard in a specific concrete form that has the immediacy and motivating power of direct perception.

On the basis of some researches, following characteristics are found in an ideal student, and an ideal teacher.

### Characteristics of an Ideal Student

Some students possess great qualities that made them different from others. They are termed as ideal students and become role-models for others. The characteristics are as follows:

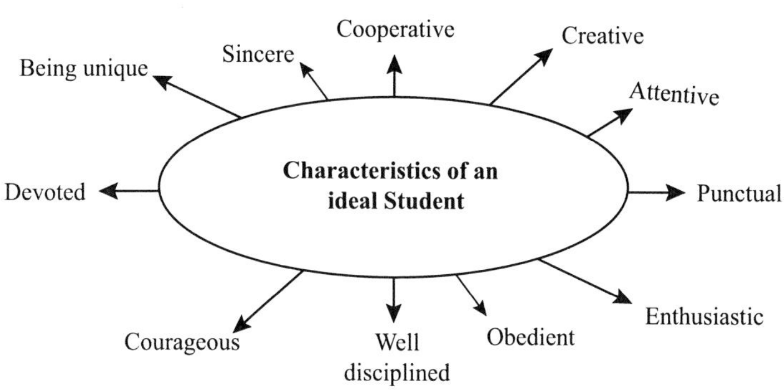


**Fig. 6.6: An Ideal Student**

- *Attentive:* An ideal student remains always attentive towards his studies. He/she understands the importance of the lessons being taught by the elders and teachers. He/she never neglects them at the cost of getting some pleasure in life.
- *Strong desire to learn:* A good student has a strong desire to learn everything either it may be from teachers, elders, administrators etc. He/she analyses everything minutely
- *Punctual:* Time is very precious. A good student knows that is why he/she tries to remain always punctual. He/she always try to do the things in time.
- *Creative:* A student loves to work out of box. His/her creative mind always inspires him/her to do something unique and do better in life.
- *Sincere:* A good student remains always sincere to whatever tasks he/she has in hand. He/she wants to complete that work with full interest and concentration.
- *Scientific outlook:* Scientific outlook means to see the things minutely and to go into detail and asks how, what and why. His/her reasoning ability is very high. He/she accepts something as true only when his/her curiosity is satisfied.
- *High ambition:* An ideal student always sets goals for himself/herself and does hard work to attain them. His/her involvement in all academic and co-curricular activities remains fully as he/has knows that these are the ladders to success.
- *Sense of empathy:* A good student is kind and sympathetic. He/she helps the needy people as well as students for the welfare of human society.
- *Good character:* A good student possesses a strong moral character. He/she has his/her own ideals. 'Simple living and high thinking' is the motto of his/her life. He is very humble, modest and polite. Apart from this he/she remains fearless and courageous

The above explained qualities represent general qualities, yet there may be some others also. An ideal student should be an embodiment of inspiration, encouragement, honesty, forgiveness, morality, spirituality, industriousness and a role model for others. He/she should always have an open mind to let in knowledge from anyone and anywhere. Rigveda says, *"Aanao Bhadrah Kratavao Yantu Vishwhah"*, means let noble thoughts/knowledge come from all directions.

## Characteristics of an Ideal Teacher

An ideal teacher is like a lamp that burns itself to bring the students out from the darkness of ignorance and fills their lives with the light of knowledge. He shows them the right path to get success in life. He is like a role-model in the life of every student. He/she is one, whom a student fondly remembers him even after leaving the institution. To be an ideal teacher, one should have:

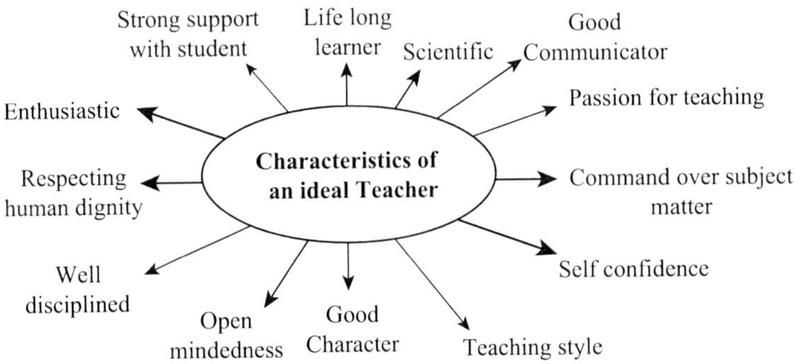


**Fig. 6.7: An Ideal Teacher**

- *Knowledge of learners:* An ideal teacher should have the understanding of pace and capacity of students. He/she should have the knowledge of cognitive, social and emotional development of learners. He/she should have an understanding that instructions should be tailored to meet each learner's needs.
- *Strong communicator:* An ideal teacher should be a strong communicator. His/her communication should be understandable by the students, teachers and others. If a teacher's communication (verbal, non-verbal, which include speaking, writing, imagery, body language) is good, he/she can convey knowledge with better results.
- *Command over subject matter:* An ideal teacher should possess a strong command over his/her subject. He/she should always keep himself/herself updated with the latest developments in the subject he/she is teaching.
- *Management skills:* An ideal teacher should have good classroom management skills. It will help him to grow better learning habits among the students.
- *Good listener:* An ideal teacher should be an excellent listener also. As the Turkish proverb says, *"If speaking is silver, then listening is gold."* The teacher can provide good environment in the classroom for the student to speak or to express their views without any hesitation.
- *Strong relationship with students:* An ideal teacher needs to be able to build caring relationship with his students. It is the caring student-teacher relationship that facilitates the exchange of information. Caring about the students is what inspires teachers to teach out, do better, communicate more, ask more, learn, refine and improve.
- *High expectations for the students:* An ideal teacher have high expectations for all of his/her students. These expectations are both challenging and realistic. He should know what each student is capable of individually and strive to help each one attain their best.

# 7

# Education and Socialization

*"The highest education is that which does not merely give us information but makes our life in harmony with all existence."*

–Rabindra Nath Tagore

The word 'Socialization' has different meanings. The social scientific usage of the term embraces two aspects of the designated process. The first aspect derives from the point of view of society. In this sense, socialization means transmission of the culture of the society to individuals. The second aspect derives from the point of the view of the individuals. In this sense, socialization means the process of becoming human in one's social environment.

When a newly born baby comes on this earth, he knows that what is happening in surroundings. He becomes a member of society when he interacts with other individuals. For living in society he requires some specific methods and techniques. The child must learn the expectations of the society so that his behaviour can be relied upon. He must acquire the group norms. So, it is the socialization process which molds a baby into a social person of the society.

Socialization is a process with the help of which a living organism is changed into a social being. It is a continuous and life long process till the end of life. An individual learns language, culture, values, norms, attitudes, and behaviours which molds his/her personality. This is the only process through which a person develops his/her self and personality when he interacts with his/her family and community. They transmit the norms of the society from one generation to the other.

## Meaning of Socialization

Socialization is a process through which individuals acquire the knowledge, language, social skills and values to conform to the roles and norms required for integration into a group or community. It is a combination of both self-imposed and externally imposed rules, and the expectations of others. The process operates at two levels, the one within the infant called the internalisation of objects around and the other from the outside. Social rules become internal to the individual, in the sense that they are self imposed rather than imposed by means of external regulations and thus become the part of individual's own personality.

Secondly, it may be in viewed as essential elements of social interaction, the individuals become socialized when they act in accordance with the expectations of others.

In the words of Horton and Hunt, *"Socialization is the process whereby one internalise the norms of his groups, so that a distinct 'self' emerges, unique to this individual."*

In the words of Lundberg, 'Socialization consists of the complex processes of interaction through which the individual learns the habits, skills, beliefs and standard of judgement that are necessary for his effective participation in the social groups and communities."

In the words of MacIver, *"Socialization is the process through which social beings develop relationships and association with each other."*

In the words of Ogburn, *"Socialization is the process of learning the norms of the group and society."*

According to Collins Dictionary, *"Socialization is the process by which people, especially children are made to behave in a way which is acceptable in their culture or society."*

In the words of Bogardus, *"Socialization is a process of learning to live and work together."*

In the words of Ross, *"Socialization is the development of 'we' feeling in associates and their growth in capacity and will to act together."*

In the word of Schaefer, *"Socialization is the process whereby people learn the attitudes, values, and actions appropriate to individuals as members of a particular culture."*

In the words of M.M. Johnson, *"Socialisation is a process of learning, that enables the learners to perform social roles."*

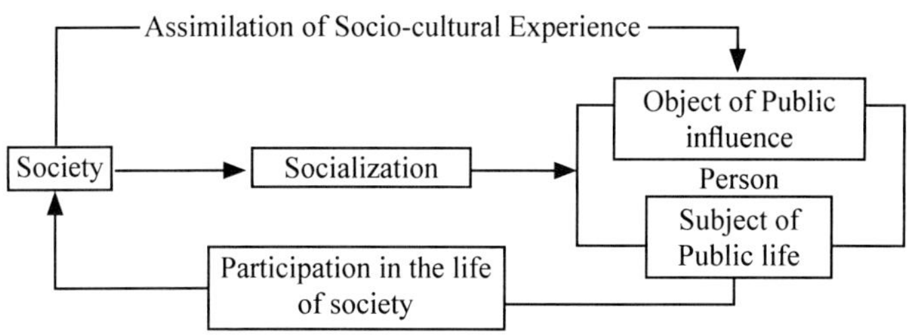


**Fig. 7.1: Process of Socialization**

Thus, on the basis of above definitions we can conclude that socialization is the process of fitting individuals with particular forms of group life. It transforms human organism into social beings and transmit established cultural traditions.

## Characteristics or Features of Socialization

Following are some of the important characteristics of socialization:

1. It is a life long process. It starts from birth and continues till death. It never stops, however, the speed and nature can be different at different stages of life.

2. It inculcates basic discipline. Through socialization an individual learns to control his impulses. When he interacts with the other persons, he may show a disciplined behaviour to gain social approval.
3. It transmits rules of the society from one generation to other.
4. It takes place formally through the formal agencies as schools and other educational institutions. They provide instructions directly to their students.
5. It takes place informally through the informal agencies as family, peer group, society, media etc. The family is the primary and the most influential source of socialization. The members learn their customs, norms and values in the family.
6. It involves changes. Nature never remains static. The person also undergoes changes from inception to death. The process of socialization changes according to the changes coming in the society.
7. It is often predictable. Psychologists have observed that each phase has certain common socialization traits and characteristics. As a result it is possible for us to predict at an early age the range within which the child is likely to fall.
8. It may differs from society to society and thus culture to culture.
9. It takes out the hidden qualities of a child and so, develops him mentally, physically and socially.
10. It helps to control human behaviour. The behaviour of an individual is controlled in various ways, as he/she gets training.
11. It is the most influential learning process one can experience.
12. It is the means by which social and cultural continuity are attained.
13. It has three primary goals: teaching impulse control and develops a conscience, preparing people to perform certain social roles and culturally shared sources of meaning and value.
14. It is definitely a matter of learning and not of biological inheritance.
15. It is a product of interaction of the organism and its environment. It is not possible to indicate exactly in what proportion heredity and environment contribute to the individual's socialization. Both work hand in hand from conception.
16. It proceeds from general to specific responses. The early responses of the child are very general in nature which is gradually replaced with specific ones.
17. It is unique. It is a fact that if the two children are of same age or even from the same family, they can't be expected to behave in an identical manner.

Thus socialisation is the means by which the infants begin to acquire the skills necessary to perform as functioning members of the society. It can be a two way process also as not only adults socialize the children, but sometimes adults can also be socialized by the child. For example an educated child can socialize an uneducated father in some skills. Socialization as both process and an outcome, is not better or worse in any particular culture or sub culture.

Socialization is very important for an individual. Social interaction provides the means through which we gradually becomes able to see ourselves through the eyes of others, we start learning who we are and how we fit into the world around us. In addition, we have to learn basics of both material and non-material culture to function successfully in the society. We learn how to dress ourselves, what is suitable attire for a specific occasion, what is considered appropriate to eat for dinner etc. Most importantly, we have to learn language—whether it is the dominant language or one common to a sub culture, whether it is verbal or through signs, in order to communicate and to think. If new generations of society don't learn its way of life, it ceases to exist. Whatever is distinctive to a culture must be transmitted to those who join it in order for a society to survive. For Indian culture to continue, for example, children in India must learn about cultural values related to democracy. They have to learn the norms of voting. They have to learn to respect all the religions, languages, customs etc. related to secularism and socialism also. In fact, there are many ideas, skills and values that Indians teach children in hopes of keeping the society's way of life going through another generation. Without socialization, we are unable to function socially.

## Types of Socialization

Socialization is a life long process and it continues from infancy period to adulthood. The different types of socialization are as follows:

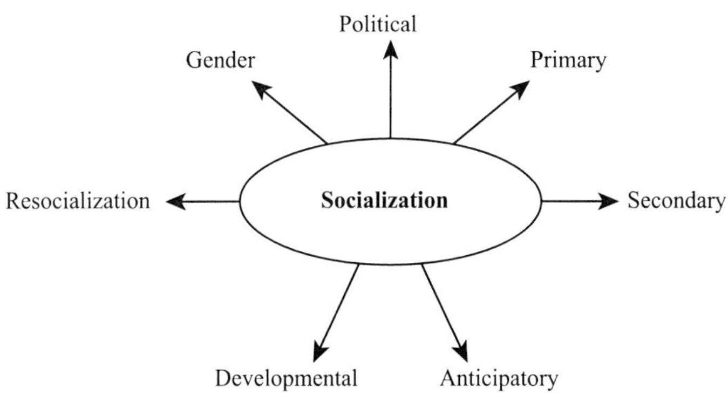


**Fig. 7.2: Type of Socialization**

1. *Primary Socialization:* Primary socialization starts from the infancy period because it sets the ground work for all future socialization. It is a process by which the infant learns language and cognitive skills, internalises norms and values. He learns the ways of a given grouping and is molded into an effective social participant of that group. At this stage,

the child does not have a sense of right and wrong. He gradually learns the norms relating to wrong and right things on the basis of direct and indirect observation, as well as through experience. It is mainly influenced by the immediate family and friends. It becomes a part of the personality of the child. For example, if a child saws his/her mother expressing a co-operative behaviour towards everyone, then that child may think that this behaviour is acceptable and could continue this behaviour towards the society members. It is the most crucial stage of socialization for later development.

2. *Secondary Socialization:* Secondary socialization refers to the process of learning what is the appropriate behaviour as a member of a small group within the larger society. It takes place outside the family. It takes place throughout one's life, both as a child and as one encounters new groups that require additional socialization. It is the behaviour pattern which is reinforced by socializing agencies of society. When the child goes to school, he is to behave according to the rules framed by the school. The teachers also to learn the new rules of the educational institutions.
3. *Anticipatory Socialization:* Anticipatory socialization occurs between the childhood and adulthood. Adolescence begins to establish independence from their parents. It refers to the processes of socialization in which a person rehearses for future positions, occupations and social relationships. A person learns the culture of a group with the anticipation of joining that group. As a person learns the proper beliefs, values and norms of a status to which he aspires, he is learning how to act in his new role.
4. *Professional or Developmental Socialization:* It occurs during the adulthood. This depends on the primary and anticipatory socialization. During these stages an individual has acquired the skills, attitude has developed and the goals for future are established; which have prepared him for the position that he is likely to hold as an adult. During this socialization, an individual enters roles as an employee, a husband or wife, etc means he/she is to take on new duties. It is more likely to change the overt behaviour.
5. *Re-socialization:* Re-socialization is the process by which an individual's sense of social values, beliefs, norms etc. are re-engineered. The basis of this socialization is to unlearn and relearn. It occurs when an individual changes his group and becomes the part of a new group, he has to abandon his old way of life. For example when a person joins the military, he enters a new social realm, where he becomes socialized as a military member. So, it is defined as a process where in an individual defined as inadequate according to the norms of dominant institution(s) is subjected to a dynamic programme of behaviour intervention aimed at instilling and or reinventing those values, attitudes and abilities which could allow him/her to function according to the norms of said institution(s) It often includes learning new norms and values that are

different from those associated with the culture in which the individual was raised. This process can be voluntary.

6. *Gender Socialization:* Gender socialization is the tendency for boys and girls to be socialized differently. Boys are raised to confirm to the male gender roles and girls are raised to confirm to the female gender roles. A gender role is a set of behaviour, attitudes and personality characteristics expected and encouraged of a person based on his or her gender.
7. *Political Socialization:* Political socialization is the process by which norms and behaviour acceptable to a well running political system are transmitted from one generation to the other. It is the process by which people of all ages and adolescents acquire political cognition, attitudes and behaviour.

Thus, on the basis of above explained different types of socialization, we can conclude that socialization is used by sociologists, social psychologists and educationists to refer to the process of learning one's culture and how to live within it. For the individual, it provides the resources necessary for acting and participating within their society. For the society, it is the means of maintaining cultural continuity.

Now we will discuss the relationship between education and socialization.

### Role of Education for Socialization

Education is derived from the word 'Educere' means to bring out the potentialies and abilities of the child. It is one of the intervening variables in the phenomenon of social change. Durkheim conceives of education as 'the socialization of the younger generation'.

In the words of James Welton, *"Education consists in an attempt on the part of the adult members of human society to shape the development of the coming generation with its own ideals of life."*

In the words of Samuel Koenig, *"Education is a process whereby the social heritage of a group is passed on from one generation to another."*

Both socialization and education involved learning. To be a well rounded person, we must be able to make solid decisions, figure out problems and think about solutions. From the time, a child is born, he/she is shaped and molded socially. Socialization and education can't be separated from each other. They overlap and intermingle from the first step in the classroom.

The main purpose of education should be to promote socialization. Socialization refers to the act of inheriting and spreading standards, customs, and ideologies, providing an individual with the skills and habits necessary for contributing in the society. Education effectively develops individuals into people who can contribute wealth and ideas in a society. It makes the people aware about the present situation and broadens one's perspective. The perspective and awareness has the muscle to enhance multiculturalism and lesson wrong attitudes.

**I. Aims of Education**

In has already been made clear that the basis of socialisation is the attainment of social and cultural continuity. Real socialization can be done of all our citizens when we make available suitable opportunities for that. Hence, from this view point education must have the following aims:

1. *To develop abilities and strengths:* The aim of education should be to develop people's abilities and strengths so that they can be assets with in the society. A nation's progress is not possible without education. An education system that seeks invest equally in the potential of all, is working towards making a powerful society that is fully maximizing its resources and functioning at its best. Education should function in such a way that every child should reach his/her highest potential and contribute to society with skills developed in the class.
2. *To create independent individuals:* Education should make the provisions so that the opportunities to get the education be made available to all. The skills learnt by the students in school gives them better opportunities outside the classroom. These skills create independent individuals who learn how to utilize their resources, making them competitive in society and the world. Education should be based on productive activities in order to enable the people to earn more wealth. To make the people efficient, scientific and technical education should be imparted along with general education. Each individual should be in a position to equip himself with the ability-which is necessary to make him well placed in the society in terms of necessary wealth for having both ends meet. When people make money, they are also creating monetary gains for the organisation they work for, as a result the government earns taxes also. It is cyclical system. The more that we put into education and the development of people, the society will be richer more and more. They will become able to bring changes in the society.
3. *To make the people aware:* Education should make the people awared. Basically, education is meant to teach individuals to read and write. Students obtain knowledge from different sources. The knowledge has the power to awaken and enlighten the sprit and mind. The people will be able to apply that knowledge in solving different problems not only of individuals but also of the society. They will be able to understand who they are and how they came to be. As a result education should be inclusive and provide a holistic view of the past for each and every person of every background. Education also provides knowledge about the other cultures and encourages students to see cultures and identities in a new way. All become sensitive and appreciative while learning about others.
4. *To develop democratic values:* Education should develop democratic values so that each person can play the role as good democratic citizen.

The democratic values as liberty, equality, fraternity and cooperative living are to be developed. True socialization stresses the dignity of individual and the sacredness of human personality.

5. *To develop sympathy:* Sympathy simply means to feel with another individual. It binds us more closely with our fellow men. Education should help in providing such opportunities in which with sympathetic reactions the children enter into a fuller understanding of the feelings and motives of others.
6. *To develop culture:* Education has an intrinsic value as the hallmark of a civilised society and the foundation of our culture. Now a days high quality education is essential—a love of learning is not sufficient. With the advancement in technology, awareness about right and wrong, enhancement in knowledge, the educationists brings change in the culture. We must resist attempts to divide culture from knowledge or to suggest that a focus on a core academic curriculum in schools makes it more difficult to develop our young people into creative, and engaged citizens.
9. *To prepare for adult life:* Adult life today is complicated, and we owe it to young people to ensure that they have the character and sense of moral purpose to succeed. Education can make a significant contribution by providing opportunities to instil key character traits, including persistence, grit, optimism and curiosity. It is a fact that the key attributes as resilience, self control, and social intelligence are powerful predictors of success in adult life.

Thus education and socialization are interrelated. E. Durkheim, a French educational sociologist has explained the role of education in socialization of child as *"Education is the influence exercised by adult generation on those that are not yet ready for social life. Its object is to arouse and to develop in the child a certain number of physical, intellectual and moral traits that are demanded of him by the society."*

## II. Socialization and Curriculum

The curriculum should be such which will help in proper socialization of the child. It should translate the aforesaid aims into practice. The following principles should be kept in mind while constructing the curriculum:

- The curriculum should be such that it helps in achievement of socialization of an individual as an individual as well as a society member.
- Through curriculum the cultural values should be brought to light and through it the high ideals of the society should be transmitted to the new generation.
- It should develop a sense of dignity of labour.
- The stress should be on the futuristic role also.
- The curriculum should be dynamic and flexible in nature.

Thus in the curriculum not only the topics like democracy, freedom, equality, social justice, secularism, social reforms etc. should be studied but a number of co-curricular activities should also be included so that the students might understand the practical implications of these ideas. It will help is making students self-reliant, socially sensitive and democratically oriented personalities.

### III. Socialization and Methods of Teaching

Educational sociologists advocate the use of project method, socialized techniques, group discussions and techniques of group dynamics. The teachers should also use cooperative learning, problem solving and democratic methods of teaching. While adopting different approaches and techniques of teaching, the teacher should keep in mind the following aspects:

- While teaching more stress should be on the social behaviour.
- The skills and knowledge acquired by the individuals should have practical implications.
- The social and cultural programmes should be organised which will help in doing socializations.
- The teacher should develop constructive thinking and problem solving ability among the student. For this socialized techniques will be more fruitful.
- By playing with other children, they learn skills that stick with them their whole life.
- Children react better to cooperative learning in which they learn sharing, setting boundaries and problem solving.

Thus with the help of using different methods and techniques the teacher can socialize the individuals. They learn to have empathy for other people. As they develop and pick up social cues they learn what behaviours or reactions are appropriate and which one aren't.

### IV. Socialization and Teacher

The teacher should take care of his duties. He should provide intellectual and social leadership. He should set himself as an example before the children. He is a symbol of high caliber and high ideals. He should mould the personality of the children in such a way that they may be able to become the makers of prosperous society. He should pay a pivotal role in achieving the objective of socialization. A teacher should know the process of socialization among students, the methods of interaction and programmes for social development.

The teachers have to activate the mind as well as the body of students. They have to prepare the students for the life of purity and sincerity. The teacher can help the students in choosing the right path for their future life. They open the mind of their students about their future life that how they will survive in the society. They can set an example in front of the students. Good behaviour of teacher with students would promote the positive effect among students. They have to develop the feeling of love, care, help, brotherhood, broadmindedness, cooperation, collaboration, respect etc., which create a special bond of affection. In this way they can contribute in socializing the students for every aspect of life.

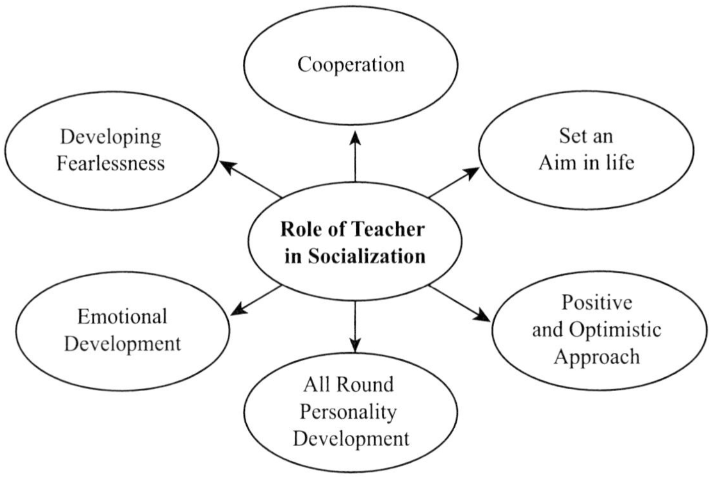


**Fig. 7.3: Teacher and Socialization**

Thus the most important function of education is socialization. The people have no knowledge about the culture of their society. They must learn them and they must learn the way in which their society is functioning. Dewey says: *"Though people learn a great deal from their parents or in clubs and among group of friend yet they learn more of the culture of their society through educational system. Through education, the child is able to develop reasoning in social relations, cultivates social virtues and thus becomes socially efficient."* When he speaks about social efficiency, he call it 'socialization of individual.' In this way, we can conclude that education may not be only part of the process of socialization, but it is a very important part.

- A small economic unit
- Means for rearing the children.
- Provides companionship.
- A religious, political and recreational unit.
- A complex and complicated structure.
- Standard of living is becoming high.
- Living in great security.
- Establishes a set of values.
- Its social life is becoming increasingly complicated, anonymous and impersonal.
- Provides emotional stability and security.
- Affords basic learning in the childhood.
- Transmission of culture.
- Provides Adequate Educational Guidance.
- Provides proper feelings of affection and attention.
- Develop better social intelligence.
- Better social—personal conditioning is afforded,
- Develops proper communicative abilities.

The child remains mainly with the mother, the father, and other siblings up to the age of 5 or 6. Childhood or infancy is the most impressionable period just like a clean slate on which anything can be written. A child's behaviour during the early years can be moulded and shaped in a desired form and direction provided that suitable socio-psychological environment is made available. If negative impressions are provided at home to the child, it is very difficult to remove these during the years of schooling of the child. And if the child is reared in an open, affectionate and free environment with due care and attention, later developments of the child is healthy. Home, therefore, plays the most significant role in laying the foundation of child's personality in terms of cognitive, social, character, emotional, religious and moral development.

Different educationists have highlighted the importance of family in different terminology:

In view of Pestalozzi, *"Home—a centre of love and affection, is the best place and the first school of the child."*

In the view of Froebel, *"Mothers are the ideal teachers and informal education given by home is most effective and natural."*

In the words of Prof. K.G. Saiydain, *"The education of man depends on the environment that he enjoys. If these environments are based on good customs and traditions of the family, they will spread beneficial influence on his ideas and development and his education will be useful not only to him but to the whole community."*

Using the formulation of psychoanalytic theory, Freud attempted to explain the impact of parent behaviour, parental attitudes and early childhood experiences on the development of the personality and the social behaviour of the child. Freud observed, *"The family is the society in miniature."* This statement highlights the crucial role of the family in the socialization process. There are enough evidences to show that the socialization process at home during early childhood years leaves an indelible impression and influence on the adult social behaviour of the child.

The opinion expressed by different educationists clearly reveal the importance and value of home in his education, socialization and development of the child. Family has some important functions in relation to the development of the child a social being as well as educational functions related to an overall development of child's personality.

***Functions of Family/Home***

1. *Preservation of Social Inheritance:* Family is the first social institution which attempts to socialize the child. This means developing in the child components and capacities essential for future role performance. Every society relies upon a number of social institutions for the performance of one or both of the social functions viz:
   (i) To help in perpetuating the culture of the society and
   (ii) to facilitate the process of social change.
   Of these two basic functions of social institutions preservation of social inheritance is the most crucial function of the home. Human life, as we know, has ground in an organised cultural history as well as cultural transformation. In regard to the former function, family performs the most pivotal role.
2. *Development of Sense of Belongingness:* The child observes his parents in particular way in day-to-day living and because of the sense of belongingness, it easily retains and internalizes those behaviour which are appreciated by the family. In fact, it is the we feeling which is a characteristic feature of the family that makes internalization possible.
3. *Primary Place of Learning:* As Pestalozzi has rightly remarked, "Home-a centre of love and affection, is the best place and the first school of the child." Home is the primary place of learning. Rousseau has also described, *"Education begins at birth and the proper nurse is the mother."* The mother is rightly said to be the first teacher of the child.
4. *Proper Care of Physique:* The first and foremost function of the home is to develop the child physically sound. For this purpose family members provide physical experiences. In other words physical exercises, habits of cleanliness and vigorous living are fostered in the child. Apart from this balanced diet is provided to the child for the proper physical development.

We all understand that socialization function relate to an overall development of child's personality which comprises development of worth while skills, attitudes, values, behaviours and above all the social abilities of the child. Social abilities mean development of good habits what is worth while and who can supplement and appreciates the activities of society. Thus even in the modern times the lap of mother is considered as the first school of the child. Raymont has rightly remarked the importance of family as, *"Two children may attend the same school, may come under the influence of same teacher and the same organisation, may pursue the same studies and performs the same exercises, and yet may differ totocoelo as regards their general knowledge, their interests, their speech, their bearing and their moral love, according to the home they come from."*

In rural societies children have most of their early social content with the family. Today, however the importance of family in the child's life is changing, because most children growing up will spend a great deal of time with people other then members of their families, but this does not mean that the participation of families in socialization has ended. Still the family continue to be a major means of passing on values, attitudes and behaviours.

## 2. Peer Group

After family/home the individual comes in to contact with peer group during the early childhood, later childhood and adolescence. As per dictionary peer is one who is equal in rank. Boys and girls form group of their peers called peer groups. Much of the social learning takes place in association of peer group. Many social interests, social customs and traditions, social prejudices and the like are learnt during peer group association. The members of the peer group may be classified as the infant peers, the childhood peers and the adolescence peers.

The peer groups are the activity groups of young children and it is very significant one which also plays the socialization role in their own way. They come next to the family. They are the associations framed spontaneously for the purposes of recreation or play and such other common interests. Generally they are formed without the interference of the elder generation, either the family member or outsider,

Peer groups help for the socialization of the child. The group life of the peer provides social facilitation to learn many social roles as group leaders or followers. The leaders of these groups serve as models for the followers. These groups satisfy many social and personality needs of the children. In peer groups, there is better learning. Sometimes it is seen that what the students can not learn from the teacher, the same thing he/she can learn easily and effectively in a short span of time in the peer group.

### *Characteristics of Peer-Group*

Peer groups help in socialising and providing recreation to the child. Its characteristics can be described as follows:

- They are of two types—primary and secondary.
- They may be social or anti-social.
- There is inborn type of motivation which ensures good learning by all in the group.
- They are formed more or less spontaneously without the help or interference of the elder generation.
- The age or play or other common interests bind them together.
- There is neither external guidance nor influence in the formation of these groups.
- The secondary associations are organised in a planned manner either by the youth or an external agency like the government or any voluntary organisation.
- The primary associations may carry out either the constructive or destructive activities.
- They care for the welfare of the youth, their physical, social, mental and emotional health.
- They programme for creational and recreational activities.
- They are meant to benefit the society and to be profitable to the individuals.
- They help in the formation of good conduct and character, and
- They help in the development of wholesome personality.

***Classification of the Peer-Groups***

The peer-groups may conveniently be classified as the primary and the secondary peer groups.

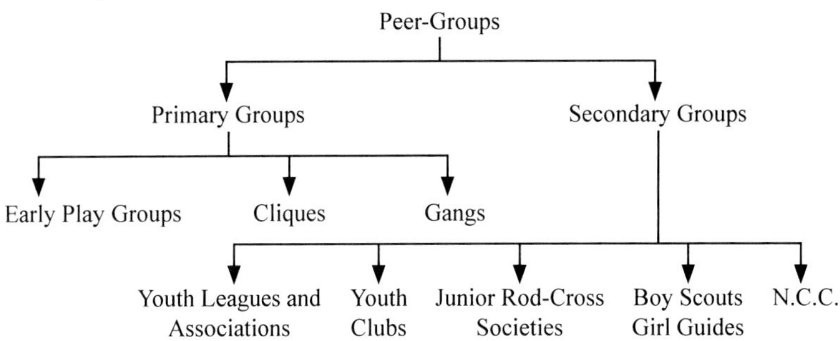


**Fig. 8.3: Classification of the Peer Groups**

1. *The Early Play Groups:* When the child comes in to contact with society members, his social environment extends. The members of the society form the members of the primary group. In the early childhood, the children make friendship with other children of the same age group in the vicinity of their homes. The chief purpose of framing this group is play. Three are no differences on the basis of caste, creed, colour. sex, religion, language etc. since social attitudes and prejudices are not formed by that time. The children come to learn and play many roles as leaders, sub-

group leaders. followers etc. They learn many good habits as pleasure, cooperation, love, affection etc. They carry out many life responsibilities in the form of play rehearsals.

2. *The Cliques:* The cliques are next to the early play groupings. Their membership is limited. They co-operate and conflict with each other. Common interests like castes. communities, play, studies and other cultural and social activities are responsible for the formation of the cliques. In these peer groups children learn both good as well as bad habits.
3. *The Gangs:* The gangs are more conscious peer groups. They are usually formed during the later childhood and continue during the stages of adolescence and may also be carried over to adulthood. They are peculiar of adolescence stage. In its formation sex differences are found. They may be constructive or destructive. The constructive groups are those social-service groups that carry out constructive activities like adult education programme, cleanliness drive etc. The destructive -groups are those that carry out antisocial activities.
4. *The Secondary Groups:* The youth organisations of different kinds come under the secondary groups. They, are not formed spontaneously but consciously. They are purely constructive organisations formed by external agencies like the government or welfare organisations. In the absence of these organisations the youth are likely fall prey to anti-social organisation.

### *Functions of the Peer Croups*

Peer-groups help in socialising the child. In these children perform constructive as well as destructive activities. In schools the students of different sections of different classes form peer groups. They perform the following functions:

1. *Learn How to Behave:* Like schools, community, family and other agencies of socialization the foremost function of peer-group is to socialize the child. In it the child learns how to behave with others, how to live with others and how to make their group strong. This means developing in the child components and capacities essential for future role performance, The child observes the behaviour of peers and because of the sense of belongingness, it easily retains and internalize those behaviours which are appreciated by the peers.
2. *Changes in Behaviour:* Peer group brings changes in the behaviour of the child. They may be desired or undesirable. There is free and frank atmosphere in the group. Sometimes free atmosphere brings undesirable changes in the behaviour of the child. This is the reason that there is need of some restrictions of the family and community members on the child and on the other hand the child should live in good peer-group.

3. *Development of Feeling of Belongingness:* In the peer group there is no place for 'I' feeling. They bind with each other. Feelings of belongingness, brotherhood develop in the members of the peer group. They feel more secured. They understand that they belong to one another. They become ready to sacrifice their individual interests for the group.
4. *Development of Healthy Attitude:* All the members in the group work for one another with cooperation and every work look easy to them. Every individual work according to his/her capabilities and potentialities. Everyone learn to live in cooperation so the healthy attitudes as cooperation, patience, love, affection, sacrifice, brotherhood etc. are developed in the peer group.
5. *Development of Creative Ability of Free Expression:* In the peer group every individual is free to express his feelings, thoughts, views, opinions without any fear or stress. Every body has his own individuality. Development of this habit will help him in future life. They can think independently and make their own judgements.
6. *Development of Personality:* In today's complex society, the peer-group plays a vital role in the development of child's personality. The child's intellectual abilities, aspirations and commitments are also acquired in the peer-groups. For the proper development of a child's personality, parents should take care that the child should remain in good friends. The peer-group provides opportunities to the individuals for mixing with each other. They are able to learn together, play together and better interaction with one another. All this help in the development of the personality of the individual.
7. *Diffusion of New Knowledge:* In 21st century there is huge explosion of knowledge due to the new findings of the scientists, technologists and other investigators. This knowledge must be acquired by the youth to cope successfully with a society different from their ancestors' society. The individuals in the peer groups while discussing transmit new ideas to one another. This would help them understand the changes.
8. *Self-Dependence:* Peer groups also help in developing the habit of doing work independently. They help in developing a sense of responsibility, discharging their duties and solving problems with the help of the members of the group. The children become self dependent in making decisions regarding various issues.

Thus undoubtedly, peer-group is an important agency of socialization. Sometimes individuals develop study habits with the help of it. During the interaction of these groups, the individuals of different regions and religions, castes and communities, loyalties and languages etc, come closer and closer according to their interests and aptitudes. Sometimes if they remain unchecked it may result in to immeasurable loss. So formation of code of ethics by the student population itself and inflicting of punishment by themselves through the formation of students courts etc. will lead in due course to the development of right behaviour and self-discipline among the students.

### 3. School

In most small, simple societies socialization may be almost entirely by informal agencies. Group way was learnt by observing behaviour of adults. The family provides the child with all the activities and experience he needed for inter-personal and inter social relationship with his group. Subsequently religious places like temple, the mosques and church began to serve this purpose. In ancient period our society was divided in to four varnas—Brahman, Kshatriya, Shudra and Vaishya. So long as occupations were centred around home or village, the family, the church and the local community performed the function of socialization. The children learnt by initiating the work and model of living of their parents and neighbours. In this way socialization was first of all a family affair and then religious affair but as the society becomes more complex and differentiated, informal institutions become less effective. With the passage of time, social complexity and need for socialization becomes so great that school and teaching get more or less embedded in to the social structure

The concept of school also underwent a tremendous change. There is a vast difference between ancient and modern school.

#### *Ancient School*

Ancient school or traditional school can be summed up in one sentence i.e. 'Limited responsibility for limited population.' By limited population we mean that everyone was not allowed to go to school i.e. instructions provided to only the children of priestly class and noble families and not for masses. In the same way limited responsibility means that the activities of school were confined mainly to the field of highest cultural attainment through the study of different subjects as philosophy, languages, mathematics and religion. In fact, the ancient schools imparted only liberal education. This process results in developing a 'dualism in civilization' between the ways and behaviour pertaining to everyday business of life and higher aspects of culture preserved in books. It was teacher centred education. Students are to respect the teacher as 'Guru'. The teachers lived in more or less isolation. Socialization was chiefly a one way process.

#### *Modern School*

The school in modem times is rightly concerned as a part of social system. It is part of the system of education, which itself is a social system. The schools has its obligations to the fulfilled and objectives to be achieved for the sake of the betterment of the society, A time has come when the school has to discharge the functions of home, community, church and its own specific functions. Drastic changes have upset everything and the school has to work as a balancing factor. It is considered as a part of the social system as it is concerned with social role and status as per the existing social model and ensuring the process of socialisation and individualisation, while effecting the acculturation process also.

***Origin of the Term School***

In the words of A.F, Leach, *"The discussion forums or talking shops where the youth of Athens spent their leisure time in sport and exercise, in training for wars, gradually crystalized in to schools of -philosophy and in fine arts. In the leisure spent in the trim gardens of the academy, schools developed."*

What is the origin of school? There is no definite answer to this question. In ancient period, there were schools to provide Vedic knowledge. During the early stage of humanity also we see that there was some type of education or the other but it seems that the schools as formal agencies have started after the stone age. The term school has been derived from the Latin word 'SKHOLE' which means 'Homes of Leisure.'

It seems that in ancient Greece the leisure was devoted to the development of spirit and people started practising it at a definite place. This was termed as 'Leisure' by them. 'Leisure' or 'Holiday' is closely related to socialization. Gradually these words become synonyms of whole education and thus the term 'Homes of Leisure' or 'place for education' or 'school' was derived. In Hindi school is known as 'Vidyalaya' which means a place of 'Vidya' (education) or 'Pathshala' which means a 'a place of lessons'.

***School can be Interpreted in Different Ways***

1. For a better informed man, *'School is a unity of interaction personalities', a field of social forces, a system of formal, informal control, a special cultural world and an image of society which it is called upon to serve.*
2. The most right and modem definition of school is, *'school is a place where teaching learning process in life and through life, that there are certain functions which has been assigned by the society to perform.'*

With the progress of civilization and culture, man began to think that his experiences are being broadened. By trial and error he was gaining new experiences. He wants that the errors of man should not be repeated by new generation. He wanted to take more progress of civilization. In order to carry the chariot of civilization forward and to bring development in the future, man took the help of definite methods, curriculum, teachers, time and place. The school, while it is related to society as a whole, represents a little society by itself. Teachers, students and other members of the little society interactively participate in their own distinctive ways. The school has its own mores, its own social settings and its own culture. In a way, it represents a 'total institution' in the sense that any student coming from any social culture has to abide by the rules and regulations of the school and adjust to the distinct social milieu of the schools for that period during which he stays at school. School can be treated as an agency of the society for socialising the younger generation. It is an agency through which individuals are trained to be motivationally and technically adequate to the performance of adult roles.

1. *"Schools are institutions developed by civilised man for the purpose of aiding in the preparation of the young to be well adjusted and efficient members of the society."* –J.S. Ross
2. *"School is a special environment where a certain quality of life and certain types of activities and occupations are provided with the object of securing child's development along desirable lines."* –John Dewey
3. *"School is a foregoing place or manufacturer of humanity"* –Comenius
4. *"School—the modest temple of wisdom."* –Franklin
5. *"A school is not a market place where knowledge is dumped upon unwilling consumers. It is a seedbed of culture. It is a symbol of unity. It is an arsenal of democracy. It is an epitome of the world. It must lay in youth proper and secure foundation in the spring time of their lives."* –S, Balkrishna Joshi
6. *"The school may be regarded as a social invention to serve society for the specialised teaching of younger ones."* –Ottaway

***Need and Importance***

In modem age the role of school is very important. Schools are formed in every country of the world. S. Balakrishna has rightly said, *"The progress of a nation is decided not in legislation, not in court, not in factories, but in schools,"* School education is becoming the major source for socialization and the organization and direction of school has become the principle task of state and society. As H.G Wells has aptly remarked, *"A world whose schools are unreformed is an unreformed world."* The need of establishing school arise due to the following reasons:

1. To lead the child for all round development.
2. To transmit the huge treasure of knowledge to the next generation.
3. Inadequacy of the informal agencies for socialization in the complex society.
4. To provide a simple, interesting and well organised environment to the child for his mental, emotional, physical and social development.
5. For the complete socialisation of the child, with the development of socially desirable values, they prove useful citizens.
6. School is obliged to conserve and promote society's culture which otherwise might pass in to an oblivion.
7. There is economy of energy and time.
8. All homes are not good homes which may socialize the child in right direction.

9. Schools provide the desired solution for all the problems of society,
10. To propagate ideals and ideas of each state in the shortest possible time.

***Functions of School***

School is a socializing agency and has real autonomy of its own. It acts on its own initiative and its own judgement in view, precisely of expert knowledge which led to its becoming such agent. The function of school is to help the child to live fuller and happier life in adjustment with the changing environment, to develop the best elements in his own culture and to achieve the social and economic progress in the later life which will enable him to take his place in the modern world and to live together in peace. The general functions performed by the schools are socialisation of the child and acculturation. The major functions of the school can be grouped in two categories—A. Manifest Functions B. Emerging Functions

A. *Manifest Functions*

1. *Transmission and Promotion of Culture:* The central role of the school i.e. transmission of culture from one generation to the other is usually done through formal teaching of history, literature, art and craft etc. The celebration of national, historical and other significant events is also a good means to transmit the culture to the young child. But It not only transmits the culture, but also trains children in a manner that they enrich and modify that heritage through their own efforts and this helps in the establishment of a better and happier society.
2. *Teaching Basic Skills:* Some attention at secondary level of schooling has been given to occupational education. It is the function of school to impart vocational and industrial education to children.
   Gandhiji believed that education should provide economic security to the child, Recommendation to this effect were made by the Secondary Education Commission in 1956, then by Education Commission in 1966, later by Adisesiah Committee as well, and now by National Education Policy 2020. Work experience is introduced in the schools with a view to develop in students a respect for manual and practical work. It will help in developing the feeling of dignity of labour. The students will be able to support themselves and serve the society with sincerity.
3. *Development of Character:* It is a very famous saying that if wealth is lost, nothing is lost; if health is lost, something is lost; but if character is lost, everything is lost. In early times family and religious institutions develop the character of children, but now it has become the function of school. It implies that children understand that they ought to do in a situation and they actually behave the way they ought to behave even if it involve personal inconvenience. In the school, the child is to participate in such moral, ethical and social activities which may inculcate in them

the socially desirable values and lead to the formation of a strong good character.

4. *Promotion of Mental Health:* Mental health is in no way less important than physical health. The mental health of the students can be restored to a large extent by providing a reasonable balance between curricular and co-curricular activities. If the student is not able to adjust in the school, it is the responsibility of the school to find out its causes. After finding out the cause of disturbance, the school can devise proper means to give positive guidance. It will help in solving the problem of wastage and stagnation.

B. *Emerging Functions of School*

The functions of school as stated above are established facts whether or not they are satisfactorily achieved. The emerging functions depend on the prevailing situations in the society and hence they may be better named as socialization issues. If the circumstances and needs of the society change, emerging functions will also change. Some functions are as follows:

1. *Personal and Social Problem Solving:* The school is fundamentally an experience giving institution. The development of general ability for independent thinking and judgement should always be placed as foremost aim of school. Real education must help the child to solve difficult problems relating to personal life. The children should no longer emerge as helpless. It is the function of the school to enable children to solve personal and social problems.
2. *Diffusion of New Knowledge:* There is a wide explosion of knowledge in the 21st century due to the multi-findings of scientists, technologists and other investigators. It is the major function of the school to impart a wide variety of knowledge to the students. If the youth is to cope successfully with the modern-society, he is to acquire the new knowledge. His advanced knowledge imparted by the school would help children understand the changes and adapt themselves to the growing demands.
3. *Increased Functional Literacy:* A few days back we consider literacy as knowledge of 3Rs (Reading, Writing and Arithmetic). But at present for the dynamic and democratic society, the literacy of 3R is inadequate. A more comprehensive concept called functional literacy—has been accepted as essential for the development of the society. A new R i.e. computer has also been added to this 3R. The term functional literacy represents meaningful and relevant ways of social survival. It involves worthwhile knowledge, skills, attitudes and values which provide empowerment to the common man for effective personal growth.
4. *Sex Education:* In the traditional Indian society, sex education was not at all systematic, but only incidental. Parents were hesitant to provide sex education. But due to the incidence of ghastly diseases like AIDS, this area needs immediate attention. It is for this reason that now a days due

attention is being paid to include sex education as a part of curriculum at school level. It will help in providing systematic sex education to the students. They will become aware of the dangers of unsafe sex.

5. *Social Competence:* Secondary Education Commission in his report recommended that we would like the school to become a centre of actual social life and social activities. Today the whole society is changing in its various fields as—political, social and economic. Society is fast heading towards urbanisation, industrialisation and westernisation. Life seems backward without the use of computers. There is need of behaviour competencies for effective social interaction. Advancement results in personal and social problems. Such problems require social competencies to solve them. For this schools are to encourage children to come in contact with social centres, social institutions and also participate actively in various social functions.
6. *Development of Democratic Outlook:* Our society is multi-cultural, multi-religious and multi-lingual. The schools today badly need to educate children to enable them to live and to cope with a secular, global community by developing harmonious relations with open-mindedness and respect need to be developed in children in schools. This, in fact, is the most important function of the school which alone can bring the society to peaceful co-existence. The school is to provide democratic environment so that each child may learn to live democratically.
7. *Reorganisation and Reconstruction of Human Experiences:* The human beings gain experiences in the past and the function of school is to transmit these experiences from one generation to the other. But due to advancement in the society, it has to meet social problems, to reform the society. For this, a continuous process of research in all the branches of knowledge is must and the schools are to be equipped to do it.
8. *Moral Development:* It is the crucial need of present day society because it is deteriorating day by day in the field of morality. It is not possible through bookish knowledge. For this a school can chalk out a programme of moral and religious education and give it a practical shape. Now a days every school is organising different activities like morning assemblies, mass prayers, celebration of religious days, talks by eminent persons to give a moral boost to the students.

Thus Schools socialize children in several ways. The students learn a formal curriculum, informally called the '3R's' reading, writing and arithmetic. Through this they become the productive members of the society. Apart from it, they interact with peers, so, ideally strengthen their social interaction skills. They interact with authority figures, their teachers, who are not their parents and learn a lot. Thus the child is formally introduced to the love and the learning, the arts and the science, the values and the beliefs, the customs and taboos of the society from a wider circle.

The schools are also places of learning cultural content in which one can be made aware of their society's history, tradition and norms.
Schools and classroom rituals, led by teachers serving as role models and lenders, regularly reinforce what society expects from children. Sociologists describe this aspect of school as 'hidden curriculum', the informal teaching done by schools. For example, schools have built a sense of competition with the way the grades are awarded and the way teachers evaluate students. Students learn to evaluate themselves within a hierarchical system as 'A+', 'A', 'B+', 'B' etc. When children participate in a relay race or a science contest, they learn that there are winners and losers in the society. They practice teamwork with other students in cooperative situations when they work on a project. Thus the latent functions of competition, teamwork, classroom discipline and time management are the features of hidden curriculum. After family, schools play an important role in hidden socialization of the child.

### 4. Media

The term 'media' comes from Latin word 'medi' meaning 'middle' suggesting that the media's function is to connect people. The word media is the plural form of Latin word 'medium' means middle ground or intermediate. Media used for the masses to communicate something is known as mass media. The 20th century advancement in information technology led to tremendous revolution in communication in the shape of multi media system which are vital for our understanding of the modem world. With the help of mass media new forms of socialization and new types of individuals and collective identities are being created. The expansion of information technology and network is tending to encourage communication with different people with in or outside the country. The media which makes interactive communication with different people possible has wider implications as an agency of socialization.

The media affects us in many ways: as a major socialising influence, a carrier of culture, a source of information, education and entertainment, an important factor in political communication and participatory democracy, and a communicator of ideological values and norms, attitudes and beliefs. The media also represents and constructs conceptions of what constitutes a successful and valued life, along with what is considered to be deficient, deviant, marginalised or undesirable. In all these ways, the media exert an influence on identity formation and associated issues to do with stigma, self-esteem, social relations, economic and political positions. For instance, the way in which socioeconomic status is framed in the entertainment and news media significantly influences how audience feel about social equity and how they treat those who are impoverished, homeless or unemployed.

Communication is the function of life and as a function it is extricably linked with it. Life is impossible without communication. It is, therefore, said that communication begins with life and ends only when life ceases to exist. Communication can take place only through media. Communication involves sharing of information, attitudes and experiences. It is a process of transmitting a message from a source to an audience through a channel. Another example is the news item in a newspaper. The message is everything the news says or everything a reader might understand from it. This type of communication can only take place through certain media.

A mass media says Wilbur Schramm, "is essentially a working group organised around some device for circulating the same message, at about the same time, to a large-number of people."

Such a definition excludes the folk media, group media and natural communication such as rumour, education and preaching, where communication is not mediated by a device Further the term mass suggests that the modern media are mass and mass culture.

Mass Media means the media used for the masses to communicate something. It may be defined as any medium, means or agency through which ideas, attitudes or impressions are simultaneously communicated to a large number of people.

***Types of Media***

The following types of media can be used for socialization:

Types of Media

| Print Media | Non-print/Electronic Media | Digital Media |
|---|---|---|
| 1. Books | 1. Radio | 1. CD-Roms |
| 2. News paper | 2. Television | 2. DVDs |
| 3. Magazines | 3. Computer | 3. Internet facilities as www, e-mail. |
| 4. Journals | 4. Video-disc | |
| 5. Pamphlets | 5. Motion pictures | |
| 6. Atlas | 6. Tape recorder | |
| 7. Dictionaries | 7. Slide projector | |
| 8. Encyclopaedias | 8. Film projector | |
| 9. Flash Cards | 9. Video-text | |
| 10. Pictures | 10. Teletext | |

**Fig. 8.4: Classification of Media**

Of the different agencies of socialization, media in today's context plays the most vital role in socialization, acculturation or information dissemination. The media have found their rightful place in formal, informal and non-formal socialization of children and adults. For development of worth while knowledge, skills and attitudes in people of all ages, the media seems to possess great potential. In the last quarter of 20th century and beginning of

21st century there was a rapid development in information technology with the help of which tremendous amount of knowledge can be gained, processed and disseminated in most desired and effective manner. Mass communication systems opened up new directions to the horizon of human world. They brought a revolution in man's behaviour in gaining of knowledge.

Mass media have pervasive effects on our personal and social life. Its role in our society is in the following areas:

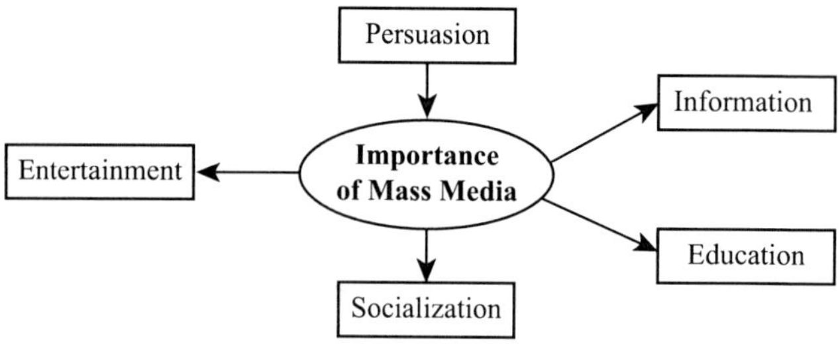


**Fig. 8.5: Effects of Mass Media**

### *Importance of Print Media*

The role of print media in the process of socialization is of special importance. Print media like newspapers, journals etc. are the basic and oldest channels of communication between one source to the other. Because of development of roads and communication newspapers are being circulated in every small village in India even if situated in a very remote area. Print media are being printed in every regional language to facilitate the readers to get information and knowledge in one's own mother tongue. In India where more than 30% of the people are living below poverty line, where they cannot afford to have expensive devices like television to get information, for them newspaper is the cheapest medium.

Before independence, print media played a missionary role of helping in creating public opinion against the foreign rule. This they did for more than half a century. The whole country was up against the foreign rule which eventually ended in 1947. The achievement of independence brought in a real challenge for those in power and also those not in power. This meant an altogether different role for the press.

In the present situation, the press has to play the role to maintain the integrity of the country by highlighting the consequences of separatist and fissiparous tendencies. Those agitating for the division of the country on linguistic and parochial basis have to be exposed through the press. Our country is wedded to the concept of secular state where people belonging to all religions and faiths have a right to live as Indians. The press had to help to form public opinion in favour of secular state on the plea that every Indian, irrespective of his/her religion, has right to live in this country.

Print media is the chief instrument for socialization throughout the world. Thousands of books, journals, magazines are being printed throughout the world in different languages for different purposes. Print media is the reliable and economical source of information and knowledge. Even in the present age of computer and satellite communication, the print based material is the most powerful and pervasive technology.

1. Newspaper is printed and distributed in almost all the languages in the world. It is the most important means of communication of the civilized man. It brings all the important happenings of the world with in the reach of the public with in hours. Now-a-days it is a powerful medium influencing the minds of general public and shaping and moulding the tastes, opinions, attitudes, aptitudes and interests. They attempt to socialize the people in the desired manner.
2. Print media excellently is a basis for intelligent class-room discussion and problem-solving situations.
3. Periodicals serve as the efficient socialising agencies because they help to transmit the social and cultural heritage of the society. There are special children's periodicals that cater to the needs and demands of the budding generation,
4. Both students and teacher are equipped to become researchers. Teachers can coach their students to evaluate and to use effectively the information they have gathered for themselves. In this way, a new partnership can develop in the classroom.
5. They are very economical. They save the time of the pupil and teacher.

### *Non-Print Media or Electronic Media*

The rapid progress of information technology may offer new prospectus for development by opening up a large number of isolated regions and enabling people to communicate with the whole world in the vital field of scientific research. According to Delors Commission, the inventions that have left their mark on the 21st century—records, radio and video recording, cable and satellite broadcasting—have not only added a technological dimension but also achieves economic and social significances as well. Most of these technologies have become sufficiently miniaturized and cost-effective. They have reached a majority of homes in the industrialized countries and also a number of people in developed countries. The non-print media/electronic media is of special value as it can reach millions at home, overcoming the barrier of illiteracy. They do not depend on the physical facilities, of roads and communication for reaching their target. Because of the introduction of electronic media, urbanisation is no longer an essential conclusion for mass communication. In India where 70% of the population are living in rural areas having 74% of the literacy rate and where people cannot read newspapers, electronic media have played a significant role. The newspaper is undoubtedly powerful but it is less direct than the broadcast media and certainly less intimate. The effect of television on the children and adolescents is considerable. It is of great help in socializing the children and others and in informing people on national programmes and development efforts. Democracy needs widespread understanding by people of the national objectives and attitudes, the details of welfare programmes and the methods of selection of representatives of people, the working of different political parties. All these aspects can be dealt with effectively by electronic media.

Children also learn about current themes and issues both from newscasts and dramas—issues as kidnapping, the homeless, spread of AIDS, currently spread of COVID-19 etc. Most of these issues are not the happy one, and many are very frightening especially when children watch programs that are intended for adults. Research also suggests that young children obtain considerable political and social information from television.

***Digital Media***

The children can get every type of information and communicate through mobile, internet, computers etc. This communication media has an important effect in encouraging children to support the existing norms and values or oppose or change them. They are the instruments of power. They influence us with their messages.

Thus print, non-print and digital media has a great effect while socializing the individuals. Non-print media communicates directly to our ears and eyes and thus leaving a strong impression. The importance of these influences varies from individual to individual. Different people read to the same suggestion differently. The media has a great impact on children from a very young age and affects their cognitive and social development. People learn about objects of material culture (like new technology) as well as non-material culture-what is true (beliefs), what is important (values) and what is expected (norms).

## 5. Community

The community is the next socializing agency of the informal type. It is with the community that the child comes into contact as he-enters in to life outside the home after the pals and clan.

The word 'community' is sum of two words i.e. 'COM' + MUNIS'. 'COM' signifies 'togetherness" and 'MUNIS' indicates 'to serve'. So community means 'to serve together'. Generally community indicates a group of people living together on a geographical piece of land having common ways of working. As we define government of the people, for the people and by the people, in the same way, we can define the working of community as of the community, for the community and by the community.

The essential ingredients of a community are—a source of land, group of people living more or less a common life, having a common spirit with common aims and ideals. Each individual naturally becomes a member of the community in which he is born and during the course of its development, he has to learn to adjust in the social environment and to its cultural heritage. In the words of Cook and Cook, *"A community is a group of people who dwell in given place and by means of efforts, build a social system which supports them. People include everyone, all the ages."*

According to Brownell, *"By a community I mean, a small diversified group of people; young and old, male and female; with different skills end abilities, together as kin neighbourers. It is face to face, primary group, in which many of the major functions of life are carried on co-operatively with in the group itself."*

In view of K. David, *"A community is the smallest territorial group that embraces all aspects of social life."*

In the words of Ginsberg, *"By community is to be understood a group of social beings living a common life including all the infinite variety and complexity of relations which result from that common life which constitute it."*

On the basis of definitions described above we can say that community is a population aggregate living in a contiguous geographical location characterised by consciousness of local unity—the community sentiments. It is a part of large society with common cultural and social linkages.

***Characteristics of a Community***

The characteristics of a community may briefly be described as follows:

- The members of the community are conscious of its existence and feel pride of their membership.
- They are fully aware of their ideals.
- They have a clear idea of the organised body which they constitute.
- They have devotion to common territory, traditions and culture.
- They have we-feeling.
- They have feeling of affinity.
- They have love, interest and loyality for the community
- They are fully conscious of their relationships.
- Their co-operation on conflict with others intensifies their group consciousness.
- Collective recreation, amusements etc. help to foster national solidarity.
- A well-knit population.

Thus in a community people of different groups are tied in bonds of unity and they take interest in each other and preserve each other's interest.

***Role of Community in Socialization***

Since the community is a relatively larger social unit as compared to the home, the functions of the community are the continuation and furtherance of the function of family. Every community has its various needs. When the needs are met and the problems are solved, the standard of community rises higher. On the contrary, a community which is unable to that, remains cramped up and stagnant with the results that its progress is blocked. Community is an informal and active agency of socialization. It modifies the behaviour of the child through social contracts, group activities and group dynamics in such a way that he begins to participate in all the desirable activities of that community of which he is an integral part. In fact, the child does not develop in the environment of his family alone, the environment of community also moulds and modifies the behaviour of the child according to its ideas, ideals and goals.

The community is a socializing agent because it is where children learn the role expectations for adults as well as for themselves.

**Fig. 8.6: Community Wheel**

The inter-relationship of community, school, media, etc is quite obvious in modern times. The functions related to the socialization of the child can be illustrated as follows:

1. *Moulds the Child in Different Areas:* The child is moulded in skills, concepts, habits, motives and values by the forces in the community that bear effectively upon his development. In some communities the skill in agriculture for example, is given such an emphasis that these become much more important than that of reading and writing.
2. *Mental Development:* In community children get opportunities for the development of their mental powers. They meet different people, they face various situations, reason out various facts and results in mental and intellectual developments. The enlightened communities often, organise reading rooms and libraries for the use of children and adults. Some communities organise exhibitions, fairs, symposiums and conferences on various subjects which help in mental development of the child.

3. *Social Development:* Community is a social unit in which people have we-feeling and all of them live together and meet their needs with the help of one another. When the child enters in the community from family then he got love, affection, cooperation of the members of the community. The community organises fairs, festivals and many other functions and they stimulate children to imbibe social ideas and a spirit of social service with the result that they learn about the social customs, traditions and beliefs in a rational way and also learn the socially desirable values as sympathy, tolerance, co-operation, sacrifice and adjustment.
4. *Cultural Development:* The children learn language, rituals, traditions, beliefs, ideals and values from the family but their scope is limited in comparison to community. When the children come in to contact with community, their learning sphere becomes wider, They act and react as their elders do. Culture is the result of accumulation of values, customs and traditions. The respect of the elders, love for the country, social service, folk music, folk dances etc. are better cultivated in the community and are important ingredients of socialization.
5. *Moral and Character Development:* The foundation of moral and character development lays down in the family. If the child gets suitable environment in the community then it makes their character and morality more stronger otherwise they learn other things from the community. They are to adjust in the community, if morality and good character is significant for adjustment, they follow it and vice versa. Thus it becomes the responsibilities of the community to take care that only good moral ethics are transmitted to the children and they are saved from the influence of lower values.
6. *Spiritual Development:* Community also plays an important role in spiritual development of the child. If community is religion oriented then it helps in development of spiritual power of its people, they think about God and soul, but if there is no place for religion in the society then the religious attitudes of the people will start vanishing day-by-day. Religious insipiration is very helpful in fulfillment of one's duties and a person following his religion in its true sense will be sober, tolerant, selfless and patriotic. He will be imbued with the feeling of brotherhood and he will always come forward to share the miseries of others.
7. *Adult Education:* Besides children, most of the adult population of the country is illiterate. It is the function of the community to give them knowledge of the rights, duties and responsibilities of a good citizen by educating them. Literacy does not mean education. Adult education means educating a person for the responsibilities of daily life as health, agriculture, vocation and other things related to the country and other nations.

# 9

# Culture and Education

*"Culture is a pursuit of the total perfection by means of getting to know on all matters which most concern us, the best which has been thought and said in the world"* –Mathew Arnold

Culture is not a given, but a human creation dependent on particular geographical, temporal and sociological contacts and therefore vulnerable to issues of power and control. The term culture can be problematic because it has different meaning to different people in different contacts. For instance, culture is sometimes used as it is pertained only to those with formal education and privileged social status, employing activities such as attending the opera once a month. In the present day, generally it is acknowledged that culture is not just what an elite group of people may do in their spare time. but there are still various and conflicting ideas of what is actually meant in everyday life. Sometimes, culture is used interchangeably with ethnicity as if both simply were passed down constant and eternal from one generation to the next. At other times, it can mean the traditions, one celebrates within the family; less often, it is thought of as the values one holds, or the way one looks at and interacts with the world.

## Meaning of Culture

The word 'culture' derives from a French term, which in turn derives from the Latin 'colore' which means to tend to the earth and grow, or cultivate and nurture. It shares its etymology with a number of other words related to actively fostering growth.

In English Dictionary, *"Culture is the way of life especially the general customs, beliefs, of a particular group of people at a particular time."*

Edward Taylor, *"Culture is that complex whole which includes knowledge, belief, art, law, morals, customs, and any other capabilities and habits acquired by man as a member of society."*

Franz Boas, *"Culture may be defined as the totality of the mental and physical reactions and activities that characterise the behaviour of individuals composing a social group collectively and individually in relation to their natural environment, to other groups, to member of the group itself and to each individual to himself. It also includes the products of these activities and their role in the life of the group. The more enumeration of these various aspects of life, however, does not constitute culture, It is more, for its elements are not independent, they have a structure."*

Ruth Benedict, *"What really binds men together is their culture in the ideas and the standard they have in common."*

Margaret Mead, *"Culture means the complex whole of traditional behaviour which has been developed by the human race and is successively learned by each generation. A culture is less precise. It can mean the form of traditional behaviour which are characteristics of a given society, or of a group of societies, or of a certain race, or of a certain area, or of a certain period of time."*

Krocbcr and Kluckhohn, *"Culture consists of patterns, explicit and implicit, of and for behaviour acquired and transmitted by symbols, constituting the distinctive achievement of human groups, including their embodiments in artifacts."*

Richard Shwedcr, *"Culture is the constituted scheme of things for intended persons."*

Bruno Latour, *"Culture is the set of elements that appear to be tied together when, and only when, we try to deny a claim or to share an association."*

Geert Hofstede, defines culture as, *"the collective programming of the human mind that distinguishes the members of one human group from those of another."*

Campbell on his part defines culture as, *"a complex web of information that a person learns and which guides each person's actions, experiences and perceptions."*

Banks defines culture as *"the behaviour pattern, symbols, institutions, values and other human made components of the society."*

Patrica Marshall defines it as *"consistent ways in which people experience, interpret and respond to the world around."*

Harris, *"A culture is the total socially acquired life way or life-style of a group of people."*

Culture has been variedly defined by the different authorities in the field of social science especially sociology. *Linton* defined it as the configuration of learned behaviour, and the result of behaviour, whose component elements are shared and transmitted by the members of a particular society. *Kasper* referred to culture as a collective term for patterns of essential and normative assertions taken from literature, language or drama or sounds or music, or symbols in sculpture and art, or movement in dance and ballet of fashion in clothes and so forth.

Right from the time immemorial, human being lived together at a given place and at a given time. A society was formed in this way. Set of individuals organised themselves to lead group life. In their social interactions, the people had common interest which made them to have a common pattern of behaviour. They do everything in common to achieve desired objectives. Their values, standards and norms are affected in their ways of thinking and feelings. In their relationship they acquire 'a way of life which was known as culture'.

Thus it is certainly hard to define culture. There are as many definitions of the word as there are authors who wrote about it. *Raymond William* writes, *"Culture is one of the two or three most complicated words in the English language."* All the above definitions can be summarized as follows:

- Culture refers to the cumulative deposit of knowledge, experiences, belief, values, attitudes, meanings, hierarchies, religion, notions of time, roles, spatial relations, concepts of the universe, the material objects, possessions acquired by a group of people in the course of generations through individual and group striving.
- Culture is sum total of learned behaviour of a group of people that are generally considered to be the tradition of that people and are transmitted from generation to generation.
- Culture is symbolic communication. Some of its symbols include a group's skills, knowledge, attitudes, values and motives.
- Culture is a collective programming of the mind that distinguishes the members of one group or category of people from another.
- Culture is communication, communication is culture.
- Culture in its broadest sense, is cultivated behaviour, that is the totality of the person's learned, accumulated experiences which is socially transmitted, or more briefly behaviour through social learning.
- Culture is the systems of knowledge shared by a relatively large group of people.

Thus we can say in sociology the meaning of culture is as the product of human experiences. It is the sum of what the group has learned about living together under the particular circumstances, physical and biological, in which it has found itself. By picking up the culture and by tapping the heritage of his past, man becomes distinctively human. Man has, therefore, been called the culture-bearing animal.

## Characteristics of Culture

On the basis of above discussion we may point out the following characteristics of culture:

1. *Culture is Dynamic:* Culture does not exist outside of human beings. Cultures are always changing as a result of political, social and other modifications in the immediate environment. When people with different backgrounds came in contact with one another, such change is expected even more. Culture is dynamic, active, changing, always remain on the move.
2. *Culture is Multifaceted:* Closely related to the dynamic nature of culture is that cultural identifications are multiple, eclectic, mixed and

heterogeneous. This means, for one thing, that culture cannot be conflated with just ethnicity or race. Because culture is not simply ethnicity, even among specific cultural groups, there are many and often conflicting cultural identities. Skin colour, time of arrival in different countries, language use, level of education, family dynamics, place of residence, and many other differences in the group, may influence how one interprets or 'lives' a culture.

3. *Culture is embedded in context:* It means culture is invariably influenced by the environment in which it exists. The culture of a student living in India is different from that of Indian immigrant student in the United States or of Indian immigrant student in Australia.
4. *Culture is influenced by Social, Economic and Political Factors:* As is evident from the above, intimately related to the fact that culture is bound to a particular contact is that it is greatly influenced by the political, historical and economic conditions in which it is found. It exists not in isolation but through concrete relationships characterized by differential access to power. As a result dominant groups in a society often determine what counts as culture. The tastes,, values, languages and dialects that pave the greatest status are associated with the dominant social class not because these are inherently better but because they have higher social prestige as determined by the group with the greatest power.
5. *Culture is created and socially constructed:* It is a reality that culture is constantly evolving, and the reason that it evolves is because human beings change it. The actions of people on culture takes place in big ways and small, by middle class people and by those who have power. Culture changes as a result of the decisions that we, as cultural agents, make about our traditions, attitudes, behaviours and values. As *Frederick Erickson* rightly says, "Culture can be thought of a construction .... it constructs us and we construct it." Thus, culture is not a passive legacy, but an active operation that takes place through contact and interactions with others. It is a social construction because it cannot exist outside of social contact and collaboration.
6. *Culture is Learned:* Culture is not handed down through our genes, nor it is inherited, but it is learned. For example, when children from a particular ethnic group (for instance Indian) are adopted by families from another ethnic group (usually Korean), although the children may still be considered ethnically and racially Indian. They will in all likelihood be culturally Koreans, unless their parents made a conscious and deliberate effort to teach them the culture and history of their heritage while bringing up them, or the children themselves later decide to educate themselves. Thus culture is learned through interaction with families and communities. It is neither consciously taught, nor consciously learned.
7. *Culture is Dialectical:* A culture is neither good nor bad in general, but rather embodies values that have grown out of historical and social

conditions and necessities. Culture is dialectical leads to an awareness that there is no special virtue in preserving particular elements of culture as if they existed outside of social, political and historical spaces.

Thus culture exists as a continuous process. It is a product of history what ever form and content it has in the present, has been handed down from the past and is carried to the future. Culture is the social heritage of man and the memory of the human race.

### Relationship between Culture and Education

Education and culture are closely related to each other. In fact it is impossible to say whether the education influences culture or the culture influences the education system within that society. In this era of globalisation, society becomes more multicultural than ever before and education system is challenged with the issues of cultural diversity of students in a schooling contact. Culture and education arc inseparable, as they are simply two sides of the same coin. Both the concepts can in fact be said to be indistinguishable, as the primary definition of Education is Acculturation.

Dr. SS Bhatti has described role of education as:

E - Excellence
D - Determination
U - Understanding
C - Creativity
A - Awareness
T - Truthfulness
I - Intelligence
O - Open mindedness
N - Nationality

On the basis of it. we can say that education plays a vital role in bringing cultural change by changing values and attitudes of the pupils.

In the report of Indian Education Commission it has been rightly pointed out, *"The most important and urgent reform needed in education is to transfer it; to endeavour it to the life, needs and aspirations of the people and thereby make it a powerful instrument of social, economic and cultural transformation necessary for the realisation of national goals."*

Every society has a culture or a method of operating which is unique to it. To live harmoniously in a given culture, its members must be aware of the various modes of conduct which are acceptable to that culture. It is through the process of education that children and new members are appraised of these facts. Also, in order to survive, the individual must become acquainted with the nature of these things in his environment with which he may have to cope. In general terms, we can say that the purpose of education is to inform the individual about the nature of his culture and the acceptable methods of coping with it.

The relationship between culture and education can be discussed in the following way:

**Culture and Different Aspects of Education**

Education, however in many forms may assume, has to maintain a dynamic interrelationship with culture. In order to perform its role efficiently as an agent of cultural development and prepare individuals for life in a society that is being enriched by different cultures, education needs freedom of expression, freedom of participation, free exchange between people, scientific knowledge and cultural creativity. Education requires equal access to the learning process and a democratic cultural life. The culture has its influence in different aspects of education as follows:

1. *Aims of Education:* The culture of a social group is reflected in the aims of education. The society expects from its educational institutions to fulfill following aims of education:
   - An introduction to knowledge and appreciation of the cultural heritage and an introduction to contemporary cultural life.
   - Familiarization with the processes by which cultures spread and evolve.
   - Recognition of their equal dignity and the indissoluble link between cultural heritage and contemporary culture.
   - Artistic and aesthetic education.
   - Training in ethical and civic values
   - Media education, and
   - Intercultural/Multicultural education

   Taking one from the culture of the society, education refines physical, moral, and internal aspects of individual's personality. Education makes use of the experiences of the race to produce an educated and cultured human being.
2. *Curriculum:* The aims of education can be achieved through viable content of education. The curriculum must become the mouth place of the society's culture. The curriculum should include different subjects as - social sciences, moral education, languages, science and technology. The progress of all societies is profoundly made by science and technology whose development is strongly influenced by social and cultural factors. In order to be truly free and less subjective to constraining factors arising from their natural and social environment, people need science and technology. But, to be liberating, scientific and technological culture has to be linked to, ethical and humanistic values. The end goal remains the self-fulfillment and future of humanity, in other words each and even one of the people forming the human community. The syllabus of

various disciplines, including science and technology, should therefore be prepared with the participation of cultural and educational specialists as well as anthropologists, sociologists, psychologists and others.

The choice of one or more languages, the mother tongue or a national or foreign language, as a separate subject is determined by the educational and cultural policy of each country. History teaching should include elements concerning the development of universal culture, thoughts and creativity and should avoid a presentation exclusively in terms of power conflicts and confrontation. The study of religion in a spirit of tolerance could be one of the components of studies of cultural creativity.

The education system should give greater prominence to media education. This form of education could be assigned a double function:

(a) Creating a better understanding of the role, functioning and effects of the media on individuals and on society, and in the development of the capacity to interpret independently and critically the message conveyed by the media, and

(b) as an educational tool designed to improve the quality of teaching,

3. *Methods of Teaching:* The teaching of various disciplines should give rise to interdisciplinary and co-operative activities conducive to cultural and inter-cultural education. To ensure closer interaction of cultural, intercultural and interdisciplinary practices, schools will find it useful to adopt a project approach. The purpose of a project is to encourage team work with a view to achieve common objectives. Teaching could be made more effective by organising cooperation with artistic and cultural partners through thinning arrangements between educational and cultural establishments. When choosing the language of instruction, in particular at the level of basic education, account should be taken both of the efficiency of the educational process and the rights of individuals and various ethnic groups to preserve their cultural identity, of which their language is one of the most important vehicles. When teaching different disciplines, a proper place should be reserved for the history of scientific and technological development in the context of overall socio-cultural development.

4. *The Teacher:* In the promotion of the contribution of education to cultural development, the teacher plays the most vital and unique role. In this context, a true sense of commitment on the part of the teacher is very necessary. The teacher is the conservator and transmitter of culture. He is the architecture of the culture of the society. It is his duty to infuse the best values, which he has imbibed himself, among the members of the younger generation. He is the spokesperson of the cultural values of the society.

5. *Discipline:* Culture also influences the discipline of educational institutions. The ancient and medieval society was authoritative, as a result the discipline was authoritative but in the present scenario we believe in democratic values. The democratic way of discipline is accepted. Children

in Indian schools are taught to respect their elders and love their peer group. They arc also taught to be on the side of justice. These values are infused in them by persuasion and examples, not by rod.

## Co-curricular Activities

Co-curricular activities are integral part of educational system. The culture of the society is reflected in the co-curricular activities in which children take part. Morning assemblies, debates and discussions, clubs and societies all are the part of the cultural programmes.

Apart from it different activities can be organised:

- Exchange of pupils, children, young people, teachers, youth leaders, etc. in different cities and states.
- Exchanges between schools and youth organisations.
- Learning of modern Indian languages.
- Exchange of teaching and audio-visual material, scientific equipments etc.
- The promotion of educational and cultural programmes of general interest.
- The school should prepare pupils to participate in socio-economic and cultural life of the community and act as a centre for community educational and cultural activities.

In order for the school to become a useful instrument of communal integration. particularly in rural areas, a process of consultation and agreement should take place between the educational authorities and all other partners: parents, local authorities and associations, cultural institutions which will help schools to set up their cultural activities in favour of the community.

Thus the total pattern of society determines the pattern of education.

## Functions of Education towards Culture

Education plays an important role in the transmission of culture from generation to generation. The progress of civilization in a society is closely related with the transmission and through this only the uniqueness of a society and the dignity of its people can be truly maintained.

### *1. Education Preserves Culture*

The education is responsible to take good care of the culture and keep it safe for the future generations. How far has education succeeded in its role as the preservative society's culture shall be determined whether it is expressed in the behaviour of the society's group to which it belongs. Pandit Nehru has rightly remarked. *"The core of our cultural heritage is love of beauty and truth, spirit of tolerance, capacity to absorb other cultures and work out new synthesis. Education must help in preserving the vital elements of our heritage."*

Preserving culture includes aspects of human rights, tolerance, development and protecting cultural sites and artifacts, as well as intellectual property rights for culturally specific languages and art. The United Nations Education Scientific and Cultural Organisation (UNESCO) is the primary body to protect and preserve the culture. Respect, tolerance and protection of culture are central to the UNESCO mandate of 'advancing, through the educational, scientific and cultural relations of the people of the world, the objectives of peace and common welfare of mankind.' The 1966 Declaration of the Principles of International Cultural Co-operation states that 'each culture has a dignity and value which must be respected and preserved' and that 'every people has the right and duty to develop its culture.'

The Constitution of India guarantees every single citizen of India has the rights to education and culture. All minorities, religious or linguistic, can setup their own educational institutions to preserve and develop their own cultures.

As evidenced by the educational efforts of UNESCO, education is a primary key to promoting, understanding and pleasure of cultural diversity. Education leads to consensus on the issue of protecting and preserving the cultural identities of all people. Community education, education in the school system, education to teach rural population and education about one's rights and responsibilities are all necessary steps towards respect for cultural diversity. When the people receive the information about different cultures and their belief systems, it helps in recognition of the values of different culture.

Preservation of culture include documenting and studying languages; preserving and restoring historic relics significant to a culture or heritage; and emerging the preservation and use of indigenous or tribal languages and rituals. Educational philosophers argue for preservation of the culture, by fostering children's development of autonomy and introducing them to new and different ideas. Thus, education can play an important role in preservation of culture both material and non-material. Material or 'built' aspects of culture includes sites, building, landscapes, monuments and objects and non-material or 'living' heritage embodies in social practices, community, life, values, beliefs as well as expressive forms such as languages, arts and handicrafts, music, dance and poetry.

***2. Transmission of Culture***

Education not only conserves the culture but also transmits to the generations. Ottaway has rightly said, *"The function of education is to transmit the social values and ideals to the young and capable members of the society."* The human being can't progress without the knowledge of culture, if it is not transmitted, cultural values get degenerated and this leads to chaos and confusion in the society.

An education system is the reproductional organ of every culture. Education includes both formal system and informal transmission of culture by transmitting knowledge, skills and developing attitudes. Individuals grow and die, while new members are born and grow to maturity, but a society and culture is a living entity which transcends all the individual members of the society. The culture of a society can survive for a longer period than the life span of any of its member, because its educational system passes the knowledge of one generation to subsequent generations. A culture is dynamic, but has a recognizable continuity of basic values and behavioural patterns that distinguish it from other cultures. The education system provides that continuity.

The education system is also dynamic, so, it can be a very effective way to change a culture. It is extremely difficult to make rapid, deliberate changes in the informal education that occurs incidentally and in the homes spontaneously from day to day, but media can be manipulated fairly quickly to influence short-term public opinion.

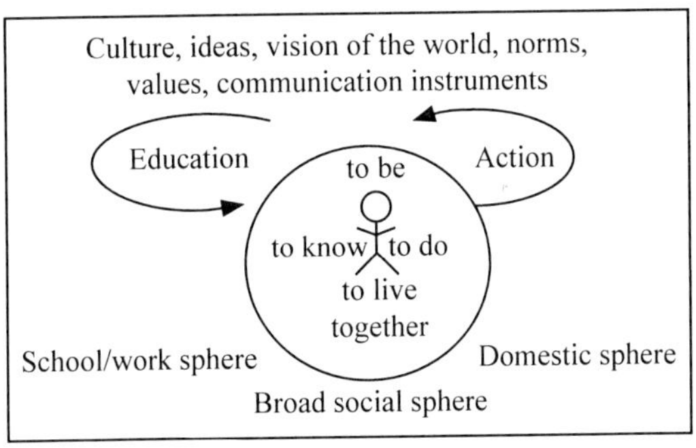


**Fig. 9.1: Process of Cultural Transmission**

It is a fact that the roles and responsibilities of the education systems have changed dramatically. The growth and development of the world have forced the educational institutions to assume new and different posture. Schools are now expected to develop the social, personal and intellectual capabilities of individuals with in the existing framework of highly developed, diversed and technological society. If the educational institutions are to assume the role of transmitting the cultures of all learners in our society, then the curricula must reflect the cultural diversity of their students. Multicultural education should be viewed as a process.

Multicultural education is a process through which individuals are exposed to the diversity that exists in the society and to the relationship of this diversity to the world. This diversity includes ethnic, racial minority population as well as religious groups and sex differences. The exposure to diversity should be based on the foundation that every person in our society has the opportunity and opinion to support and maintain one or more cultures.

The teachers can plan an important role in transmission of culture from one generation to the other. They can fulfill this responsibility through teaching of languages, social science, art, science in an integrated way. Thus the schools or educational institutions can be effective in transmitting the culture to all learners. Curriculum planning is essential approach to a multicultural and that will meet the cultural needs of the students. From learning about other cultures comes tolerance, tolerance promotes respect, respect leads to open-mindedness which results in civic reasonableness and equality.

***3. Promotion of Culture***

Education helps in the promotion of culture. Cannon has rightly said. *"If each generation has to learn for itself what has been learned by its predecessors. no sort of intellectual or social development could be possible and the present state of society would be little different from the society of stone old age."*

The success of any culture is based on modern inventions of the society. It plays a very important role in the development of culture. Education teaches about the social and cultural values. It prepares the students to deal with cultural ethics and norms. Various elements of culture help the individual in adopting natural and social environment in a positive way. Each person of the society has his or her own behaviour, attitude, qualities and mentalities to perceive the world around. Education changes the perspective of the individual towards different cultures. The current example is that the institutions have started to provide online education in the period of lockdown due to COVID-19. After the advancement of modern inventions and technology, day-by-day new scientific methods are being used in the transmission and promotion of culture. As a result of this advancement, culture is changing and adopting new ideas to survive in the society.

Every society needs to refine the culture as we find that caste system, untouchability, child marriage, child labour, home sexuality, girl foeticide, etc. are hindrances in the development of the society. Through education only we can create favourable attitude towards change as growth of culture is the purpose of education. We are to bring changes in the curriculum, methods of teaching, text books etc. to promote the culture throughout the world. Education develops youth's awareness and understanding of issues related to the promotion of a culture of non-violence and peace, such as non-discrimination and respect for diversity, violence prevention, inter-cultural dialogues, social inclusion and gender equality. Education should not lay stress on cognitive development only, or tell youth what to do, but it should encourage youth to change perspectives, to realize that there is no 'black and white truth' and to develop their own position. This is favoured through a non-cognitive methodology, meaning that feelings, experience, or the physical body, rather than intellectual analysis, are the entry points for learning and transmission through games, role-plays, visualizations, art, music, sports and theatre.

The function of education is to give a desirable direction to culture which comes automatically. It prepares the individuals for culture.

## Culture and Ideology

### *Culture*

Culture is an abstract concept. Different educationists, sociologists, behaviourists, constructivists have different concept of culture. We can't efficiently summarize the word. It is the knowledge, beliefs, traditions and customs of a society of people. Right now, you live in the culture of the country you reside in. You may have a sub-culture with in your local region. You should not forget the religious culture, and anything else that may have a cultural influence on you.

Indian culture varies like its vast geography. People speak in different languages, dress differently, follow different religions, eat different food but are of the same temperament. So, whether it is a joyous occasion or a moment of grief, people participate whole heartedly, feeling the happiness or pain. India is a diverse country, a fact that is visibly prominent in its people, culture and climate.

### *Ideology*

Ideology is not as abstract concept as culture. It is a system of ideals that form the basis of a belief. Like culture, you probably have many ideologies you support. The ideology is the basis of what all your opinion stem from.

As culture is transmitted, learned and shared throughout the society or group, but ideology is discovered. It is something that you grow into and choose from logical reasoning and evaluating your values.

As societal culture can also be incredibly hard to adopt too, as seen with many immigrants, some just are unable to adopt, on the same way ideology can be hard to change. It is hard to move from a hard line stance as a particular issue, especially if it holds sentiments or personal significance.

Many times the ideology you support is directly related to the culture you align too. As the people from India consider cows holy and they worship them. The reason behind it is that millions of Indians are peasants who rely on their farms for their food and thus their existence. Oxen and water buffaloes are the way they plow their fields. Oxen are made by cows, it thus becomes essential to preserve cows at all costs. In India, cows also act as an essential source of fertilizer in the form of cow manure.

It shows that culture and ideology go hand in hand. A strong culture can bread a strong ideology. A lacking culture can foster numerous derivatives of an ideology.

According to Manfred Steger and Paul James," Ideologies are patterned clusters of normatively imbued ideas and concepts, including particular representation of power relations."

Eagleton considers ideology as "a body of ideas, characteristic of a particular social group or class."

Christian Duncker defines ideology in terms of a system of presentations that explicitly or implicitly claim to be absolute truth.

Sociologists define ideology as "cultural beliefs that justify particular social arrangements, including patterns of inequality."

According to Richard W. Sterling. "Ideology is a set of ideas that purports to give meaning to the past, to explain the present and to prognasticate the future."

In the words of Padelford and Lincoln, "Ideology is a body of ideas concerning economic, social and political values and goals which posit action programmed for attaining these goals."

Thus an ideology can be thought of as a comprehensive vision, as a way of looking at things (compare world view), as in common sense (ideology in everyday society), and several philosophical tendencies (political ideology, social ideology) or a set of ideas proposed by the dominant class of a society to all members of that society (products of socialization). The main purpose behind an ideology is to offer change in society, and adherence to a set of ideals where conformity already exists, through a normative thought process.

*Characteristics of Ideology*

On the basis of above explanation of ideology. We can find some of its characteristics:

- An ideology provides a window to see the world.
- Every ideology has its own base.
- An ideology is averse to change.
- It is never created in vacuum. Every ideology is a reaction to some existing ideology.
- An ideology tries to interprets the reality in a new way.
- Ideology inspires and motivates people.
- It is a coherent system of ideas that rely on a few basic assumptions about reality that may or may not have any factual basis.
- Ideologies are patterned cultures of normatively imbued ideas and concepts, including particular representatives of power relations.
- Ideology has power over cognition.
- It provides guidance towards actions.
- It is a process that converts social life in to a natural reality.
- Ideologies are forms of thought motivated by social interests.
- It is stated in different forms—complicated and simplified. There are books and treaties explaining the theory, there are slogans and symbols.
- Examples: Socialism, Communism, Fascism, Gandhism, Liberalism.

*Types of Ideology*

There are mainly two types of ideologies:

- Political ideologies
- Epistemological ideologies

*Political ideologies* are sets of ethical ideas about how a country should run. In social studies, a political ideology is a certain set of ethical ideals, principles, doctrines, myths or symbols of a social movement, institution, class or large group that explains how society should work and offers some political and cultural blue print for a certain social order. There are different types of political ideologies as—communism, socialism, capitalism, anarchism, democracy, fascism, liberalism etc. Democracy is a political ideology which we see in practice in India.

*Epistemological ideologies* are sets of ideas about the philosophy, the universe, and how people should make decisions.

It is uncertain how many different ideologies there are and what they are, because different parts of the world have different beliefs and therefore different norms and values.

## Difference between Ideology and Culture

| *Ideology* | *Culture* |
|---|---|
| 1. It is a part of culture. | 1. Culture in itself is whole. |
| 2. It is a set of ideas under culture. | 2. It is an enormous term contain a variety of ideology as political ideology, social ideology, cultural ideology etc. |
| 3. It is homogeneous. | 3. It is heterogeneous. |
| 4. It is unilinear. | 4. It is multi linear. |
| 5. It is a thought or a collection of thoughts and founded by a thinker or a person. | 5. It is founded by plurality of ideas and people. |
| 6. It leans more towards political theory. | 6. It leans more towards religious. |
| 7. It is what an individual express or claims according to his own understanding and thinking of his culture and this could be mixed with other cultures also and a persons beliefs and morals. | 7. It is a life style of a group of people connected together in one place and one language. Your culture affects how you view the world and interact with it accordingly. |
| 8. It is when you try to claim that everything you do is consistent, virtuous and correct, and is conformity with some set of ideas that ensure that everything you do is right. | 8. Culture is everything you do. |
| 9. Ideology of China is communism. | 9. Culture in China is free market capitalism. |

Thus ideology and culture are interrelated. Ideology is the way culture is seen by society. If you are cultured, you are better than others. If you are cultured you are the ideal person. There is an integral relationship (dialectic) between structure and ideas, between the socio-economic and the ideology, between the institutional and cultural. 'Ideas' and 'Culture'–are a product of time and space. If you live in a country that had the best financial system and realistic freedom; no poverty, no death, no war, no diseases; would you ever seek to change it? Of course not. Your ideology would match the ideology that the culture fostered.

None of us can predict the new world that culture and ideology will lead us too. But this is inevitable. Traditions, people, lifestyle, and geopolitical aspects are ever changing. We can't prevent that. We can't stick with the nuclear family system of 20th century. It must change, but how it will change, depends upon us. We can make it better or worse. Our choices and the culture we instill in our children, are what will inevitably determine which way this change goes. The future in the hands of those, who control the culture. At the end of the day, we are the ones that determine our beliefs and opinion. All of us need to support a culture that helps us all.

# 10

# Constitutional Values

> *"The constitution declares India a secular, socialist, secular, democratic, republic assuring its citizens justice, equality and liberty and endeavours to promote fraternity."* –Ministry of Law & Justice

Constitution is a set of rules, generally written, which defines and regulates the structure and functioning of an organisation, institution or a company. When it is used in the context of a nation or state, it means a set of fundamental principles, basic rules and established precedents.

A constitution may be written or unwritten, but it contains fundamental laws. It is the supreme and ultimate authority. It is not a static, but a living document, because it needs to be amended as and when required to keep it updated. Its flexibility enables it to change according to the changing aspirations of the people, the needs of the time and the changes taking place in the society. Constitutional morality provides a principled understanding for unfolding the work of governance. Its elements are—

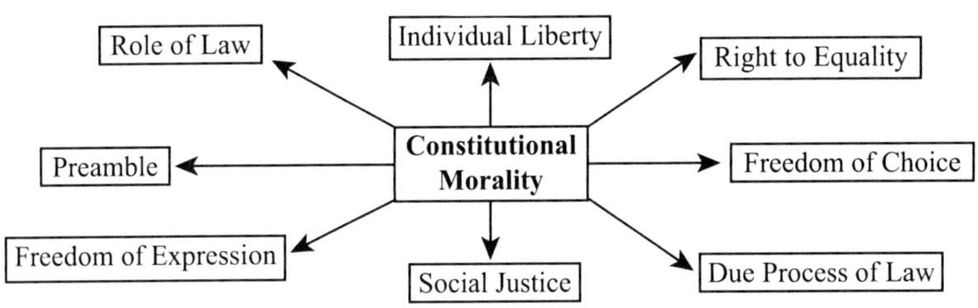


**Fig. 10.1: Constitutional Morality**

## Preamble

> *'We, the people of India having solemnly resolved to constitute India into a Sovereign, Democratic, Republic and to secure all its citizens—Justice, Liberty, Equality and fraternity'.*

The Constitution of India is one of the best constitution in the world. It is certainly a unique one. It has certain values. The constitutional values are those values which safeguard the human rights of every Indian citizen. These values ensure that there should be no unfairness or injustice towards anyone.

The emerging Indian society upholds a set of basic values that should guide individual life and group functioning. The values expressed in the preamble are expressed as objectives of the constitution. These are sovereignity, socialism, secularism, democracy, republic character of Indian state, justice, liberty, equality, fraternity, human dignity; and the unity and integrity of the nation.

15th August 1947 is a red letter day in Indian history when India got freedom. The constitution was adopted on Nov. 26, 1949 and came with force on January 26, 1950. It has provisions for bringing about social change and defining the relationship between individual citizen and the state.

Let us discuss the constitutional values enshrined in the Constitution of India.

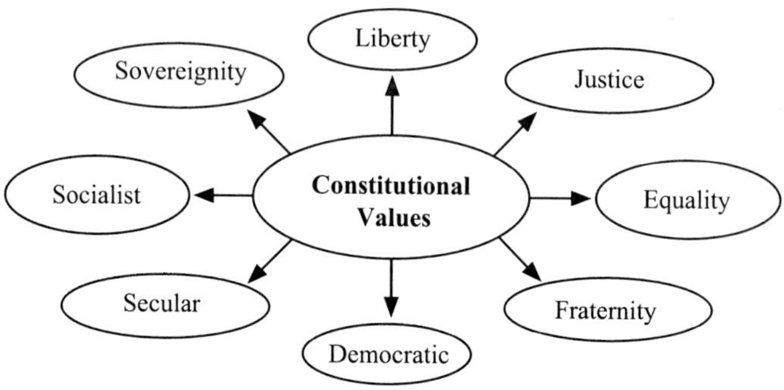


**Fig. 10.2: Values in Constitution of India**

## 1. Equality

Equality has several dimensions and it cannot be defined or described at a single glance.

In the words of H.J. Laski, *"No idea is more difficult in the whole realm of political science than equality."*

According to Collins Dictionary, *"Equality is the same status, rights and responsibilities for all the members of a society, group or family."*

According to Merrian Webster Dictionary, *"Equality is the quality or state of being equal."*

India is a democratic country and liberty and equality are the basic principles of democracy as well as they are interrelated. In the Constitution of India, fundamental rights are guaranteed to protect the basic human rights of all citizens of India. One of such fundamental right is Right to Equality. It refers to the equality in the eyes of law, discarding any unfairness of caste, creed, religion, place of birth, sex.

Various articles related to right to equality are as:

- *Equality before Law:* Equality before law is well defined under the Article 14 of the constitution which ensures that every citizen shall be likewise protected by the laws of the country. It states "The state shall not deny to any person equality before the law or the equal protection of the laws within the territory of India.

This mean that no person or groups of people can demand for any special privileges.

- *Social equality and equal access to public areas:* The right of social equality and equal access to justice area is clearly mentioned under the Article 15 of the Constitution of India."

Article 15:. Prohibition of Discrimination on grounds of Religion, Race, Caste, Sex or Place of Birth

Art. 15 (1) — 'The state shall not discriminate against any citizen on the grounds only for religion, race, caste, sex, place of birth or any of them.'

Art. 15 (2) — 'No citizen shall, on grounds only of religion, race, caste, sex. place of birth or any of them, be subject to any disability, liability, restriction or condition with regard to —

(a) access to shops, public restaurants, hotels and places of public entertainment, or

(b) the use of wells, tanks, bathing ghats, roads and places of public resorts maintained wholly or partly out of state funds or dedicated to the use of general public.

Art 15 (3) 'Nothing in this article shall prevent the State from making any special provision for women and children.'

Art 15 (4) 'Nothing in this article or in clause (2) of the article 29 shall prevent the State from making any special provision for the advancement of any socially and educationally backward classes of citizens or for the SC and ST.'

The constitution provides for reservation of seats in the Parliament and State Assemblies, seats in educational institutions/courses, and posts in govt./ quasi govt, services for SC and ST for a specified period; such provisions for certain minorities and backward communities are also indicated.

The educational corollary of these constitutional guarantee is equality of educational opportunities - the provision of opportunities for every child to obtain education suited to his ability and interest irrespective of caste, colour, creed, sex or the financial ability of his parents.

- *Equality in matters of Public Employment: Article 16 of the Constitution of India mentions:*

  Article 16. Equality of opportunity in matters of Public Employment

1. There shall be equality of opportunity for all citizens in matters relating to employment or appointment to any office under the State.
2. No citizen on grounds only of religion, race, caste, sex, descent, place of birth, residence or any of them, be ineligible for, or discriminated against respect of, any employment or office under the State.
3. Nothing in this article shall prevent Parliament from making any law prescribing in regard to a class or classes of employment or appointment

to an office under the govt, of, or any local or other authority within, a State or Union Territory, any requirement as to residence within that State or Union Territory prior in such employment or appointment.

4. Nothing in this article shall prevent the State from making any provision for the reservation of appointments or posts in favour of any backward class of citizens which, in the opinion of the State, is not adequately represented in the services under the state.
5. Nothing in this article shall prevent the State from making any provision for the reservation in matters of promotion to any class or classes of posts in the services under the State in favour of the SC and ST which, in the opinion of the State, are not adequately represented in the services under the State.
6. Nothing in this article shall affect the operation of any law which provides that incumbent of an office in connection with the affairs of any religions of denominational institution or any member of the governing body there of shall be a person professing a particular religion or belonging to a particular denomination.

Thus the constitution provides equal opportunities for the public employment to all the people except in the case of SC and ST. The appointment in different offices are given only on the basis of merit.

- *Abolition of Untouchability:* The untouchability offence Act of 1955 (now Protection of Civil Right Act in 1976) states punishments for not allowing a person to enter a place of worship or from taking water from a well or tank. Article 17 of Constitution of India abolishes the practice of untouchability in India.
- *Abolition of Titles:* Article 18 of the constitution prohibits the state from granting any titles. Citizens of India are not allowed to accept titles from a foreign State. Nevertheless academic and military distinctions can be conferred upon the citizens of India.

Thus basic premise of right to equality is equals should be treated equally and unequals should be treated unequally. Treating unequals equally would further perpetuate inequality. So, special provisions have been allowed by the constitution in favour of weaker sections of society like women, children, SCs, STs. Equality is one of the most important value of our constitution, which gives strength to all those people who belongs to Indians nationality. It is necessity of the upcoming generations to secure their rights, develop this value and change our developing nation in to developed India.

### 2. Freedom

Freedom of thought and action is a fundamental value embedded in our constitution, since it recognise the vital truth that man cannot develop his personality in the absence of this value. it is the basis for creativity and exploration of new ideas and experiments that can help in the advancement of society. Consequently Article 19 assumes the freedom regarding.

- *Freedom of speech and expression:* Article 19(1) (a) implies that every citizen of India has the legal right to express his or her views, opinions and beliefs freely by the medium of words spoken orally, or by writing, by printing, or by picturization in any manner.
- *Freedom to assemble:* Article 19(1) (b) empowers the Citizen of India with the freedom to assemble peacefully and without arms, arms as ammunition, or melee weapons etc.
- *Freedom to form association:* Article 19(1)(c) provides the freedom to form association or co-operative societies.
- *Freedom to move:* Article 19(1)(d) guarantees the freedom to move throughout the territory of India. The purpose is to promote national feeling among the people.
- *Freedom to reside and settle:* The constitution also provides freedom to reside and settle in any part of the territory of India.
- *Freedom to practice any profession:* Article 19(1)(g) granted the freedom to practice any profession but it should not be immoral
- *Freedom of protected life:* Article 21 provided the freedom to life. No person will be deprived of his or her life or personal freedom except according to the procedure established by the law.
- *Freedom of education:* Act 21 A declares that the state must provide free and compulsory education to all children of the age group six to fourteen years.
- *Freedom of religion:* Art. 25(1) provides freedom of conscience and the right to profess, practice and propagate religion.
- *Freedom to get information:* Article 19(1) of the constitution implicit the freedom to get information in 2005. He/she has the freedom to know how the government works, what roles does it play and what are its functions. Article 19 (2) also states that if the disclosed information affects the integrity or security of the country then government can impose restrictions on such subclause.

Thus freedom is a necessary condition for the harmonious development of the personality of the individual, without which no social progress is possible. It is plainly unethical to deny an individual his freedom which is her birth right (All human beings are born free —says under Universal Declaration of Human Rights) and prevent him from accomplishing what he is capable of. Freedom is a spiritual necessity. It does not mean doing whatever one likes. It means accepting constraints of law and convention. Laws are necessary to secure equal freedom for all and to protect the weak from exploitation by the strong.

### 3. Justice

As a corollary to the above constitutional values, it is natural that an individual has the right to justice. He/she cannot be deprived from any opportunity nor he/she be debarred from getting his/her dues in all walks of life. Individual cannot be discriminated on grounds that are unfair or illegal.

The term 'justice' in the preamble embraces 3 distinct forms—social, economic and political, secured through various provisions of fundamental rights and Directive Principles. Social justice denotes the equal treatment to all citizens without any social distinction based on caste, creed, colour, religion, sex and so on. Economic justice denotes the non-discrimination between people on the basis of economic factors. It involves the elimination of inequalities in wealth, income and property. Political justice implies that all citizens should have equal political rights, and equal voice in the government. The 42nd Amendment Act by introducing the word 'socialist' in the preamble has strengthened the constitutional ethos of economic and political justice.

The Constitution of India recognizes and seeks to realise the various components of justice as Article 14 guarantees to every person 'equality before law or equal protection of the laws within the territory of India'. Article 15(1) prohibits discrimination against any citizen on grounds of religion, low caste etc. Article 16(1) provides equality of opportunity in matters related to employment, and by Article 17 'untouchability' the age-old practice has done away all its manifestation. According to Article 46, the state shall promote with special care the educational and economic interests of the weaker sections of the people, and in particular, of the scheduled castes and the scheduled tribes, and shall protect them from social injustice and all forms of exploitation. The Supreme Court declared 27% reservation legal for socially and economically backward classes of the society under central services. It is a part of corrective and compensatory justice. The court also has held that for the object of compensatory justice, limit of reservation should not be more than 50% in India.

There is a wide planning of justice according to the necessity in the constitution. Under Article 41, it is expected that the state shall, with in the limits of its economic capacity and development, make effective provisions for securing the right to work, to education and to public assistance in cases of unemployment, old age, sickness and disablement, and in other cases of undeserved want. Article 42 states that the state shall make provisions for securing just and humane conditions of work and for maternity relief. Article 43 denotes that the state shall endeavour to secure, by suitable legislation or economic organization or in any other way, to all workers, agricultural, industrial or otherwise; a living wage, conditions of work ensuring a decent standard of life and full enjoyment of leisure, social and cultural opportunities. The state shall endeavour to promote cottage industries on an individual or cooperative basis in rural areas.

We can summarize the constitutional provisions in Part II and Part IV for Justice as follows:

a. Equality before law (Article 14)
b. prohibition of discrimination on grounds of religion, race, caste, or place of birth (Article 15(1))
c. Equality of opportunities in matter of public employment (Article 16)
d. Abolition of untouchability (Article 17)
e. Abolition of titles (Article 18)
f. Protection of certain rights against freedom of speech (Article 19)
g. Protection in respect of conviction for offenses (Article 20)
h. Protection of life and personal liberty (Article 21)
i. Protection against arrest and detention in certain cases (Article 22)
j. Protection of trafficking in human beings and forced labour. (Article 23)
k. Prohibition of employment of children in factories or mines or in any of the hazardous employment (Article 24)
l. Freedom of religion (Article 25-28)
m. Protection of interests of minorities. (Article 29-30)
n. Judicial remedies for enforcement of rights conferred by Part III of the constitution (Article 32)
o. Provision of welfare of the people (Article 38)
p. Adequate means of livelihood; equal distribution of material resources; equal pay for equal work; promotion of health and strength; protection against childhood and youth (Article 39)
q. Equal justice and free legal aid (Article 39A)
r. Right to work, education and to public assistance in certain cases (Article 41)
s. Just and humans conditions of work and maternity relief (Article 42)
t. Living wages for workers (Article 44), uniform and code (Article 41)
u. Free and compulsory education for children of the age group 6 to 14 years (Article 45)
v. Special care for educational and economic interests of weaker section of the society, and the particular SCs and STs, and protection from social injustice and all forms of exploitation (Article 46)

Thus the fundamental rights emerged in Part III of the Constitution of India has a tremendous contribution in rendering justice to the country at large and till date it thrives to maintain its constitutional goals, in guiding legislation aimed at social welfare for the common good and common interest of people.

### 4. Secularism

Indian society is a multi-religious society. Democracy in a multi-religions and multi-cultural society like India can grow only in a secular framework. For this reason, we decided to create a secular state. India has chosen to build itself in to a democratic and secular state in which different groups and communities can flourish side by side in confidence and goodwill. Different social and cultural traditions might grow in freedom. All citizens might be able to make the best of their capabilities for personal fulfilment and social progress.

When the Constitution of India was adopted, the 'secular' word was not included in it. It was formally inserted in the preamble by 42nd Amendment of 1976 as well as the words 'Socialist' and 'Integrity of nation' were also added. The basic aim is to promote fraternity while ensuring unity and integrity of the nation along with individual dignity. Fraternity is a very significant tool to combat the divisive factor. Religious harmony is must to promote fraternity particularly in Indian context. So, it is a constitutional mandate upon the state to combat the factors which curtails religious fraternity. It is also incumbent upon the state to take positive as well as negative actions to promote fraternity.

*Meaning of Secularism*

The word 'secularism' was first used in the 19th century by George Jacob Holyoake. He derived it from the Latin word 'saeculum' meaning 'this present age'. He used it in the context of social and ethical values or system. Thus secularism came to be known as a social and ethical system. According to Oxford dictionary, secularism means *"the doctrine that morality should be based solely in regard to the well being of mankind in the present life, to the exclusion of all considerations drawn from belief in God."*

Chambers dictionary defines secularism as *"the belief that the state, morals, education etc. should be independent of religion."*

Webster's Dictionary says that secularism is *"the belief that religion and ecclesiastical (clergyman) affairs should not enter into the functions of the state."*

Webster gives an alternative definition, *"A system of doctrines and practices that rejects any form of religious faith and worship."*

In the words of Pt. Jawahar Lal Nehru, "Secularism is the affirmation of the values of science and technology, the acceptance of the integration of man and welfare of mankind as the standard of all religions and secular creeds the society."

Thus the term 'secularism' actually implies lack of any relationship with religion, and hence, in a secular state, there is no place for religion of any kind, as is the case with communist societies. The Indian concept of secularism requires that there shall be no state religion and the state shall treat all religions equally.

The fact that many religions were existing simultaneously in our country made it incumbent upon the state to clarify its attitude towards religion. It was with in this end in view that, by the 42nd constitutional amendment the word 'secular' was added as an adjective before the word 'society', although the concept and spirit of secularity was already implicit in the constitution, since the preamble secures to every citizen the liberty of thought, expression, belief, faith and worship. The new amendment only sought to make this view even more explicit.

The first President of India, Dr. Rajendra Prasad, clarified the issue beyond doubt when he said, "There are some who think that because we are a secular state, we do not believe in religion or spiritual values. Far from being so, it really means that, in this country, all are free to profess or preach the faith of their liking and that we wish well of all religions and want them to develop in their own way without any hinderance".

Gandhiji said, *"My veneration for other faiths is the same as for my own faith." "We believe in Sarvadharma-samantva—having equal regard for all faiths and creeds."*

Thus it was envisaged that our society would be one in which every individual would be free to have faith in the religion of his own choice, to propagate it and to conduct himself according to his tenets. The Indian constitution guarantees individual and corporate freedom of religion and equal citizenship right for members of all religious groups. It prohibits any discrimination on grounds only of caste, colour or creed. The state is neither constitutionally connected with any particular religion, nor it seeks to promote religion or interfere with it.

Even when the secular word was not present in the constitution, there were various provisions which show the secular nature of India. The list of those provision are as follows:

As per Article 15, the state cannot differentiate its people based on religion, caste, birth place and gender. Article 16 says that there is an equal opportunity for everyone in the recruitment under the state and state cannot differentiate based on religion.

As per Art. 25(1) of the constitution of India, all citizens are equally entitled to freedom of conscience and the right freely to profess, practice and propagate religion, This article contains mainly three phases as follows:

(i) *Freedom of Conscience:* This is inclusive of the liberty by virtue of which the individual is free to establish relation with deity he worships in the manner and faith of his own choice.

(ii) *Faith in and Practice of Religion:* According to it, an individual is free to observe the duties, rites and religious performances enjoined upon him by the religion of his choice, provided that these strictly conform to the general law and order in society, harmonious relations and the health of society.

(iii) *Propagation of Religion:* It implies the individual's right to express his views and communicate them to others, to publish his views, to persuade others to believe in or accept his religion, but it does not allow him to attempt harmful conversion.

As per Article 25(2)(a), the State may interfere with freedom of religion for the purpose of regulating or restricting any economic, financial, political or other secular activity which may be associated with religious practice. It is important to note that only those religious practices need be regulated or. restricted which are regarded as integral part of the religion, others can be banned without affecting religious freedom, if they are undesirable.

Article 26 implies the following:

- establishment and maintenance of institutions for religious and charitable purposes,
- management of affairs relating to religion,
- possession and acquisition of movable and immovable property for the fulfillment of the purpose stated above.

Article 27 'provides freedom as to payment of taxes for promotion of any particular religion.'

Article 28 makes the following provisions —

- religious instruction of any kind will not be imparted in any educational institution maintained wholly out of state funds;
- any person attending an educational institution recognised by the state or receiving aid out of state funds will not be compelled to take part in any religious worship or religious instruction.

Art 28 mentions four kinds of educational institutions—

- Govt., institutions wholly maintained out of state funds,
- Institutions recognised by the state,
- Institutions receiving aids out of state funds
- Institutions established under an endowment or trust.

In institutions of first kind, religious education of any kind, will not be imparted, second and third kind of institutions may provide religious instructions provided that the students and their parents give their consent and the fourth kind of institutions are free to impart religious education.

Article 29 and 30 protect the religious minorities from conserving their educational institutions.

In Directive Principles of State Policy, Article 44 orders the government to bring the Uniform civil code as per their continence.

In the view of Education Commission (1964-66) the adoption of a secular policy means that no religious community will be favoured or discriminated against and that instructions in religious dogmas will not be provided in state schools. But secularist policy is not an irreligious or anti-religious policy. It does not belittle the importance of religion. It gives every citizen the fullest freedom of religious belief and worship. It promotes not only religious toleration but also an active reverence for all religions. We have to make a distinction between 'religious education' and 'education for religion' The former is largely concerned with the teaching of tenets and practices of a particular religion in a particular form, and it would not be practicable to provide this type of religious education in respect of any religion to pupils belonging to different faiths. But it is necessary for a multi-religious democratic state to promote a tolerant society to all religions so that its citizens can understand each other better and live amicably together.

On the basis of the above analysis, the following important features of our secular society become evident —

(i) The state does not patronize or support any religion.
(ii) Considering all religions as equal, it gives the individual—the freedom to profess, practice and propagate any religion,
(iii) It allows every person to believe in any religion without any restraint, to practice it and to propagate it.
(iv) It provides freedom to manage religious institutions.
(v) It permits religious institutions and trusts to impart religious education.
(vi) It does not allow government institutions or institutions funded by the state to provide religious education of any kind.

Thus secularism develops a rational outlook. It fosters scientific spirit by emphasizing objectivity, spirit of free enquiry, and freedom from undue exaltation of the past. It glorifies material needs and promotes reverence for earthly life, without rejecting spiritual values.

Secularism has helped in improving life in India by —

- fostering religious tolerance,
- encouraging democratic values,
- promoting healthy pluralistic outlook which has led to the autonomous growth of science, art, religion and philosophy, and
- breaking age old rituals and dogmas.

The constitution have made every conceivable provision to make the Indian society a perfect secular society so as to ensure that a harmonious social order can be created through equal respect for all religions in our society which hosts a large variety of religions.

Thus secularism undoubtedly helps and aspires to enable citizens to enjoy fully the blessings of life, liberty and happiness, but in the pursuit of this ideal, those who believe in secularism must be inspired by a sense of ethical purpose in dealing with their fellow citizens. The present scenario of secularism in India is indeed a cause of concern but it is indeed a fact that India and its people, though have entered the globalized era, but still maintain the deep religious values at the core.

*Article 2:* Everyone is entitled to all the rights and freedoms set forth in this Declaration, without distinction of any kind, such as race, colour, sex, language, religion, political or other opinion, national or social origin, property, birth or other status.

Furthermore, no distinction shall be made on the basis of political, jurisdictional or international status of the country or territory to which a person belongs, whether it be independent trust, non-self-governing or under any other limitation of sovereignty.

*Article 3:* Everyone has the right to life, liberty and the security of person.

*Article 4:* No one shall be held in slavery or servitude; slavery and the slave trade shall be prohibited in all their forms.

*Article 5:* No one shall be subjected to torture or to cruel, inhuman or degrading treatment or punishment.

*Article 6:* Everyone has the right to recognition everywhere as a person before the law.

*Article 7:* All are equal before the law and are entitled without any discrimination to equal protection of the law. All are entitled to equal protection against any discrimination in violation of this Declaration and against any incitement to such discrimination.

*Article 8:* Everyone has the right to an effective remedy by the competent national tribunal for acts violating the fundamental rights granted lo him by the Constitution or by law

*Article 9:* No one shall be subjected to arbitrary arrest, detention or exile.

*Article 10:* Everyone is entitled in full equality to a fair and public hearing by an independent and impartial tribunal, in the determination of his rights and obligations and of any criminal charge against him.

*Article 11*

1. Everyone charged with a penal offence has the right to be presumed innocent until proved guilty according to law in a public trial at which he had all the guarantees necessary for his defence.
2. No one shall be held guilty of any penal offence on account of any act or omission which did not constitute a penal offence, under national or international law, at the time when it has committed. Nor shall a heavier penalty be imposed than the one that was applicable at the time the penal offence was committed

*Article 12:* No one shall be subjected to arbitrary interference with his privacy, family, home or correspondence, nor to attack upon his honour and reputation. Everyone has the right to the protection of the law against such interference or attacks.

*Article 13*

1. Everyone has the right to freedom of movement and residence within the borders of each state.

2. Everyone has the right to leave any country, including his own, and to return to his country.

*Article 14*

1. Everyone has the right to seek and to enjoy in other countries asylum from persecution.
2. This right may not be invoked in the case of prosecutions genuinely arising from non-political crimes or from acts contrary to the purposes and principles of the United Nations.

*Article 15*

1. Everyone has the right to a nationality.
2. No one shall be arbitrarily deprived of his nationality nor denied the right to change his nationality.

*Article 16*

1. Men and women of full age, without any limitation due to race, nationality or religion, have the right to marry and to found a family. They are entitled to equal rights as to marriage, during marriage and at its dissolution.
2. Marriage shall be entered into only with the free and full consent of the intending spouses.
3. The family is the natural and fundamental group unit of society and is entitled to protection by society and the State.

*Article 17*

1. Everyone has the right to own property alone as well as in association with others.
2. No one shall be arbitrarily deprived of his property.

*Article 18:* Everyone has the right to freedom of thought, conscience and religion. This right includes freedom to change his religion or belief, and freedom, either alone or in community with others and in public or private, to manifest his religion or belief in preaching, practice, worship and observance.

*Article 19:* Everyone has the right to freedom of opinion and expression. This right includes freedom to hold opinions without interference and to seek, receive and impart information about deals through any media and regardless of frontiers.

*Article 20*

1. Everyone has the right to freedom of peaceful assembly and association.
2. No one may be compelled to belong to an association.

*Article 21*

1. Everyone has the right to take part in the government of his country, directly or through freely chosen representatives.
2. Everyone has the right of equal access to public service in his country.
3. The will of the people shall be the basis of the authority of government. This will shall be expressed in periodic and genuine elections which shall

be by universal and equal suffrage and shall be held by secret vote or by equivalent free voting procedures.

*Article 22:* Everyone, as a member of society, has the right to social security and is entitled to realization, through national effort and international co-operation and in accordance with the organization and resources of each state, of the economic, social and cultural rights indispensable for his dignity and the free development of his personality.

*Article 23*

1. Everyone has the right to work, to free choice of employment, to just and favourable conditions of work and to protection against unemployment.
2. Everyone, without any discrimination, has the right to equal pay for equal work.
3. Everyone who works has the right to just and favourable remuneration ensuring for himself and his family, an existence worthy of human dignity, and supplemented, if necessary, by other means of social protection,
4. Everyone has the right to form and to join trade unions for the protection of his interests.

*Article 24:* Everyone has the right to rest and leisure, including reasonable limitations of working hours and periodic holidays with pay.

*Article 25*

1. Everyone has the right to a standard of living adequate of the health and well-being of himself and of his family; including food, clothing, housing and medical care and necessary social services, and the right to security in the event of unemployment, sickness, disability, widowhood, old age or other lack or livelihood in circumstances beyond his control.
2. Motherhood and childhood are entitled to special care and assistance. All children, whether born in or out of wedlock, shall enjoy the same social protection.

*Article 26*

1. Everyone has the right to education. Education shall be free, at least at the elementary and fundamental stages. Elementary education shall be compulsory Technical and professional education shall be made generally available and higher education shall be equally accessible to all on the basis of merit.
2. Education shall be directed to the full development of the human personally and to the strengthening of respect for human rights and fundamental freedom It shall promote understanding, tolerance and friendship among all nations, racial or religious groups, and shall farther the activities of the United Nations for the maintenance of peace,'
3. Parents have a prior right to choose the kind of education that shall be given to their children.

*Article 27*

1. Everyone has the right to freely participate in the cultural life of the community, to enjoy the art and to share scientific advancement and its benefits.

2. Everyone has the right to the protection of the moral and material interests resulting from any scientific, literary or artistic production of which he is the author.

*Article 28:* Everyone is entitled to a social and international order in which the right and freedoms set forth in this Declaration can be fully realized.

*Article 29*

1. Everyone has duties to the community in which alone the free and full development of his personality is possible.
2. In the exercise of his rights and freedoms, everyone shall be subject only to such limitations as are determined by law solely for the purpose of securing due recognition and respect for the rights and freedom of others and of meeting the just requirements of morality, public order and the general welfare in a democratic society.
3. These rights and freedoms may in no case be exercised contrary to the purposes and principles of United Nations.

*Article 30:* Nothing in this Declaration may be interpreted as implying for any State, group or person any right to engage in any activity or to perform any act aimed at the destruction of any of the rights and freedoms set forth herein.

A glance at the forgoing list of human rights make it explicit that almost all the rights have been included in the Indian Constitution. The foundation of all these rights is provided by the idea of respect for individuality and dignity of each person as a human being.

Human rights are intimately connected with democratic ideals.

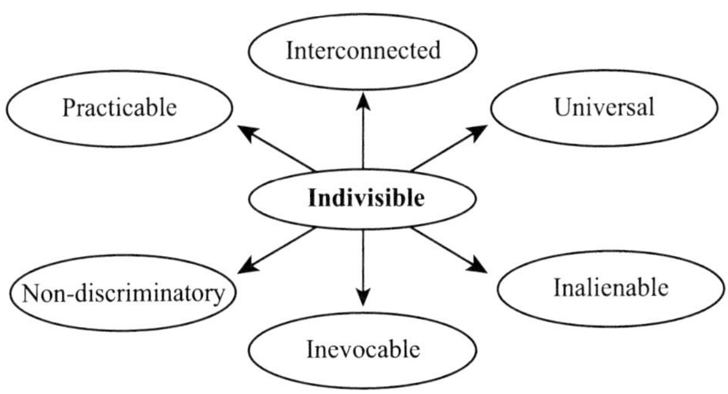


**Fig. 10.4: Human Rights & Democratic Ideals**

Following provisions exist in Indian Constitution to safeguard Human Rights.

- Equality before law (Art. 14)
- Non discrimination on grounds of religion, race, caste, sex and place of birth (Art. 15)
- Equality of opportunity (Art. 16)

- Freedom of speech, expression, assembly, association, movement, residence, acquisition and disposition of property, practising of any profession, carrying out any occupation, trade or business (Art. 19)
- Prohibition of forced labour (Art. 23)
- Freedom of religion (Art. 25)
- No provision for religious instructions in any educational institution, wholly maintained out of state funds (Art. 28)
- Conservation of language, script and culture (Art. 29)
- Right of minorities to administer educational institutions (Art. 30)
- State guarantee of a social order (Art. 38)
- Adequate means of livelihood, equal pay for equal work for both men and women, non abuse of health of the workers, opportunity to children to develop in a healthy manner and in conditions of freedom and dignity. (Art. 39)
- Right to work, to education and to public assistance in specific case (Art. 41)
- Provision for free and compulsory education of children up to 14 years of age (Art. 45)
- Ensuring education and economic development of scheduled castes, scheduled tribes and other weaker sections of the society (Art. 46)
- Art. 28 and 29 of the United Nation Convention deal with the rights of the child. (Art. 28)

State parties recognize the right of the child to education and with a view to achieving the right progressively and on the basis of equal opportunity they shall in particular.

(a) Make primary education compulsory and available free to all.
(b) Encourage the development of different forms of secondary education including general and vocational education.
(c) Make higher education accessible to all on the basis of capacity by every appropriate means.
(d) Make education and vocational information and guidance available and accessible to all children.

- Article 29: State parties agree that the education of the child shall be directed to —

(a) The development of the child personality, talent, mental and physical abilities to their fullest potential.
(b) Development of respect for the natural environment.
(c) The development and respect for human rights and fundamental freedom for the principles enshrined in the charter of United Nations.
(d) The development of respect for the child's parents; his or her own cultural identity, language, values; for the national values of the country in which the child is living.

(e) The preparation of the child for responsible life in a free society, in the spirit of understanding, peace, tolerance, equality of sexes, and friendship among all people, ethnic, national and religious groups and persons of indigenous origin.

Tolerance has been defined by Symonider and Voldin 1995 as the recognition and appreciation of others, the ability to live together and to listen to others, to respect as formulated by UNESCO Declaration on Race and Racial Prejudices of 1978, the right of all individuals and groups to be different. The importance of development of spirit of tolerance among individuals has been highlighted by the United Nation declaring 1995 as the year of tolerance.

*Formal Education and Human Rights* : The best method would be to infuse the environment in society with these values and norms which occupy an important place in man's behaviour. In the sphere of formal education, this can be done by introducing cooperation, love, tolerance, brotherhood freedom and equality into the atmosphere prevailing in schools.

# 11

# Ancient Indian Goals: Purusharthas

*'Purusharthas are values which human beings seek either for their own sake or as a means to the achievement of a further end.'*

'*Purusha*' means either God or a human being. '*Artha*' means an object or objective. Purushartha means objectives of a human being. In order to explain what constitutes the right way of living or what is generally referred to as 'The good life', Indian philosophers make use of the concept of Purushartha.

The concept of Purushartha is based on the realization that desires constitute the source of human action. The life of man centres around certain basic desires. Each of these desires or aspirations is distinct from the other in its object and each stimulates man to a particular mode of activity in order to satisfy it. Each individual, for example, has in him the sexual and parental urges, lure of power and wealth, desire for the common good, and a hunger for communication with the unseen. They function in interdependence in man's life.

The purusharthas serve as pointers in the life of a human being. They are based on the vision of God which is evident in the creation. He manifested and which can be followed by man to be part of that vision and in harmony with His aims. The world is filled with the abundance of material and spiritual beings and energies, who seek fulfillment by achieving their desires and liberation. Since man is God in his microcosmic aspect, he too should emulate God and manifest the same reality in his own small world. He should pursue the same aims, experience life in its fullness and be an instrument of God by serving the purpose to which he has been created.

If life is considered as one whole then there is one master science of life which recognises its four supreme ends (goals) i.e. the Purusharthas:

- Artha (Wealth)
- Karma (Physical well being or desire)
- Dharma (Righteousness); and
- Moksha (Spiritual freedom or salvation).

Purushartha is translated to mean a human goal, an object of desire, consciously pursued. The scheme can be elaborated in the form of a diagram:

**Human Needs/Pursuits**

Material well-being

- Bodily Needs (Karma)
- Needs of Material well-being (Artha)
- Needs for social and moral order (Dharma)

Spiritual well-being

- Needs to overcome suffering and realise oneself (Moksha)

The purusharthas have a gradation, with each value constituting a preparatory stage for the realisation of the succeeding one. Artha, an economic value (Need of material well-being) is only helpful as a means for satisfying one or the other of the diverse needs and desires of life. Their satisfaction is Kama (Bodily needs or pleasure) which is not only physical but psychological; in that it satisfies the natural impulses and cravings of a person. The value of money is only to an extent it serves as a means to get goods. It is not desired for its own sake except, perhaps by a miser. Artha thus is an instrumental value as it acts only as a means to the realisation of Kama which is an intrinsic value, for it is desired for its own sake. Further artha and kama are sought not only by man but by all living beings. Thus both wealth and pleasure are goals only perusable in society, but they can be successfully pursued only if society has at least some amount of stability and harmony.

The appeal of Dharma, which is the moral value among the four, is restricted to man. It is value which raises man above the level of animals; in this sense it is a spiritual value. It determines what one ought to do in different life situations; in accordance with the best moral code. Thus dharma acts as a regulating principle in life deciding the right and wrong karma. That kind of karma is acceptable which is in accord with the demands of dharma but not any other. As long as dharma is not thrown to the winds or ignored, the pursuit and even enjoyment of artha and karma are not bad or reprehensible. Dharma thus helps in discrimination between good and bad and had a good life. Dharma is an ethical law which prevents human beings from falling into cropped ways of the ordinary and unbridled demands of impulses, desires, ambitions and egoism.

But even higher than dharma is Moksha. The purpose of man's life on this earth is to follow the law (dharma) of God and achieve salvation (moksha) or freedom from his false self (ahamkara) by leading a balanced life in which both material comforts and human passions have their own place and legitimacy.

What the purusharthas characterize is not a life of self negation, but of balance, complexity, richness, opportunities and moderation in a cosmic drama of immense proportions in which man ultimately envisions and experiences his true grandeur and fulfill the very purpose of his creation.

marriage is not permitted except in special circumstances as laid down in Dharmashastras.

Sexual desire is an important and legitimate aspect of manav-dharma and is created by nature to perpetuate life in the material plane. While the law books draw a clear demarcation between legitimate and illegitimate sex, sex by itself is not considered unclean or sinful. Creation itself is a continuation of the union between 'Purusha' and 'Prakriti', the male and female aspects of the manifest universe, which is symbolically represented in the form of Sivalinga. Creation ends when this union ends. Sexual desire is also the last stronghold of Prakriti and the final refuse of our attachment with samsara. It is the most difficult spiritual obstacle to be overcome.

### 3. Dharma

Dharma is not only a central concept in Indian philosophy but a unique one The word 'dharma' comes from the root 'dhar' which is also the first letter of 'dharti', the earth, which is suggestive of its connection with the earthly life. In a wider sense it means 'to hold' or 'to sustain'. It is the secret glue, the binding force, which upholds and regulates this entire creation just as the gravitational force controls and holds the entire material universe as one piece. It has been variously translated as duty, faith, religion, righteousness, sacred law, justice, ethics, morality and so on. According to one school of Hinduism, dharma is an obligatory duty as prescribed by the Vedas to be performed by an individual in accordance with the rules prescribed for the caste to which he or she belongs. God is an upholder of dharma because He performs His duties even though they are not obligatory and He is without desire or preference.

Broadly speaking, dharma is right action or right conduct. It is much more than duty. It is an all pervasive complex of virtues in conformity with the true nature of things. Adharma which is the opposite of dharma is vice as it is opposition to the truth of things.

Dharma, as we have already seen, is learning in a broader sense, which can enlighten the human beings to understand the subtle niceties of living a dignified life. The values inculcated through education include a rule of prohibition regarding acquistion of wealth or securing or fulfilling of pleasure and desires of an individual. The rule is: Reject the wealth, pleasure and desires which are inconsistent with moral law (dharma). This may be termed as strategic pursuit of human needs for developing a holistic personality and same is illustrated in the following diagram:

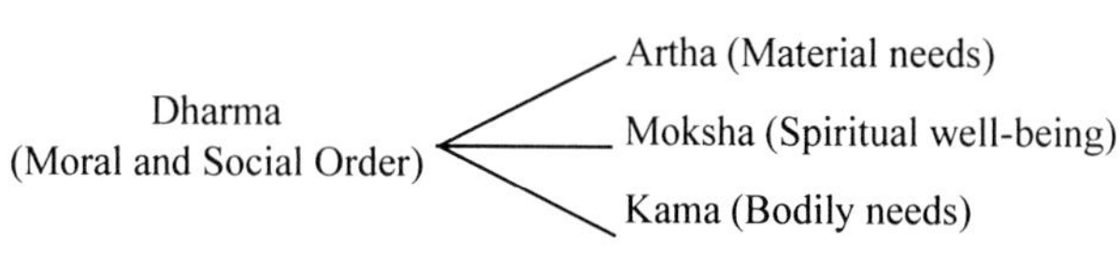

As a moral value dharma signifies, according to the sage Yagnavalkya, the cultivation of the virtues of non-injury, sincerity, honesty, cleanliness, control of the senses, charity, self-restraint, love and forbearance. This list includes both social values (values that refer to the good of others or all altruistic) and individual values (values that serve to develop one's own character and will). The aim of dharma, on the one hand, to put a check on selfish, natural impulses; and, on the other, to strive to the best of one's ability for securing the welfare of the society.

Dharma exists in all planes, in all aspects and at all levels of creation. In the context of human life, dharma consists of all that an individual undertakes in harmony with divine injunction and his own sense of morality and justice. However to comprehend the true nature of dharma is not an easy task. The source of dharma are Vadas, the Vedangas, the Sutra literature of which the most important are the Dharamshastras and scriptures such as Bhagavadgita. In ancient India Dhamishastras (law books) played an important role in guiding people on the path of dharma. It is however difficult to say how far they are relevant in the present age. One should also remember that dharma should not be viewed as end in itself but the means to a still higher end, i.e. liberation. It is not just a moral value in Indian thought; it is an ultimate metaphysical principle with certain amount of commandment built on it. "Follow Dharma or the whole structure will collapse."

### 4. Moksha

The pursuit of Artha and Kama enrich the experiences of a human being and impart to him valuable lessons. The pursuit of dharma regulates his life and keeps him on the righteous path. To understand the meaning of Moksha we should know, in the first place, that Indian philosophers make a distinction between the self as one experiences it (the empirical self) and the self as it really is (The True Self). The empirical self is characterized by narrowness of one kind or another because it is in actual relation with its physical body and the senses. But the true self is free from such limitations. Thus Moksha is realization of such true self or self realization.

The pursuit of dharma usually begins at the early age when one is initiated into religious studies. The pursuit of Artha and Kama begins in most cases when one becomes a householder. The pursuit of Moksha however is the most important of all aims and can begin at any time. However, in most cases, though not correctly, moksha becomes as important pursuit in the old age during vanaprashta or the age of retirement. Moksha is both a purushartha and a parmartha (transcendental aim) which is important not only for men but also for the divine beings.

Moksha actually means absence of moha or delusion or cultivate a sense of vairagya (detachment). Delusion is caused by the interplay of the triple gunas, the activity of the senses, attachment with and desire for sense objects.

A person achieves liberation when there is increase in the quality of sattva, suppressing rajas and tamas, increase in self control, surrender to God and offering of one's actions to God. There are many paths to salvation. The main paths are the path of knowledge, of action, of devotion, of dhyan (meditation), realization of true self, practice of nishkama karma and of renunciation. Each path has its own advantages and disadvantages. Whatever may be the path, the help and guidance of a Guru is indispensable to one's spiritual journey. A Guru is God in human form whose chief purpose is to remove the darkness hidden in the hearts and minds of the disciples and help them to find their true selves.

Thus the four purusharthas are responsible for balance in human life. They make life a rewarding and enriching experience. They cater to the spiritual and aspirations of human beings and lead them in the right direction on the path of liberation. Thus by worshipping Brahma, we can gain the knowledge of dharma and perform our obligatory duties with precision and perfection. By worshipping Vishnu we can gain material and Spiritual wealth and work for the welfare of our families and society. By worshipping Shiva, we can seek the fulfillment of our desires and overcome our delusion and finally by pursuing Brahma, or any of these Gods as Brahmans, we can achieve liberation by becoming Brahman Himself.

The direct aim of ancient Indian education was to make the student fit to become a useful member of the society. Inculcating the civic and social duties among the students was also a part of ancient Indian education system. Ancient Indian thinkers fixed for education certain life long objectives that require life-long efforts to achieve and realize These objectives were summarized in triple formula which gave a wide and lofting framework to the ancient system of education.

*asato ma sad gamaya*
*tamso ma jyotirgamaya*
*mrityorma amritam gamaya.*
*(Lead me from falsehood to truth*
*Lead me from darkness to light*
*Lead me from death to immorality)*

To them the ideals of truth, light and immorality constituted a triune unity, each subsisting in the other.

# 12

# Fundamental Bases for Formulating Aims of Education

*"An aim implies an orderly and ordered activity, one in which the order consists in the progressive completing a process."*

–John Dewey

A developing country is also known as an LMIC (low and middle-income country). It is less developed than countries classified as developed countries but these nations are ranked higher than least developed countries. These countries are characterized by:–

- Less developed industries
- Lower human development index
- Low economic status.

The most global issues most often discussed by developing countries include globalization, global health governance, 'education, health and prevention needs etc. Most of developing countries have these criteria in common:–

- High level of poverty: It is measured based on GHI per capita averaged over three years.
- Human resource weakness: It is based on indicators of nutrition, health, education and adult literacy.
- Economic vulnerability: It is based on instability of agricultural production, instability of exports of goods and services, economic importance of non-traditional activities, merchandise export concentration, handicap of economic smallness etc.

There are around 137 countries termed as developing (Based on GNI of US $ 11, 905 and less, specified by World Bank) as India, Afghanistan, Sri Lanka, Fiji, Bhutan, Chili etc.

The United Nations has set a list of sustainable development goals designed to help developing countries to overcome these challenges, specially related to education and literacy level. We must understand that education and development go hand in hand. The role of education in developing countries is very important as lack of education causes poverty and slow economic development of a country especially if the country is a developing country.

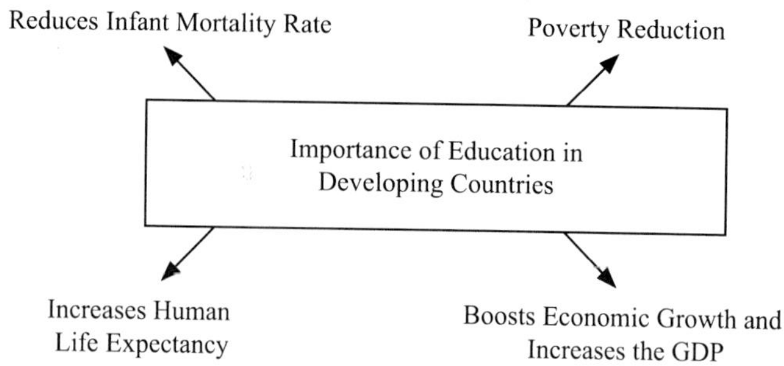


**Fig. 12.1: Education and Developing Countries**

Education is an important investment in a developing country as there are huge benefits. It guarantees lifetime income, promotes peace and reduces drop-out rates. It helps in making the right decisions at the time of conflicts.

So, we can say that only education can improve the economic and financial lifestyle of citizens and determine the prospects of future generations, especially in developing countries.

## Bases for Formulating Aims of Education

Education is fundamental to development and growth. The human mind makes possible all development achievements. For developing countries to reap these benefits fully, they need to unleash the potential of the human mind and there is no better tool for doing so then education.

Aims of Education are based upon certain fundamental aspects of human life and the different aspects of his life serve as important bases of education. The whole process of education consists of transforming the animal being into a social being in the light of his instincts, urges, needs and temperament.

> *'The new born baby is not really a human being, but is a candidate for humanity.'*

Education is viewed as a psychological, philosophical, ethical and sociological process. These serve as the fundamental bases for formulating aims of education. The most important aspects or bases for formulating aims of education in developing countries are:

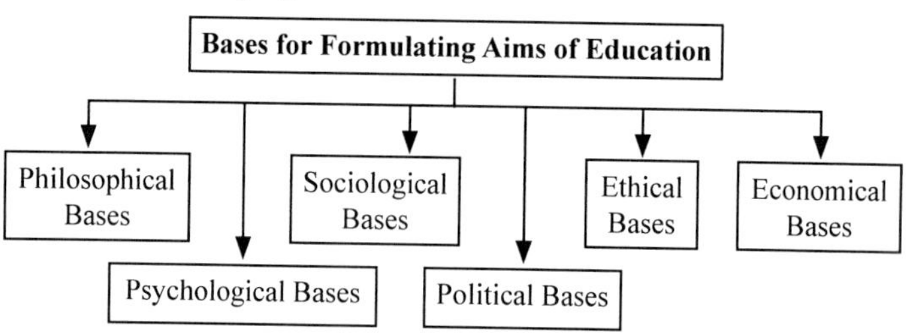


**Fig. 12.2: Bases for Formulating aims of Education**

### *Philosophical Bases*

> *"Philosophy formulates what it conceives to be the end of life, education offers suggestions how this end is to be achieved."* (Rusk)

Philosophical Bases give direction to education by providing certain guidelines. It attempts to establish coherent meaning within the whole domain of thought. These are only philosophical bases that the school officials, teachers and even parents can co-ordinate their efforts towards formulating and achieving the aims. Philosophy is fundamentally a belief or an opinion. There should, therefore, be a consensus among different beliefs. This consensus will lead to co-ordination and evolve a desirable philosophy of education based upon certain criteria. Thus philosophical bases is the living and unifying force behind the educational aims.

In the words of John Dewey, *"Education is the laboratory in which philosophical distinctions become concrete and are tested. In fact, it is other way round. It is the philosophy which serves as laboratory for testing educational distinctions, theories and practices."*

Fichte's view, *"The art of education will never attain complete clearness in itself without philosophy"*

In the words of Ross, "Philosophy and education are the two sides of the same coin present different views of the same thing; one is implied by the other; the former is contemplative while the other is the active side.

According to John Adam, *"Education is the dynamic side of philosophy."*

Philosophy deals with the abstract, education deals with concrete. Both of them go together. One is science and other is art. One is speculative while the other is practical. Philosophy determines the supreme aim of life and sets standards and values that should guide and direct man's educational efforts to achieve them. Philosophy inquires in to the significance of education in life. Philosophy gives purpose and orientation to the educational endeavour, although it depends on education for formulation and classification. Philosophy represents a way of life, education is as understanding of and preparation for it. Philosophy is wisdom and education transmits and disseminates it. Thus both education and philosophy are integrally and interdependently related to the other.

Education sets itself into operation to realize some aims i.e. why education is a purposeful activity. Philosophy includes a critical evaluation of the different aims of education held and propagated from time to time such as character building, human development, preparation for adult life, training for international living, evolution of democratic society and finally self realisation and spiritual emancipation. The aim of education is directly related to the aim of life and aim of life is always dependent on the philosophy that prevails. Generally philosophy is concerned with the general and universal aims rather than any specific and particular aim of education. The aims of education have been changing with the changing philosophy of life. In ancient days attainment of knowledge was considered to be the aim of education. The aim of education is determined according to the view-point of the members of society. Those who believe in worldly pleasure, want to relate education with vocational aims. Those with spiritual views want to make education as a means or basis of spiritual development

The contribution of philosophy in determining the aims of education is quite significant It provides valuable advice regarding the aims of education by studying the view-points of various persons and groups. At present, all nations of the world are organizing their educational systems according to their needs and ideologies. In countries where the philosophy of democracy is strong, the aims of education is the inculcation of democratic values and promotion of democratic principles. Rusk has pointed out, *"Every system of education must have an aim and the aim of education is relative to the aim of life"*

Education and philosophy are both related to the life of man. Attitude of man towards life is called philosophy and the aim of education is determined on this basis. Spencer and Pestalozzi recognize 'complete living' and 'harmonious development of Indian', as the aim of education. According to modern thought spiritual development is considered not as an aim but an aspect of education. Thus philosophical process is comprehensive and total. Therefore, philosophy of education aims at presenting a synthesis of various aims and ideals of education.

Currently, most of developing countries give importance to the economical and political basis of education because they want to become self-sufficient. For this purpose, the resources must be exploited and education must be related to productivity to increase national income. But, we need to start thinking about cultivating the whole of the human being, not just filling students memories with facts and information. This type of education is useless because a good education should help us to live well by teaching us how to deal with our emotions, how to build relationship and how to live well and only philosophical bases of education provides this type of education. Without a philosophy of education we get nowhere at all. All our efforts prove useless. There is an enormous loss of time, energy and finance. Moreover, there is an immense waste of human resources. Pactice, unguided by theory, is aimless, inconsistent and inefficient. Therefore, there is a need for philosophical bases for formulating aim of education.

## Psychological Bases

Psychology is known to be the study of human behaviour based upon the systematic and scientific study of human mind. It is the development of child's innate process and modification of human behaviour. Pestalozzi, a well known modern educationist, was the champion to enunciate the movement for psychologising education. It was a time when psychological movement gained momentum with the advert of psychology and its application to education, the whole process of education has been revolutionised. Educators like Rousseau, Froebel, Montessori, Dewey, Tagore and T.P. Nunn have also given full support to this movement. They have advocated the psychology of an individual should be the basis for formulating aims of education.

At present the aims of education throughout the world are based upon psychological bases.

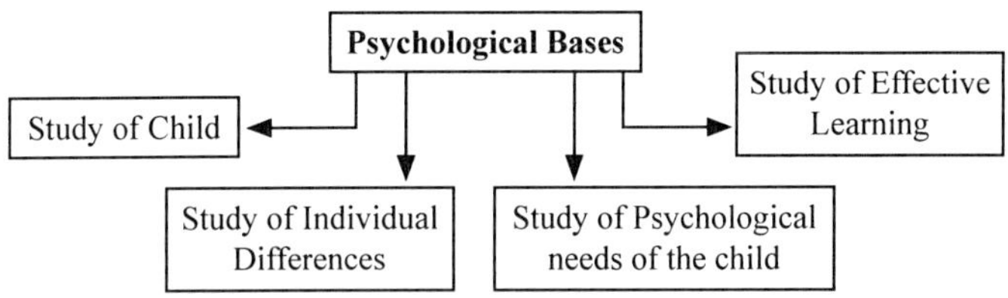


**Fig. 12.3: Psychological Bases and Aims of Education**

(i) *Psychology is the study of child:* It is believed that every child is a unique entity. The main purpose of education is to study the nature of child in terms of his instincts, urges, motives, needs, aptitudes and interests.

(ii) *Study of Individual differences:* Individual differences refers to the fact that no two individuals are alike. They differ in age, interests, achievements, aptitudes, intelligence, potentialities and other traits. Psychology plays an important role regarding this because the knowledge of individual differences helps the teacher in developing right attitude towards the pupils and helps him to devise ways and mean for achieving the attitude.

(iii) *Study of the Psychological Needs of the child:* The entire process of education centres around the child. Now a days the education is for the child and not child is for education. So the whole programme of education has to be so geared as to fulfil the needs of the child. It has to take full notice of child's potentialities, his age, stages of development, his capacities, possibilities and limitations. Thus the psychological bases forms the fundamental bases of education.

(iv) *Study of effective learning:* The science of education revolves around the child because the main purpose of research in education is that 'How to change the behaviour of a child?'. This is very essential to ensure harmonious development of the child as well as to make learning effective. Psychology provides the necessary knowledge in this regard. With the help of this knowledge, the teacher creates situations, conditions and the environment which are conducive to learning. Successful education results into effective learning.

Early period of child's life, motivational factors, freedom and discipline, direction of child's study, various modes of discipline, activity and play are also some other factors that provide the psychological base to educational thought and practice.

Developing countries like India, Sri Lanka, Fiji etc. look towards educational agencies for its onward growth and progress and a developed country looks back to streamline its education in order to sustain and confirm its progress. The awakened mind, correct knowledge, appropriate skills and desirable attitudes are the important aspects of development. The destiny of a country is now being shaped in its classrooms because the student of today is the citizen of tomorrow. He is the pivot around which the development of nation revolves. Through psychology youth power should be given constructive and creative direction. Many educationists and psychologists consider national development as a psychological process. It is development of inherited qualities. Psychological researches and findings have certainly changed the entire process of education. They have their impact on educational aims, curriculum, science of pedagogy, textbooks, concept of discipline and role of the teacher. So we can say that the psychological basis play an important role in formulating aims of education.

## Sociological Bases

Education is a sociological process, that is, education is a process oriented towards the society. The existence of education depends on the existence of society. The structure of education, its nature and principles depends on a society's norms, values and principles i.e. why education and society cannot be regards as being separate from one another.

> *"Education is the consciously controlled process whereby changes in behaviour are produced in the person and through the person with in group."* *(Brown)*

Sociology is the science of society. It is the study of human behavior in groups. It has further been described as the study of the different forms of human interrelations. John Dewey has given the sides of education: (i) Biological or psychological and (ii) Sociological. Dewey says, *"the function of education is to help in growing of helpless young animal into a happy, moral and efficient human being."* The function directly signifies psychological and sociological bases of education and it is the most important consideration of education.

Psychological basis help a teacher to understand an individual, whereas sociological basis of education provide a general background of society, its constituents, ideologies, problems and other aspects. Through this we can properly understand the human nature in action.

The three main parts of education are parts of the society:–

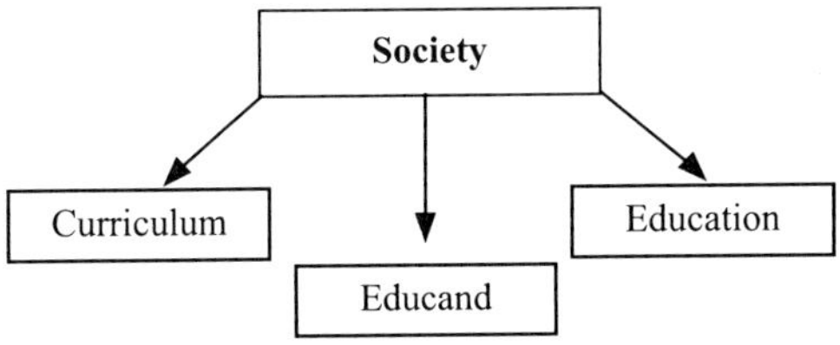


**Fig. 12.4: Parts of Education & Society**

So education is considered as sociological process.

- *Components of Education*—influenced by the Non-static society
- *Principles of Education*—Founded on the needs of the society.
- *Rules of Education*—Depends on the norms of the society within which it operates.
- *Educational Curriculum*—According to the present and future sociological needs.
- *Education Discipline*—The social point of view is given more importance.
- *Education Process*—Guided by the society's prevailing culture.
- *Resources spend on Education*—Comes from society.

The sociological basis means that education should be footed on society's needs, aspirations and principles. Education from sociological point of view, is considered as a social necessity. It becomes a great socialising factor. It strikes a balance between individual and society and makes their functioning complementary to each other.

The child cannot be educated in isolation. All education takes place in the social milieu. Child's personality development is the result of the interaction with the environment, groups and other social factors and a new direction to education. Man has always shown a liking for living in groups. With the help of group life man has not only been able to survive against heavy odds but group life also led to the development of some qualities and ways of behavior which form the basis of human civilization. Man is a society-loving individual. He does not want to get away from his group. This group life is grounded in certain fundamental, ethical, moral and behaviouristic patterns. There is need to impart education with regard to these group values which bind them together.

The present and future social needs and circumstances continuously influence the aims of education. Education obtains its new form from society itself because of the changing nature of society. The sociologists should analyze and study the gaps in society and gain knowledge on how to rectify the situation and this is sociological basis to formulate aims of education. In developing countries these basis of education help in the actual control of human behavior and ultimately leading to an individual towards socialization. Through social education, students should make remarkable progress in:

- achievement of social values.
- fulfil their duties.
- use their rights and duties.
- be valuable, awakened, productive and complete citizens of tomorrow.

Every human society operates at different levels as global, national and sub-national. They have different needs, challenges and opportunities i.e. why the desires and aspiration of the society cannot be same at all levels.

The expectations of the global society are reflected in the U.N.O, charters and its specified branch like (UNESCO) United Nations Educational Scientific and Cultural Organisation, declarations and revolutions adopted by the General Assembly of United Nations, and the report of Director Commission on Education. U.N.O. Charter aim at achieving international cooperation in solving problems of economic, social, cultural and in promoting and encouraging respect for human rights as well as for fundamental freedom for all without differentiation in race, gender, religion or language. Human rights emphasis that all human beings are born free and equal in dignity and rights. The General Assembly of the United Nations in 1979 condemned discrimination against women in all its forms and emphasized the need to adopt the principle of equality of men and women in their national contributions. In 1989, it emphasized that every child shall have the right to freedom of thought, conscience and religion and on the other hand every disabled child has the right to special care on account of his/her special needs. It enjoins on the national governments to take all appropriate social and educational measures to protect the child from all forms of physical or mental volumes, injury or abuse including social abuse.

B. Lindquist observed, *"All children and young people of the world with their individual strength and weaknesses, with their hopes and expectations, have the right to education. It is not our education system that have a right to certain types of children. Therefore, it is the school system of a country that must be adjusted to meet the needs of all children."*

United Nations has also adopted a number of declarations regarding environmental pollution and protection, global warming, sustainable development etc. These efforts have emphasized that the present generation is responsible to leave behind the resources and kind of earth worth living for the future generation. The Sustainable Development Goals (SDGs) also known as the Global Goals, were adopted by all United Nations Member states in 2015 as a universal call to action to end poverty, protect the planet and ensure that all people enjoy peace and prosperity by 2030. The 17 SDGs are integrated—that is, they recognize that action in one area will affect outcomes in others and that development must balance social, economic and environmental sustainability.

The International community has moved a step closer towards defining the education agenda beyond 2015, to be part of the global post 2015 development agenda. The proposed overarching education goal is to 'ensure equitable and inclusive quality education and life long learning for all by 2030.' The goal is being translated into seven global education targets:—

- Early childhood care and education
- Basic education
- Youth and adult literacy
- Skills for work
- Skills for citizenship and sustainable development
- Teachers—well qualified, professionally trained
- Financing of education.

These targets are the basis of a framework for action, to be developed by UNESCO, in consultation with all EFA partners. The framework will guide the implementation of a future education agenda and identify both indicators for the global targets and country specific targets and indicators, reflecting diverse social, political, economic and cultural contexts.

The National societies are the part and parcel of global society. The aspirations of national societies are reflected in its constitution, laws and policies. A developing society may aspire to strengthen itself in different areas whereas a developed society aspire to be more developed and strengthen in technology as well as production. A democratic society may strive to develop democratic values while an authoritative society may expect citizens to conform to the established norms. A multilingual, multi-religious and multi-cultural society may aspire to promote national and emotional integration to develop feeling of cooperation and respect for diversity. Thus a national society on the one hand wants to preserve its national and cultural identity as well as on the other hand tries to promote its world view,

In the world, different nations are divided in geographical regions with concentration of people belonging to a particular culture as well as language. We can see in India, each state constitutes a distinct socio-cultural unit having their own aspirations and state specific educational goals are formulated to fulfill their expectations. Every state may desire to integrate with national stream but at the same time they want to preserve their cultural identity along with its customs and traditions as well as their language.

Thus the principles of education should be in line with a society's vision, mission, its religious, cultural, political values and economic stability. Hence such subjects and activities should be included in the school curriculum which foster social growth, fill social needs and ensure progress of the society. In this way the sociological basis of education focuses on society to be the foundation of education. The school is a social institution which purifies and idealises the existing social institutions and customs and is a living society for children. Thus sociological basis of education is undoubtedly the most important basis for aims of education in developing countries.

**Ethical Bases**

> *"We live in a world of bewildering potentialities for good and evil. A great struggle is under way to win the minds and loyalties of men and women. There are means and resources available by which we may build a more satisfying life. On the other hand, there is the possibility that we may come to live in a world that is more dangerous and cruel and regimented than any which existed in the recent past." (Titus Harold)*

Ethics is the study of human conduct. It attempts to determine what conduct is good and what is bad, or what ought to be approved and what disapproved. Ethics is a normative study of the principles underlying the desirable type of human conduct. To manage life and act responsibly is very hard without ethics. The significance of ethics cannot be disregard at any level of life. It's important that they are practiced in the area of education. Education is an ethical necessity. It is true of every evil, trouble or conflict. The rapidly changing social environment is making new demands upon education. New attitudes and a loftier social morality are needed. The school atmospheres and the attitudes reflect the conduct and the ethical ideals of the teachers and the students.

Ethical basis of formulating aims of education is appraised as the segment of the human right to education. The motive of ethics education is not directly learning ethics for its purpose. Its objective is to deploy this body of knowledge for two purposes:—

**Purposes of Ethical Bases**

1. To grow intellectual dimensions that will authorize people to recognize ethical dimensions of issues and address ethical issues in various fields.
2. To develop critical thinking skills, intentional any one's purposes particularly the ability to reflect and the theoretical and practical effect of personal and collective human action.

Education is an ethical art. One cannot view the educational endeavours of modernizing nations without becoming increasingly aware that educational decisions are at heart of moral or ethical decisions. Ethical basis for aims of education is important because:–

- It assist to run the system of a country smoothly.
- It sets the standards of what's acceptable and what's not.
- Assist students to understand norms for professional behaviour.

Ethics has an essential place in all fields of life. Education is also a basic method of human life. So in education ethics has a vital and productive role. To become a better citizen, ethics should be put as a way in the educational systems.

In developing countries the main goal of education, as such, is to train people to face the future vision, to be broad and tolerant in outlook, to be seeker after peace, and to consider the rights of others. Because we are living in a period of rapid social change, the industrial, technological and atomic revolutions are producing a society which is mechanically efficient but which threatens to destroy itself. The danger is that we have learned how to control nature and to split the atom before we have learned how to unite mankind. And only the ethical basis for aims of education can a bit. A code of ethics worthy of the name, results in the establishment of clear norms for professional behaviour. It can be extended to every professional organization. Students and school authorities should also adhere to a definite code of conduct. Any departure from this norms is an indication of unprofessional behaviour or abnormal behaviour. It is suggested that necessary change in accordance with the principles discussed above, be made in the educational aims.

> *"If teaching is a profession then the pupil is the client and professionalism requires that the treatment of the client be for his best interests."*
>
> *(Brubacher)*

**Political Bases**

Most of developing countries were governed by an imperial European power. But these developing countries have only attained full self-determination and democracy. Political systems in developing countries are diverse, but most countries had established some form of democratic government by the early 21st century, with varying degrees of success and political liberty.

Aldous Huxley has remarked, *"If your aim is liberty and democracy then you must teach people the art of being free and of governing themselves."* Democratic outlook can never be developed in the event of lack of education. In a democracy the government is composed of the elected representatives of the people and if the people are uneducated, they can never elect the right leaders and consequently can never create the right kind of government. In fact, it is impossible even to hope for the development of democratic outlook in the absence of education. It is difficult to expect a citizen to behave responsibly if he is not aware of his rights and duties. The truth of the matter is that education is a prerequisite for developing democratic outlook and without it democracy is impossible.

The principles of democracy which should be kept in mind while formulating aims of education are as follows:

(i) *Liberty or Freedom:* Nunn asserts that nothing good enters human life except through the free activities of men and women. Liberty is regarded as the basic condition for the achievements of excellence in all the fields of human activities. When one talks of freedom, one refers freedom of thought, action, speech and movement. It is an atmosphere of freedom that one gets motivation to express himself / herself and to realise his/her full potentialities. The optimum growth of man's personality is possible in an environment of freedom and flexibility. Freedom of an individual is sometimes restrained in the interest of society. But it should always be remembered that a social or political set up, which leaves no option for the individual to choose, imposes rigid uniformity and represses individuality has in no way help individuals bring out their best. As the democratic outlook it took the shape of self-discipline. Everyone understood that what he should do or don't and what will be benefited for him or vice versa.

(ii) *Equality:* All men are born equal in the sense that all share the same basic human qualities and characteristics. On the other hand, everybody is unique in his own way in terms of intelligence, aptitude, physical abilities etc. The equality is not an empirical generalization about man, but the moral command that every human being has right to equal opportunity to develop and improve his or her potentialities to the optimum. Inspite of individual differences, every individual deserves equal opportunity to live, to learn and to realise his objectives in various endeavours.

(iii) *Fraternity:* It relates with the democratic outlook of fellow-feeling. All individuals of a country share the same nationality. Unless an individual feels that he belongs to the same humanity, he cannot feel that fellow-feeling or the morale of togetherness which is an important characteristic of democracy. Therefore, there should not be any distinction of caste, colour, creed, language, place or region of birth, residence, sex in the living and development of individuals. Love, affection, co-operation, sympathy and understanding are the qualities which are essential for the democratic outlook.

(iv) *Justice:* As a corollary to the above values, it is natural that an individual has the right to justice. He/she cannot be deprived from any opportunity nor he/she be debarred from getting his/her dues in all walks of life. Individual cannot be discriminated on grounds that are unfair or illegal,

(v) *Dignity of the Individual:* Every individual has dignity which is based on the assumption of the infinite value and worth of every human being. This is applicable to everybody without distinction of caste, creed, colour, sex or race. Dignity of man can be made secured by 'inalienable' right to life, liberty and happiness. In the words of *Kilpatrick*, "Respect of personality, is of primary importance. Everybody who makes any positive contribution to society through his/her work is respected in society without consideration of his/her status or calling". Everybody is, therefore, enlisted to get full opportunity for self-development and self-realization.

(vi) *Co-operation:* In a democratic country everyone should believe in co-operative living. Every individual must extend co-operation and enlist the cooperation of other in the working of all matters concerning society. From the early stages of socialization, one must learn to live with others and appreciate the cooperation of others. Democratic civilization progresses on the premise that man cannot live by himself and can not realize his goals without the help of others. Besides, in every institutional and social work, he has to work together. Every-body has to contribute his/her bit to realise the common ideals and purposes of society.

(vii) *Sharing of Responsibility:* In a democratic country everybody must assume certain responsibility and must share community life. Freedom implies responsibility because freedom without the sense of duty and responsibility would bring anarchy. Responsibility implies performing socially relevant task with honesty and commitment and being answerable to society for the purpose.

Though rights implies duties but in actual practice, very few individuals remember their duties. They have a much keener understanding of their rights than for their obligations. They are required to be reminded of their responsibilities and duties. This shows the importance of imparting education for development of democratic outlook to classes as well as to masses. In order to promote the cause of liberty and democracy we have to give education for the development of democratic outlook. Democratic outlook is not born, but developed. Man is born as a social animal. He uses society for his personal gains and ends. An able bodied, sound-minded and self-supporting individual may not serve his society. Over emphasis on personal ends may make an individual selfish and even dangerous to society. Therefore, education must include a sense of social responsibility to train individuals to develop democratic outlook and to be useful citizens.

Thus education should frame its objectives in such a way so that it becomes an effective means for the development of the nation according to their political system.

## Economical Bases

Economists have all along taken some cognizance of the role of education in the presence of economic development. In fact, the relationship of the two for the prosperity of mankind was emphasized long back by Adam Smith and Marshall in the eighteenth century, the most versatile contribution to the discipline of Economics. In his 'Enquiry in to the Nature and causes of wealth of Nations' he said, *"Education confers great indirect benefits even on the ordinary workman. It stimulates his mental ability, it fosters in him a habit of wise inquisitiveness; it make him more intelligent, more ready, more trustworthy in his ordinary work; it raises the time of his life on working hours; it is an important means towards the production of material wealth"* Alfred Marshall took the expenditure on education as 'National Investment'.

The economists of 18th century were aware of the immense scope of treating education as an investment in human beings, and several economists noticed the value of this form of human capital when they praised the value of quality labour in to the field provided the insight that the economic contribution of education could be interpreted in terms of human capital formation through education. Several studies seeking to establish the relationship between education and economic development have received the attention of both educationists and economists.

Among the various roles which education has got to play, its role in economic development through human resource development is perhaps the most significant at present especially in under-developed and developing countries. Herbinson and Myers hold the view that educational process of human resource development is necessary for the transformation of social and political institutions, for which the modernizing countries strive.

It has, however, to be noted that education system and economic development in a given social setup are interrelated in such a way, that one cannot exist without the other. Deterioration in education therefore will affect economic development and slow economic development will affect educational system and standards. According to B.G. Tilak, the relationship between education and economic development is a 'two way process'— one of a reciprocal nature, of mutual contribution. It is like a chicken-and-egg' relationship, as John Vaizzey (1962) humorously but rightly described. Herbinson and Myers spoke of education being both the seed and flower of economic growth.

The economist may ask the educationist to produce engineers, doctors, teachers or any other category of technical personnel with the least cost. The economist goes by quantitative considerations, whereas the educationist is concerned with quality but cannot predict the future of his pupils. The sort of forecasting the economist makes it purely in term of quality. As John Vaizzey put it, *"in order to produce one graduate in a given system there have to be ten people in a secondary school, and a hundred people in the primary school."*

It is well known that the literacy rate in developing countries is far below than that in the developed countries. Illiteracy is thus concomitant with underdevelopment. As illiteracy is common feature of underdeveloped countries and is common among low income group, act as barrier in economic development. It is a general observation that uneducated people are neither motivated nor qualified to make full use of the facilities created for economic growth in the field of agricultural production, co-operative societies, family welfare programmes, the adoption of used techniques in rural and small scale industries, or the intelligent use of credit for increasing production.

Cole S, Bremback holds the view that a positive attitude towards practical work and manual work counts much in economic development. He strongly opposes the, *"situation in which education entitles one to have white bands, divorce himself from practical work, and enjoy the fruits of belonging to intelligences"* Education has a prominent role to play in affecting changes in the attitudes and habits of the people as well.

Thus, it can be concluded that education plays a very significant role in economic development and social modernization, and that it has an important place among the sources of production, and also that it provides capable and skilled individuals as well as the necessary institution for various kinds of work. While formulating aim of education, a society needs to take into account all the bases as—philosophical, psychological, political, sociological, and economic. It has to strive a balance if the aspirations and desires in different areas are at variance from each other. The main target should be to make all the human being in real terms human and to sustain all the resources for future generation while making growth of that society.

# 13

# Jiddu Krishnamurti (1895-1986)

*"Real learning comes about when the competitive spirit has ceased."*

– Jiddu Krishnamurti

Jiddu Krishnamurti was born on May 11, 1895 in a small town of Madanpalli in then colonial India (Modern day Chitoor district in Andhra Pradesh) to a family of middle class Telugu Brahmin. His father, Jiddu Narayaniah was an official of the British Colonial administration, though an orthodox Brahmin, was a member of the Theosophical Society. He was fond of his mother Sanjeevamma, who died when he was 10 years old. The frequent transfers of his father and his bouts of malarial fever interrupted his studies. He often looked around vaguely in the classroom and his teacher repeatedly punished him for his inattentiveness. Due to his generosity he would also give away his books and pencils to needy students and distribute food to the needy persons who came to his house.

In January 1909, his family moved at the Headquarter of Theosophical society at Adyar. There he first met Charles Webster Leadbeater, who noticed him on the society's beach at Adyar river, and was amazed by the 'most wonderful aura', he had ever seen without a particle of selfishness in it. He was convinced that the boy would become a spiritual teacher and a great orator. Krishnamurti was greeted as 'The Master of the Earth' or 'Lord Maitreya' by him, one of the most mysterious readers of the Theosophical Society. Ms Annie Besant, President of the Society, endorsed this view and welcomed or briefed Krishnamurti as his younger brother. Leadbeater and a small number of trustee associates undertook the task of educating, protecting and generally preparing Krishna as 'vehicle' of expected world teacher. During this time he had developed a strong bond with Annie Besant and came to view her as a surrogate mother.

In 1911, the Theosophical society established the Order of the Star in the East (OSE) to prepare the world for the expected appearance of the world teacher. Krishnamurti was named as its head, with senior Theosophists, who were assigned various other positions. At the age of 15, he accompanied Mrs. Annie Besant, the influential spirit of the Theosophical Society; to England. He hated reading a book. However, he was a great observer and when his interest was enthused, he spent long periods of time looking at trees and clouds or squat on the ground watching plants and worms. Regarding his school, he wrote: *"I can't say I was too happy at school, because the teachers were very kind and gave me lessons that were very difficult for me."*

Krishnamurti, gave his first public speech to members of OSE in London in 1911. In 1912, he wrote a script entitled "Education as Service" in which he depicted the ideal school life in which the conventions of love come in, in which students grow into admirable youth under the appearance of inspiring teachers who feel the magnitude of their love. During 1912-21, his meditation entered depth and his insight in to the causes of human pain and sufferings found expression in his utterness and writings. Now his writings came in quick successions. Krishnamurti gave lectures at major conferences in Australia, England, Holland and North and South America.

On 28th December 1925, while addressing the International Convention of the Theosophical Society under the Banyan tree at Adyar, Krishnamurti spoke of the coming of Lord Maitreya. Suddenly his voice changed to a powerful tone of penetrating sweetness, and he concluded his address as

> *'I come to those who want sympathy, who are longing to be released, who are longing to find happiness in all things, I come to reform, and not tear down, not to destroy, not to build'.*

For more than 60 years, through public talks and private interviews, he addressed millions of people saying that only through a complete change in the hearts and minds of individuals a change can come about in society and the world. The emphasis in his talks and writings was on the psychological barriers that prevent clarity of perception. With the generous contribution of his followers, Krishnamurti established several centres of philosophical studies in various countries. Lots of Great Jobs done by him:

- The Kingdom of Happiness (1927),
- The Path (1930),
- Search (1931),
- Commentaries from Unknown (1950),
- Commentaries on life: Series II (1951),
- Commentaries on Living: Series III (1952),
- First and Last Freedom (1954),
- Education and the Significance of Health (1955),
- Life Ahead (1963),
- Talks in Europe (1967).

Krishna took his last walk on January 10, 1986, requested those who had accompanied him to go ahead and wait for him at the gate. He then turned to all the four directions and paused for a minute in a reverential farewell. That day he left India for California and breathed his last on February 17, 1986 at his home, Pine cottage in Ojai. Long recognised as one of the world's foremost religious teachers, he dedicated his life to awakening man to his own sorrows and the possibility of freedom.

## Philosophical Thinking of J. Krishnamurti

Krishnamurti was an eminent writer and speaker on philosophical and spiritual issues, including psychological revolution, the nature of human mind, consciousness and evolution, meditation, human relationships, and bringing about positive social change. He summarized all the disciplines and rejected all counselors and assessors. He did not invent a new faith or doctrine. He did not claim any authority, no religion, and he did not initiate a social reform program. He gave nothing other than total human change as the solution to the conflict and suffering in the world. He advised her audience to think for themselves, to feel interested, to shed the past or future burdens and to release their minds from fear. His philosophy is based on 2 F's, i.e., *Freedom of mind* and *Fearlessness*. He laid emphasis on a mind free from self and time, in other words, the emptying of consciousness of all its content. This is the essential meaning that he gave to meditation, which is the Heart of his Teachings. According to him the understanding of 'what is' and going beyond it, brings clarity - that is the clarity of a mind that is unconfused, without distortion or sense of duality at all.

The basis of his Philosophy is to live a life, daily life - which is not a life in abstraction, not a life in speculation, not a life in acceptance of the authority of another but the daily life of pain, agony, fear and in that, to find out for ourselves the Truth.

He used to say *"I desire those who seek to understand me, to be free, not to follow me, not to make me a cage which will become a religion, a sect."*

He elaborated his approach in the following words: "All men desire to discover for themselves, with certainty, what is the purpose of life...... To do this they must be rid of all philosophies, dogmas, creeds, religions, particular rites, because no one can discover his purpose in life with all these encumbrances. So long as there is limitation, there is sorrow and it is from sorrow that all men would escape. They are trying to find a way out of suffering, out of their entanglement in the wheel of sorrow and pain. In the attainment of perfection is Liberation to be found.... Sorrow and joy, pain and pleasure, light and shade are the same thing. Only when you are absolutely undisturbed by either will true perfection abide in your heart and mind....True creation is the outcome of harmony which is perfection, the delicate poise of reason and of life....Have no fear of life and you will have no fear of death."

*Meaning of Philosophy:* To him, philosophy is not a series of theories about life, man and the world. It is not a bundle of ideas, opinions and conclusions, nor it is the academic discipline of conceiving, criticizing and interpreting concepts. Philosophy is not the speculative or the intellectual activity of system-building. It is not a logical analysis of language and meaning. On the contrary, philosophy, according to him, is the love of truth. Love means the instantaneous perception. It is understanding which is beyond the intellect. Truth means the life which is undetermined by thought. It means the mind which is unconditioned. Philosophy is living life independently of systems, images, ideals and beliefs. It is living from moment to moment in the total freedom of the mind. It is living in the 'present'. True life is what is happening at this instant. It is not what thought or intellect conceives it to be. He observed that philosophy is the understanding of the truth which is beyond the reality of thought. Philosophy is the ending of the illusion of mistaking reality for truth. It is the realization that reality can never become truth. Philosophy is the actual cessation of the ignorance and the irrationality of approaching truth through reality.

*Truth:* When man becomes aware of the movement of his own thoughts he will see the division between the thinker and thought, the observer and the observed, the experiencer and the experience. He will discover that this division is an illusion. This timeless insight brings about a deep radical mutation in the mind. Total negation is the essence of the positive. When there is negation of all those things that thought has brought about psychologically, only then there is love, which is compassion and intelligence. So the free mind is truth and truth is love and love alone transforms man and his society. Therefore the real change of the society absolutely requires the change of the mind. Truth is not a matter of logic. It is direct perception. It is being without motive, without conceptualization, choice or self- interest. It is 'pure observation' and 'choiceless awareness'. When the mind is free from thoughts only then the light of truth can be seen.

He insistent on the one point which interests him, and which he considers to be of primary importance: man must free himself from 'I'. Only he who has freed himself from his condition of slavery can act truly. 'Everyone must learn to free himself, in order to awaken oneself to discover truth, real happiness'. Truth is being from moment to moment and happiness is that state of being which is timeless. And Love is not different from truth. It is that state in which thought process as time has completely ceased, and where love is, there is transformation. Where there is love, there is revolution, because love is transformation from moment to moment.

*Empty Mind:* According to Krishnamurti, truth can come to us only when our mind and heart are simple, clear, and there is love in our heart. It will not come if our heart is filled with the things of the mind. When there is love in our heart, we do not talk about organizing for brotherhood; we do not talk about belief, we do not talk about division or the powers that create division, we need not seek reconciliation. Then we are simply a human being without a label, without a country. This means that we must strip ourselves of all those things and allow truth to come into being; and it can come only when the mind is empty, when the mind ceases to create; then it will come without our invitation. It comes obscurely, not when we are watching, wanting. It is there as sudden as sunlight, as pure as the night. If we are to receive it, the heart must be full and the mind empty.

*Importance of Self-consciousness:* Krishnamurti does not trust ideals. He stated that an ideal is what is not. A human cannot understand an ideal without knowing what the other part of it is. I cannot know what truth is without knowing what is false, and what non-violence is without knowing what is violence. One cannot 'Know' of something in the present. Even 'I' cannot know of its moment during self-enquiry other than the past, as the present shall not be understandable unless it passes into the past. Humans can only learn from their past and not from their present, as the present is this very moment. All introspection is a form of retrospection. Problems that affect our behaviour cannot be resolved without awakening the creative intelligence or the intuition within us. He stated that when you are really happy and deeply in love, the 'I' is not. Liberation is a state in which all 'I' consciousness has ceased.

*Religious Mind:* According to Krishnamurti, we all follow a religion blindly, out of past conditioning or fear. We do not question or enquire what we may believe or not believe out of fear, and who is to be responsible for this – our elders who condition us to believe without questioning. What we are doing out of fear, or so-called belief, must be questioned. He states that a true religious mind is free of fear, blind faith, and contradiction. The list of must do's in any religion should be questioned by itself. A mind should be investigative and scientific in its approach, and not bounded by something, or compelled. Religious matters make humans irrational and insane. All these build the walls of our conditioning.

*Feeling and Human Mind:* According to Krishnamurti, feeling is a part of the mind. The mind includes desires, love, jealousy, emotions, everything. It includes all that we understand and feel. What is different is its manifestation and its intensity. The problem is not about feeling right or wrong, because humans will feel. What needs to be changed is the greed to have many things. People want the good things of life and yet want to feel contented and peaceful. The former brings about the need to acquire things, have power / prestige, and be ambitious. To have both is not possible: a real mind has no place for ambition and acquisitions. Pleasure is not difficult, but with it come difficulties; but we want pleasure without difficulties. It is only when the mind is capable of living in totality that remorse, difficulty, and pain will have no meaning and feeling to it.

*Consciousness:* According to him, when one becomes aware of one's conditioning, one understands the entire consciousness. It is the total field in which thoughts, functions, and relationships exist. All motives, emotions, desires, pleasures, fears, aspirations, longings, hopes, sorrows, joys, and inspirations are in that field. It can be divided into the active and the dormant, the upper and lower levels. All daily thoughts, feelings, and activities are on the surface, and below them is the subconscious, the aspects with which we are not familiar, which express themselves occasionally through certain imitations, intuitions, and dreams. We live our life in fragments. We are one person at work, another with friends, and another at home. A mind that is fragmented shall never be aware of full consciousness.

*Awareness:* It is often that we concentrate on our own problems, our own ideas, and our own world, such that we are not objectively aware. Verbally we can only be superficial. What lies beyond cannot be put into words. One needs to be aware. Awareness about how we walk, how we speak, how we talk, and how we think, is necessary. It is with a choiceless awareness that doors shall open and one would know a consciousness in which there is no conflict and no time. Understanding ourselves marks the beginning of wisdom.

*Freedom:* Freedom is found in the choiceless awareness of our daily existence and activity. For Krishnamurti, a concept very similar to that of dharma, which I cannot help but compare it with — put simply as — Live your life the right way; do what you have to and be a good human being; and maybe that will lead to the final freedom.

*Concentration and Meditation:* When a child is concentrating on a toy, what is happening? The attention of the child is being absorbed by the toy. He is not giving his attention to the toy, but the toy is very interesting and it absorbs his attention. That is exactly what is happening to you when you concentrate on the idea of the Master, on a picture, or when you repeat mantras, and all the rest of it. The toy is absorbing you, and you are merely a plaything of the toy. You thought you were the master of the toy, but the toy is the master. Concentration also implies exclusiveness. You exclude in order to arrive at a particular result, like a boy trying to pass an examination. The boy wants a profitable result, so he forces himself to concentrate, he makes tremendous effort to get what he wants, which is based on his desire, on his conditioning.

So, to concentrate is not to meditate, even though that is what most of you do, calling it meditation. And if concentration is not meditation, then what is? Surely, meditation is to understand every thought that comes into being, and not to dwell upon one particular thought; it is to invite all thoughts so that you understand the whole process of thinking. Self-knowledge is the beginning of meditation, and as you proceed deeply into it you will find that the mind becomes astonishingly quiet, unforced, completely still, without motion - which means there is no experiencer demanding experience. When there is only that state of stillness without any movement of the mind, then you will find that in that state something else takes place.

*Art of Listening to the Inner God:* To find out what is true we must never accept, we must never be influenced by what the books, the teachers or anyone else may say. If we are influenced by them, we will find only what they want you to find. And we must know that our own mind can create the image of what it wants; it can imagine God with a beard, or with one eye; it can make him blue or purple. So we have to be aware of our own desires and not be deceived by the projections of our own wants and longings. If we are in sorrow and want to be comforted, or if we feel sentimental and romantic in our religious aspirations, eventually we will create a God who will supply what we want; but it will still not be God. So, our mind must be completely free, and only then can we find out what is true by the art of listening to the inner God not by the acceptance of some superstition, nor by the reading of the so-called sacred books, nor by the following of some guru. Only when we have this freedom, this real freedom from external influences as well as from our own desires and longings so that our mind is very clear - only then it is possible to find out what God is.

Thus Krishnamurti believed that the mind which would find truth, this extraordinary beauty and depth of life, the fullness of love, must first be free. Only the free mind can discover, and only the mind that is free can be creative. His whole fabric of thought or philosophy, based on Right Perception in its essentials, seems probably closest to that of Sankhya Sutras Of Kapil - Who does not postulate God but places all His attributes in the spirit itself which is indivisible one, the moment all the combination of thoughts are stilled within the innermost of an individual being. The three aphorisms of 'Sankhya yoga' could conveniently sum up his whole philosophy on meditation and liberation. They are:

1. 'Dhyan Heyyas Tad Vrittiah' (2-11) - All combination of thoughts cease through meditation.
2. Nirvichar Vaisharidyey Adhyatam - Spiritual Bliss follows through the transparency of thoughtlessness.
3. 'Pratibhad Va Sarvam.' (3-34) - Everything is revealed through intuitional perceptiveness.

## Krishnamurti's Educational Philosophy

Krishnamurti has explained right kind of education instead of education.

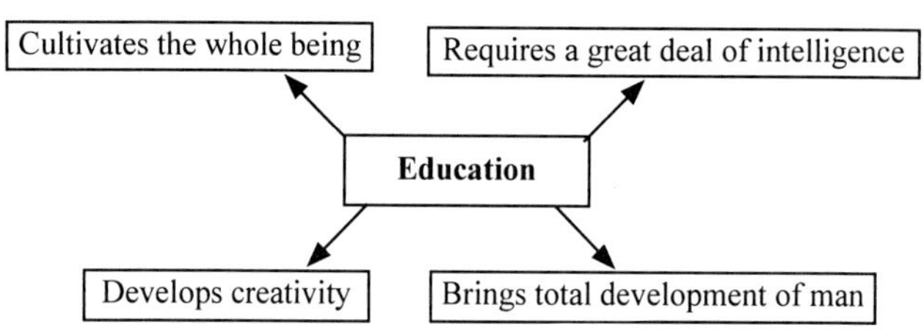


**Fig. 13.1: Characteristics of Education**

He has given some definitions, concept and characteristics of the word education as the right kind of education-

- cultivates the whole being,
- should accomplish the important things in life,

- helps to find out the problem,
- cannot be drawn into the stream of society in any circumstances,
- helps to find out what one really wants to do,
- helpful for creativeness,
- helps to find out true vocation,
- starts with students and their questions for creative pleasure,
- does not concern with any system or ideology,
- encourages thoughtfulness and consideration,
- helps to be mature,
- helps to be watchful to the influences,
- helps in understanding of oneself,
- concerned with individual freedom and brings true co-operation with the whole,
- refuses any bondage, rules and regulations of the government,
- requires a great deal of intelligence, insight,
- should help to prevent inner and outer conflict, within or without,
- avoids to become mechanical beings and pre-determined ends, and
- helps to understand all our relationships.

Traditional education makes independent thinking very difficult, it removes the dullness of the mind and heart and creates fear in our mind. Traditional education makes us sensitive to the environment. It only prepares us for getting a good job or gaining professional skills and does not help us to understand the high and wide importance of life. There is no deep integration of thought and emotion in traditional education. Traditional training has merely been grooming to attain personal gain and security and to fight for ourselves. It is the training of the mind. The current scheme of teaching makes us livelihood, mechanically and deeply unthinkable. Today's education is utterly unsuccessful as technology puts too much emphasis on current knowledge. We destroy human beings in technology of high importance. Technology specialists have produced specialists, mathematicians, bridge builders, space conquerors, but do they realize the whole procedure of Life. He criticized the technical education in these words: *"Our technological progress has been amazing, but it has only increased the power to destroy each other, and there is hunger and misunderstanding in every land. We are not peaceful and happy people."*

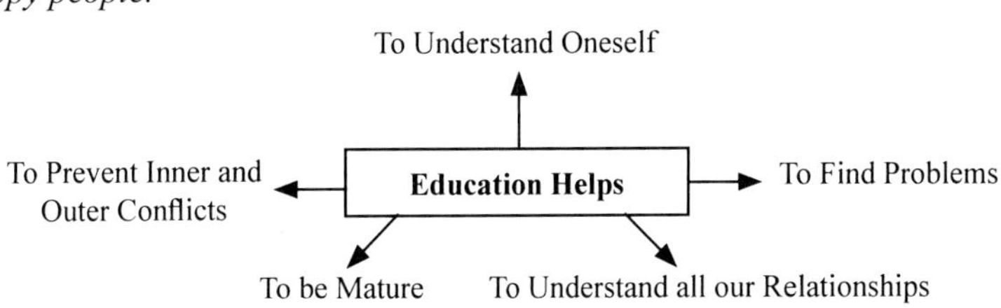


**Fig. 13.2: Functions of Education**

He sees education not with the eyes of a reformer, as a means to serve this or that end; but as an intrinsic, self-fulfilling experience requiring no further justification. The function of education, he said, is "to bring about a mind that will not only act in the immediate but go beyond…a mind that is extraordinarily alive, not with knowledge, not with experience, but alive". "More important than making the child technologically proficient is the creation of the right climate in the school for the child to develop fully as a complete human being". This means giving him "the opportunity to flower in goodness, so that he is rightly related to people, things and ideas, to the whole of life."

### *Mind*

It is essentially as a philosopher of mind that Krishnamurti looks at education. He saw the ultimate basis of all learning in the innermost working of the human mind. This is not psychoanalysis as it is commonly understood but a deep look, unburdened by any kind of conditioning, into one's own person, into one's innermost thoughts and feelings.

### *Limitations of Intelligence*

Krishnamurti says that intelligence is not the means of real knowledge. Our mind is conditioned by everything we have ever experienced. It is in the nature of the mind to store these experiences into our memory. This we call knowledge. When we have to use this knowledge practically, it can be of great benefit to us, like in mechanical operations, e.g., in driving a car. Thought originates from memory. They come on the basis of the experiences we got in our past. Intelligence also creates struggles in our life. Like thoughts, imagination also brings us far off from the reality. He does not think himself as guru or instructor. He shows us a path and it depends on our efforts to get moksha by adopting that path.

### *Learning through Observation*

Learning is pure observation–observation which is not continuous and which then becomes memory, but observation from moment to moment–not only of the things outside you but also of that which is happening inwardly; to observe without the observer. Look not with your mind but with your eyes… Then you find out that the outside is the inside...that the observer is the observed.

Thus he believed that Man can come to truth neither through any organization, any creed, any dogma, priest or ritual, nor through any philosophic knowledge or psychological technique. He has to find it through the mirror of relationship, through the understanding of the contents of his own mind, through observation and not through intellectual analysis or introspective dissection.

### *Aims of Education*

In the words of Krishnamurti: *"Without a unified understanding of life, our individual and collective problems will deepen and expand. The purpose of education is not only to produce scholars, technicians, and job hunters, but also integrated men and women free from fear; for only between such human beings can there be enduring peace."*

To understand life is to realize oneself and this is both the start and the end of education. Education is not just about acquiring knowledge, gathering facts and interacting; it is about seeing the whole of life. The task of education is to produce a human existence who is integrated.

Thus, according to him the aims of education should be as follows:

1. *To develop integrated human being:* Krishnamurti says—the right kind of education which encourages the language of technique should help man to experience the integral process of life which is of great importance. Experiencing that will put capacity and technique in their right place. The whole task of education is to awaken the individual. The chief purpose of instruction should be to encourage every student to obtain out for himself, his peculiar individual talent and grow it as fully as possible. Education is to create human beings who are integrated and therefore intelligent.
2. *To Develop Creativity:* Every person remains busy in questioning, genuine dissatisfaction, and that is called creative word. But sometimes it is really hard to hold up with inquiries and dissatisfaction, and many people do not want their children to receive this kind of intelligence. It is really uncomfortable to dwell with those who constantly question accepted value. So education, for making the individual more creative, should help the individual to understand and eliminates the problems not to help them to glorify the ways of escape.
3. *Development of spiritual preparation and education:* Dogmas, mysteries and rituals are not contributing to spiritual life. Religious instructions in the true sense means encouraging children to see their relationship with people, things and nature. Regardless of being; and without self-knowledge, all relationships, with one another and with many, bring conflict and unhappiness. In fact, it is impossible to fully explain this to a child; but if the educator and parents are deeply aware of the full significance of the relationship, they will surely be able to convey to the child through their attitude, behavior and speech, without many words and explanations; the meaning of spiritual life.
4. *To develop capacities to face challenges:* If the individual is to grapple with life's problems, intricacies, mysteries, and sudden demands, he must be free from theories and particular patterns of thoughts. If somebody is

an epic who is always fighting with life, he must be free from infinite possibilities.

5. *To develop understanding through Self-Knowledge:* An ignorant man is not the unlearned, but he who does not know himself, and the learned man is stupid when he relies on books, on knowledge and on authority to give him understanding. Understanding comes only through self-knowledge, which is awareness of one's total psychological process. Thus education, in the true sense, is the understanding of oneself, for it is within each one of us that the whole of existence is gathered. Education should awaken the capacity to be self-aware and not merely, indulge in gratifying self-expression. In this way, education is to understand oneself, in the true sense, because the whole existence of each of us is assembled.
6. *To make the individual mature and free:* In true sense, education is of helping the individual to be mature and free, to flower greatly in love and goodness. We should be interested in that, and not in shaping the child according to some idealistic pattern. According to this great teacher the main aim of education is to enable the child to develop mentally in such a way that he should know himself. Education should help one to feel freedom of mind and fearlessness
7. *Freedom from ideology:* The conditioning of child's mind to suit a particular ideology (political or religious) can increase the enimity between man and man. The right kind of education is not concerned with any ideology, however much it offers to future Utopia. It does not depend on any scheme, no matter how carefully you think. It is not a way of disciplining the individual in some peculiar direction. According to some ideal model, we should not be interested in designing a child.
8. *Re-education:* Proper education comes with transformation in us. We must re-educate ourselves not to kill each other for any reason, no matter how righteous or ideological, but it may look to the future happiness of the world. We must learn to be merciful, less satisfied, and seek the Lord, because only then there will be true salvation of mankind.
9. *To develop proper understanding of the environment:* What we need to realize is that we are not only conditioned by the environment, but by what we mean by the environment. Our opinions and reactions are governed by the values imposed on us as a part of social club. Because we receive so many entities that we never consider ourselves as the whole surroundings, all revolve around 'me', the self. The self is made of these entities, which are merely desires in various forms. In this way a division is established between 'self' and 'non-self', between 'me and 'environment' that we can call society. This division is the beginning of conflict, inward and outward.

10. *To develop wisdom:* We are losing love, diminishing our sense of beauty and sensitivity to cruelty in the desire to acquire more and more knowledge. When we concentrate on one area and become specialized in that area, means we are becoming less and less comprehensive. The mere explanation and accumulation of facts do not make man free from suffering. Wisdom cannot be replaced by knowledge. But if the mind and heart are suffocated by wisdom, and the cause of suffering is explained, life becomes vain and meaningless. Our education is making us more and more shallow and is not helping us to overcome the deeper meanings of our being and our lives are becoming increasingly meaningless, disharmonious and empty. Knowledge has no end and wisdom is infinite and it includes knowledge and the way of action. When we hold a branch and think it is a whole tree, where as in real terms it is not knowledge. Through the knowledge of the part, we can never realize the joy of whole. We are like the blind men who tried to describe the elephant after feeling different parts of the elephant. Intellect alone can never give a holistic view because it is only a segment of the whole, so, education should try to develop our wisdom, not merely the knowledge.
11. *To cultivate the attitude of love towards others:* Only love and proper thinking can bring about revolution with in oneself, but how should we love? It cannot be by chasing the ideal of love, but when there is no hate, no greed, and sense of self that causes hostility ends. A man who is caught up in things like exploitation, greed, and jealousy can never be loved. The education should cultivate the attitude of love towards others.
12. *To develop simplicity:* Awareness of the child means helping him understand freedom and integrity. In order to be free there must be order. Order can be achieved only through virtue. Integration can only occur when there is great simplicity. We must go up from innumerable complexities to simplicity. We must be compromised in our interior life and in our external needs.
13. *To develop right relationships:* Education should help an individual to cultivate right relationship between individuals and society and this is possible only if he understands his own psychological process. Conflict and confusion result from our own wrong relationship with people, things and ideas, and until we understand that relationship and alter it; mere learning, the gathering of facts and the acquiring of various skills, can only lead us to engulfing chaos and destruction. Education is a way of discovering our true relationship to things, to other human beings, and to nature.
14. *Freedom and discipline:* It is a reality that love and goodness can blossom in individual freedom. The right kind of education can offer

this freedom. One of the dangers of freedom is that this system becomes important than the human beings. Here, discipline becomes a substitute for love. We cling to discipline because our hearts are empty. Freedom can never be achieved through discipline. Freedom is not a goal or an end to be achieved. Freedom is at the beginning and not at the end. It is the responsibility of a teacher to protect and help the children towards the right kind of freedom. For this he himself should be free from ideologies and dogmas. Children always follow their teachers.

15. *To encourage thoughtfullness:* Krishnamurty said that education should encourage thoughtfulness and consideration for others which should be free from the fear of punishment and the hope of reward. It should also be free from every form of compulsion. Compulsion breeds aggression and fear. Reward and punishment in any form only make the mind subservient and dull. Generally we think that discipline may be an effective way to control a child, but it doesn't help him to understand the problems in living. If a child persists on disorderliness or is unreasonably mischievous, the educator should inquire into the cause and its solution.
16. *To prepare for right vocation:* Krishnamurti suggested that the right kind of education helps the students to discover what he is most interested in and to choose the career vocation of his choice. If he does not find his true vocation, all his life will seem wasted; he will feel frustrated doing something which he does not want to do. If he wants to be an artist and instead becomes a clerk in some office, he will spend his life grumbling and pining away. Right occupation comes through the right kind of education, and with the understanding of oneself.
17. *To create new values:* We are to develop new society, so, there is need of creating new values. Merely to implant existing values in the mind of the child, to make him conform to ideals, is to condition him without awakening his intelligence. Education is intimately related to the present world crisis, and the educator who sees the causes of this universal chaos should ask himself how to awaken intelligence in the student, thus helping the coming generation not to bring about conflict and disaster further.

The past generations, with their dreams, traditions, ideals, have brought destruction of the globe. The coming generations, with the proper sort of instruction, can end this dilemma and make a happy social order. If there is a spirit of research in the youth, and every moment they are searching for the truth - political and religious, personal and environment, then youth will be of big importance and promise for a safer universe.

### Curriculum

Krishnamurti did not believe in any prescribed fixed curriculum for the students. As he himself expresses that he does not want to be bound by any 'isms' or any specific belief about set pattern for the study or fixed course or syllabus for education. He emphasised on the growth of new technology, research work in teaching. On the basis of it we can draw 3 ideas about the curriculum as:

- *Teaching of different subjects is not enough but student's initiative should be awakened:* He suggested that the study of different subjects are necessary but if the teachers teach you merely mathematics and geography, history and science, languages, that is obviously not enough. The important thing is that students should remain alert; to question, to find out, so that their own initiative may be awakened. As society is now organized, we send our children to school to learn some technique by which they can eventually earn a livelihood. We want to make the child first and foremost a specialist, hoping thus to give him a secure economic position, but does the cultivation of a technique enable us to understand ourselves.
- *Students should be educated to live life:* Krishnamurty was of the opinion that education should be concerned with totality of life. He believed that education is the means to create new values as peace, happiness and non-violence. He did not lay stress on head (intelligent) only but he feels that heart (emotional level) in the life should also be emphasised. He was of the opinion that a child should be the lover of the nature and its elements. It means that the students should be involved in different activities to understand the environment as well as for the development of body, mind and soul. Life is pain, joy, beauty, ugliness, love, and when we understand it as a whole, at every level, that understanding creates its own technique. But the contrary is not true: technique can never bring about creative understanding.
- *With learning academic subjects, one should educate oneself:* Intelligence lies in understanding oneself and going above and beyond oneself. Education is essentially the art of learning, not only from books, but from the whole movement of life....Learning about the nature of the intellect, its dominance, its activities, its vast capacities and its destructive power is not from a book but from the observation of the world about you without theories, prejudices and values. At every moment the child should try to observe to educate himself.

Thus the ideas of Krishnamurty regarding the curriculum can be summarised as that it should not be fixed and the subject matter included should lead to live a whole life. He is the bitter critic of present day educational curriculum, so, he expresses ideas through right kind of education. He is the man who speaks complete truth in real critical words. So, he has not mentioned or forced for any specific, special subjects for the curriculum. He is not against technological or technical education, but they should not over-power human beings. The course of study should prepare the working efficiency and pass the knowledge to obtain the result of problems in students. It should encourage the patriotism, national integrity and harmony in the pupils. It should be capable to develop praise and aesthetic opinion in students and encourage curiosity in the pupils. It should develop self-expression ability in the pupils. It should offer the freedom to analyse their surroundings so they may think independently and to find himself (Atma Gyan).

### *Methods of Teaching*

In the words of J. Krishnamurti, we should not teach children to think 'what to think' and 'how to think'. Allow them freedom to think for themselves. Repetition encourages the brain to slow down so 'shock' is required to wake it up, we call it the 'problem'. Instructors should not try to resolve the problem, according to their well-worn 'explanations, justifications and rebuttal. Study the child thoroughly and employ such methods that suit him best. The pupil should be treated as an equal partner in teaching learning process. Hence, the ideas of Krishnamurti regarding the teaching learning process can be summarised as:

- Listening, Thinking and Remembering Method
- Nididhayasan Method
- Experiment Method
- Observation Method
- Discussion Method
- Explorative Method
- Illustration Method
- Self- Regulatory Method
- Problem Solving Method

He said about the right kind of teaching in these words: "Without the right kind of teaching, illusion is taken for granted, and then the person is always in conflict with himself, so there are conflicts in his relationship with others, because this is a society. One teaches because one sees that self – knowledge alone, and not to the dogmas and rituals of organized religion; can bring about a peaceful mind; and that creation, truth, God, comes into being only when the 'me' and the 'mine' are excelled." Thus Krishnamurti believed in those methods which help in developing the thinking ability, critically analyzing on the basis of experiences.

### *Role of the Teacher*

The teacher plays an important role in the life of the child but it should not be as in the traditional system that teacher is the knower of all things and the child does not know anything or teacher is a mature person and child is immature. The teacher is to be trained in such a way that he will be ready to realize the child without imposing the ideal of what we want him to be. To understand a child, we must regard him at play and study his different moods. We cannot put our own biases, hopes and fears upon him, or mould him according to the occupation of our desires. If we constantly judge a child, according to our personal likes and dislikes, we are bound to create obstacles and barriers in our relationship with him and his relationships with the world. Different levels of comfort and satisfaction are obtained under separate ownership and mastery. Human beings need to be unified to avoid any crisis, especially the current global crisis. His views about the teacher's role are as follows:

*Understanding of the Child:* If the teacher is of the right kind, he will not depend on a method. In our relationship with children and young people, we are not dealing with mechanical devices that can be quickly repaired, but with living beings who are impressionable, volatile, sensitive, afraid and affectionate. While dealing with them, the teacher should have great understanding, the strength of patience and love. When the teacher lacks these, he/she looks to quick and easy remedies and hope for marvellous and automatic results. If teachers are unaware, mechanical in their attitudes and actions, they fight shy of any demand upon them that is disturbing and that cannot be met by an automatic response, and this is one of our major difficulties in education.

*Cooperation between Teacher and Student:* There is need of mutual affection and mutual respect between teacher and student and it will be possible only with cooperation between them. When showing of respect to elders is required by the children, it generally becomes a habit, a mere outward performance, and fear assumes the form of veneration. Without respect and consideration, no vital relationship is possible, especially when the teacher is merely an instrument of his knowledge. The teacher and students, both should work cooperatively to enhance their knowledge.

*Respect for Human Life:* If the teacher demands respect from his pupils and has very little for them, it will obviously cause indifference and disrespect on their part. Without respect for human life, knowledge only leads to destruction and misery. The cultivation of respect for others is an essential part of right education, but if the educator himself don't have this quality, he cannot help his students to lead an integrated life.

*Freedom to Ask Questions:* If the teachers want to awaken and sustain the critical alertness and keen insight of the students, they should encourage the child to question the book, whatever it be, to inquire into the validity of the existing social values, traditions, forms of government, religious beliefs etc. Questioning can satisfy the curiosity of students.

*Feeling of Security for the Students:* Feeling of being secure is the primary need of the child. When the child knows and feels that he is secure, his emotional flowering not thwarted by fear. It is the feeling of being at ease, whether in his own home or at school, the feeling that he can be what he is, without being compelled in any way; that he can climb a tree and not be scolded if he falls. The teacher should provide such type of environment to the children while learning.

*No Sense of Superiority:* The teacher should not have the sense of superiority. If it will be, fear will arise on the part of the student and a sense of pressure and strain. As a result, the student will learn, from his youth, this quality of superiority; he will made to feel belittled, and so throughout life he will either become the aggressor or subservient.

*Affection towards Students:* Krishnamurti believed that the teacher should have affection towards the students. He/she may know many subjects and facts. While conveying them to the students, if there is no affection, it will result in a struggle between the two. Affection carries no pressure and it is never devious. It is direct and simple.

*Self-control in Action:* A teacher's thought must result in action. There must be no laziness, but constant activity in good work. Leave every man to do his own work in his own way. Be always ready to offer help if need be, but never interfere in other's work. For many people the most difficult thing in the world to learn is to mind their own business, but that is exactly what we must do.

*Confidence:* The teacher should have confidence. Unless there is perfect trust there cannot be the perfect flow of love and power. If they say that they know themselves too well then they do not know themselves; they know only the weak outer husk. They are spark of God's own fire, and because of that there is nothing that they cannot do if they will. Say to thyself: 'I can do this thing, and I will.' If they will have confidence, only then they will be able to develop it among their students.

From the above discussion, the ideas of Krishnamurti regarding teacher can be summarized as follows:

1. The instructor must help each student to find his inner psychological resources, recognise his weaknesses and build up his own individual strengths. For this the teacher has to provide/create the right surroundings.
2. He must be affectionate as well as the confident.
3. Dedication and vitality are needed in the teachers.
4. The instructor has to encourage creative intelligence of the pupils. He should discourage students from merely accepting statements and quotations from scripts. Questioning and critical thinking need to be made a part of the instructional procedure in the class-room. Pupils should be encouraged to be considerate of their schoolmates.
5. The instructor should not regard himself merely as a tool for imparting knowledge, only a soul who is concerned with the task of directing students to a way of spirit according to their imaginations. He, nevertheless, must not impose his beliefs, styles and ideologies on them. Let them form their own judgements. The job of the teacher is not to teach 'what to think' but to teach 'how to think and act'.

6. He should possess the power to understand the child, his emotions, thoughts, interests and potentialities.
7. He should be a facilitator for the students as providing opportunities to modernize the training.
8. He should be keen observer of child's development rather than an information or ideas giver only.
9. He should not develop the feeling of comparison among the students.
10. Student should feel secured himself with a teacher.
11. He/she should have a good conduct.

Thus the teacher should have the attitude that one must hold back one's mind from pride, for pride comes only from ignorance. The man who does not know, thinks that he is great. The wise man knows that only God is great, and that all good work is done by God alone. He/she should work as the representative of God.

*Discipline:* Every teacher believes that discipline is an easy way to control a child, but the great educationist Krishnamurti asserted that it does not help him to understand the problems involved in living. He believed that discipline means conformity, imitation, and obedience. It means to do what you are told. It is not the way of love because where there is discipline, there is fear. A child can't learn anything in fear. His mind should remain free from fear. Krishnamurti talked about doing right thing from core of his heart not just to conform a system. When we impose something from outside, you don't accept internally but follows and it creates conflict. He said one should be taught from childhood to live a righteous life. Then he doesn't need any dictated discipline to conform. Discipline means to learn, not to conform, not to suppress, not to imitate the pattern of what accepted authority considers noble.

For political and industrial reasons, discipline has become an important factor in the present social structure and it is because of our desire to be psychologically secure that we accept and practice various forms of discipline. It guarantees a result. Freedom never comes through discipline. And for centuries, age after age; we have been told by teachers, gurus, priests, politicians, kings, lawyers or by the society in which we live; that there must be discipline. It is something altogether ugly, it is not creative but it is destructive.

Learning is the freedom of perception, of seeing, and you cannot learn if you are not free. Students don't have to discipline themselves and then learn. Therefore discipline is freedom. This denies all conformity and control, for control is the imitation of a pattern. A pattern is suppression, suppression of "what is", and the learning about "what is" is denied when there is a formula of what is good and what is bad. The learning about "what is" is the freedom from "what is". So, learning is the highest form of discipline, and it demands intelligence and sensitivity.

Thus we can summarise the concept of discipline as understood by Krishnamurti:

- Discipline is not creative but destructive.
- Learning is the highest form of discipline.
- Discipline does not help the individual to understand problem.
- It means to adjust our thinking to what other people say.
- Discipline means to learn, not to conform, not to suppress, not to imitate the pattern of what accepted authority considers noble.

### *The School*

Everyone believes that school is an important place for the development of the child. Krishnamurty did not consider the school as an organization for the indoctrination of children, but rather as a place where students and teachers can flower, and where a future generation can be prepared. He emphasized on the psychological development of individuals which is as important as acquiring academic knowledge and skills. The main function of school is to help the child to discover and to see the real hindrances in the development of the child.

He believed that the education must not be bounded by four walls. Whenever, wherever the education is given, the place should be liked by the learner. It should be an ideal one concerning the elements of nature, in open space, in the lap of nature.

The following aspects reflect Krishnamurthy's thinking about an ideal school:

- Integrated personality can only be developed in a school that has a limited number of students.
- Teachers need to be vigilant, dedicated, and attentive.
- The child's abilities, difficulties and restrictions must be carefully read and interpreted.
- A school can be asserted by the spirit of selflessness.
- School performance should have no ideological impact.
- The head should not carry all responsibilities. On the reverse, each teacher should be held accountable.
- In a truly educated group, the problem of dominance should not originate.
- There should be continuous collaboration among all the instructors.
- No teacher should be intimidated by the headmaster or threatened by the head. That place should be a sense of equality and cooperation.
- A school cultivates mind to meet the challenges of life
- The purpose of the school is to make complete human being.
- The student council should be set up to discuss all matters related to the well-being of the whole group.
- It is a place where the student is basically happy, not bullied, not frightened by examination, not compelled to act according to a pattern or a system.
- The school should allow the student to discover what interests him most.

- The school must attain the confidence and backing of parents.
- Planning for proper guidance should be in a school.
- The function of a school is to help the student to awaken his intelligence to learn the importance of right relationship.

The official schools of him are:

- USA-Oak Grove School
- UK-Brockwood Park School
- India-Rishi Valley Education Centre
- India-Rajghat Education Centre Rajghat Fort
- India-The School "Damodar Gardens"
- India-Bal Anand, Mumbai
- India-The Valley School Bangalore Education Centre
- India-Sahyadri School

Thus the school is a sacred place where transformation of the child is done in the right direction. These are to equip the child with the most excellent technological proficiency so that he may function with clarity and efficiency in the modern world, and far more important to create the right climate so that the child may develop fully as a complete human being. The schools are to give opportunity to the child to flower in goodness so that he is rightly related to people, things and ideas, to the whole of life.

### *Examination*

He criticized the present education system for developing competitive spirit in students. He opposed any kind of competition and comparison in education. He believed that to help the child to learn basically and fundamentally he must cease to compete, with all its implications. We should eradicate all kinds of comparison from our life, if we want to bring out the inner potential of a student. Every child has unique personality and it is the responsibility of the teacher to recognise that.

A teacher is to keep the record of each child by observing his/her each action. He suggested that do not give the student marks but keep a record for yourself to see how he is behaving, how he is learning and the stage of his knowledge and so on, but do not grade him to compete. The reports should be as qualitative record of the students' life in school during the year and contain a review of their academic work and comments on their social and emotional life.

Thus he was against the present examination system as, for him, it breeds fear and ambition in the minds of students.

## Educational Implications

Krishnamurti spent his entire life talking about education. He considered education as being the agent not only of inner renewal but also of social change. Education has always been close to his heart. He set up nearly a dozen co-educational schools in India and abroad to translate his ideas into practice. Ten percent of these schools are reserved for recreational students. He visited students and teachers every year for discussion.

The educational implications of Krishnamurti's views in the present scenario are as follows:

*Meaning of Education:* The right kind of education is not merely to collect information but should help the individual to face the problems, understand and eliminate the conflicts, to discover the topic of interest, choice, creativc and anxicty. He defined education as to cultivate the students whole being, the totality of mind, the depth of mind and heart and understanding of beauty. It should not deal with specific ideology or system. It should encourage thoughtfulness and consideration. It is helpful to individual to be mature and free and to flower greatly in love. It should bring true co-operation with whole and many. It enriches insight. It is helpful to bring about a harmony between the inner and outer world, to achieve freedom and integration. It helps to awaken intelligence and significance of life as a whole. In the present day education system we are transferring knowledge from the mature to immature person. We dealt with only cognitive aspect and ignores psycho-motor and affective aspects. The NEP 2020 lays stress on education for the development of child's interests, capabilities and capacities.

*Purpose/Aim of Education:* For him the purpose of education is not merely acquiring knowledge, gathering and correlating facts, but it is to see the significance of life as a whole. A constant theme of education is internal freedom - the deeper freedom of the psyche and the spirit, the inner liberation that he feels is both the means and the ends of education. The aim of education for Krishnamurti was to clean off the smoke of self-centricity, fragmentation, fear, confusion, loneliness, possessiveness, envy, violence etc. Now a days our education system also believes in child centered education and its purpose is all round development of the personality. Education is to prepare the child not only for a vocation but for the whole life i.e. to make him a good human being.

*Curriculum:* Despite the common curriculum in these schools, his main aim in starting these schools was to give children the right to a reasonable opportunity and an opportunity to grow up without the national, racial, class and cultural biases that create barriers between one man and another. Along with the teaching of academic subjects, Krishnamurty wanted to have focus on the matters which teaches how to live life. Our curriculum is not so flexible and its focus is only to provide the information regarding different subjects. Many activities are included in the curriculum to provide opportunities to grow. NEP 2020 also suggests comprehensive and inter-disciplinary curriculum.

*Teaching Methods:* He was not in favour of any specific method that a teacher should opt. A teacher is to observe the child and his potentialities, interests, etc and accordingly provide guidance to him. In our institutions, sometimes we take care of it but most of the teachers opt certain methods as discussion, lecture, play way etc. NPE 1986 and NEP 2020 believe in opting the methods based on activity.

*School:* Krishnamurti believed that schools must be a centre for learning a way of life, not based on pleasure, or self-centred activities but on correct action, the depth, the beauty of relationship, the sacredness of religious life. Today's schools are more showy and fail to achieve the real goals of true education. These are not helping in developing the creative mind, so that the students may be prepared to face the real life in future.

*Discipline:* For Krishnamurti, discipline means to learn, not to bow down to a standard, a religious or a social structure. To some extent we are developing the feeling of self-discipline among the students.

*Teacher:* Krishnamurti asserted that the teacher and student should function at the same level. There is no leader and no led in this relationship, communicating through questioning and counter-questioning till the depths of the problem are exposed and understanding is revealed, illuminating the mind of both. Present day education system believes in the hierarchy and considers teacher as the mature person and student as immature person. To some extent we are providing freedom to the students to have discussion with the teachers.

Thus Krishnamurti's conception of teaching methods, school organization and the role of the teacher is really progressive in nature and is based on a good philosophy of education. Almost all thinkers have appreciated his emphasis on comprehensive personality development through a comprehensive approach to instruction. He gave completely novel, revolutionary, humanitarian ideas to the world to learn, to know, to implement and to follow. Learning, therefore in the KFI schools is not just about ideas or facts in books, but is also about feeling the earth, watching the sunset, teaming to the birds, seeing the colours of the leaves change in the different seasons and observing nature in its many colours, forms and shapes, not as a romantic naturalist but in harmony with what is being observed. From this harmony, a sense of responsibility towards the earth and a commitment towards life on earth will evolve. Modern education should follow the guidelines given by Krishnamurti, so that we may be able to develop such citizens, who will be able to understand the life as well as themselves.

# 14

# John Dewey (1859-1952)

> *"Education is a process involving continuous reconstructions and reorganisation of experiences."*
> –Dewey

John Dewey is a most renowned personality in the field of education. He was an American philosopher, psychologist and educational reformer whose ideas have been influential in education and social reforms. He can be compared with a great thinker Plato, who has influenced not only education but every area of life. He is regarded as one of the most prominent American scholars in the first half of 20th century.

## Life History

John Dewey was born on October 20, 1859 in Burlington, Vermont to Archibald Sprague Dewey and Lucine Artemisia Rich Dewey. He was brought up in rural environment. In 1879, he graduated from Vermont University. After working two years as a high school teacher in Pennsylvania and one year as an elementary school teacher in the small town of Charlotte Vermontt, he decided that he is unsuited for teaching in primary or secondary school. He received his Ph.D. from the school of Arts & Sciences at John Hopkins University. Thereafter for several years from 1884 onwards he worked as a Professor of Philosophy at the Universities of Minnesota, Michigan and Chicago. In Chicago he developed his belief in Rational Empiricism becoming associated with the newly emerging pragmatic philosophy. During that he also initiated the University of Chicago Laboratory School, where he was able to actualize the pedagogical beliefs that provided material for his first major work on education. In 1899, he was elected as President of American Psychological Association (A.P.A.). From 1904 until his retirement in 1930, he was a Professor of philosophy at Columbia University. He died in New York city on 1 June, 1952.

He never ignored social issues. He was outspoken on education, domestic and international politics, and numerous social movements. Many concerns that attracted Dewey's support were women's sufferage, progressive education, educators rights, the humanistic movement and world peace.

## Dewey's Writings

Although Dewey is known best for his publication about education, he also wrote about many other topics including epistemology, metaphysics, aesthetic, logic, social theory and ethics. The most important publication are:

- Interest as related to will, 1887.
- My Pedagogic Creed, 1897.
- The School and Society, 1899
- The Child and the Curriculum, 1902
- Relation of Theory and Practice in the Education of Teachers, 1904
- The School and the Child, 1907
- Ethics, 1908
- How we Think, 1910
- The Influence of Darwin on Philosophy, Democracy in Education, Essays in Experimental logic, 1916
- Reconstruction in Philosophy, 1920
- Human Nature and Conduct, 1922
- Experience and Nature, 1925
- The Quest for Certainty, 1929
- Liberalism and Social Action, 1935
- Logic: The Theory of Inquiry, Experience and Education, 1938
- Freedom and Culture, Theory of Valuation, 1939

In addition to a raft of important academic publication, he wrote for many non-academic audience, notably via the 'New Republic'.

### Dewey's Philosophical Thoughts

John Dewey was a leading proponent of the American school of thought known as pragmatism, a view that rejected the dualistic epistemology and metaphysics of modern philosophy in favour of naturalistic approach. The basis of Dewey's philosophy are Darwin's development concept and pragmatic theory of William James. As Darwin, he believed that the world is still in developmental stage, so the life of every human being is changeable and automatically reconstructed. As William James, he believed that every useful object is good and the object which is good is useful also. The philosophical thoughts of Dewey are as follows:

1. *Origin of Philosophy:* John Dewey thought that society creates philosophy. He stated that philosophy has a behaviouristic aim, which affects the activities of life. Philosophy does not think about the tendency of pre-determined truth, but it is an object which creates a new life. The problems of society are reflected in philosophy and it solves the different behavioural and social problems.
2. *Values:* For Dewey, there are no fixed, eternal, ultimate and absolute values. He asserted that values are changeable according is time. Human beings determine their own values. Dewey understood values as concrete practices acquired through an interaction of human organism with its

surroundings. He showed that all values start out as desires and through reflective criticism eventuate in value practices.

3. *Mind:* Dewey rejected both traditional accounts of mind as substance and more contemporary schemes reducing mind to brain states. Rather mind is activity: intellectual, affectional, volitional or purposeful. Man is supreme over other bodies due to mind. Mind is related to environment. Mind becomes vital, investigating and addressing problems, and inventing new tools, aims, and ideals. It bridges past and future, an 'agency of novel reconstruction of a pre-existing order'.
4. *Knowledge:* The intellectualists see knowledge as something absolutely certain, which is contemplatively seen, by a mind that is at most contingently embodied, working on its own. Dewey viewed the assumption that mind and material objects were inherently different kind of existence get somehow connected and that through internal mental processes the external objects could be known. He took a stand against those who held that knowing is a strictly mental thing and argued that knowing is an 'intended' thing. According to Dewey, knowledge can have two forms. One is the cognition composed of stored precepts and memories of traits, happenings, relationships, laws etc. This form contains more or less stable components being relatively independent of specific situation and challenges. For example: I know and it is also a common knowledge that water changes into ice at zero degree Celsius,, or 32° fahrenheit.

   The other form is cognition activated in a specific, challenging and/or problematic situations. It is composed of components perceived as the elements constituting that situation and by component that are stored mental elements. The human being does activities in order to meet the challenge or solve the problem created by the situation. For example; when playing with a child on the shore, I experience, and may after the fulfillment of the process have the 'knowing' or 'knowledge' that to build the sand tower, only the adding of just a specific proportion of water in relation to sand secured the cohesiveness of the building material and thus made the construction possible. Thus Dewey was interested in that knowledge which is active, problem oriented and pragmatic.
5. *Relationship between society and individual:* Dewey accepted an organic relationship between society and individual. Both are awared towards physical/natural and social environment. The development of an individual neither possible in isolation nor in contact with natural environment alone. He grows and develops in society. According to Dewey, a man without social set up is beyond imagination.
6. *Instrumental philosophy:* Dewey was an instrumentalist. Since scientific and all other ideas are but means for change, he suggests that it is possible to treat them as instrumental ideas, rather than as universals or finalities. Dewey's theory of instrumentalism does not assume that ideas are mental

entities nor that ideas are true if they somehow match or fit with the object in question.

7. *Experimental philosophy:* The philosophy of Dewey is experimental. He said that consciously or unconsciously all of us are carrying on experiments and try to solve our problems through various experiments. Out thinking follows different levels of experiment as:
   - Realisation of any problem
   - Understand the problem
   - Discover possible means—Classification of given data
   - Accepting or rejecting the hypothesis
   - To accept or reject the solution, re-observe and re-experiment that.

Thus Dewey's views, however, continue to appeal to those who aim to translate philosophy in to practice. For example, people who focus on project work, action learning, workshops, situations and community based learning.

## Dewey's Philosophy of Education

Dewey's philosophy of education is very important. It is known by various names as 'experimentalism', 'Instrumentalism', 'practicalism', 'Functionalism', 'Pragmatism' and 'Progressivism'. All these terms indicate the dynamic, ever changing and performing character of life. Dewey's influence on education was evident in his theory of social learning. He was known as the father of progressive education. He has given a new name to progress. The aim of progress changes on the basis of different ideals, truths and values in different periods, different places and different situations. So, every individual always remain active to achieve progress.

### *Meaning of Education*

Dewey considered education as necessity for life. Progress of life is not possible without education. The human being can progress only on the basis of experience, so, education is of experiences, through self-experiences and for experiences.

Deweys's ideal mirror the effects of new industrialized colonised society, fraught with the problems and aftermaths of two world wars. He was largely inspired by Marx's theory of social struggle and conflicts between classes. He had an inspiration from Haberman's thoughts which are in the traditions of Kant, and emphasize the role of education to transform the world into a more humane, just and egalitarian society. According to him, the functions of education are as follows:

- *Education as the Laboratory of Philosophy:* According is Dewey, philosophy and education are complementary to each other. The educational point of view enables one to envisage the philosophical problems where they arise and thrive, where they are at home, and where acceptance or rejection makes a difference in practice. If we are willing to conceive education as the process of forming fundamental dispositions, intellectual and emotional, towards nature and fellow men, philosophy may even be defined as the general theory of education. Education is the laboratory of philosophy.

- *Education as Reconstruction of Experiences:* According to Dewey, experience is the only source of true knowledge. Every experience gives birth to a new experience and the previous experiences are revised and changed by the new experiences. Thus experience is revised, recognised or reconstructed. In the words of John Dewey, *"We should so regulate the learning and experiencing activities of the young, that a newer and better society will arise in the end."* Education should prepare such an environment which will help in getting new experiences. Hence, there is a need of continuous reconstruction and reorganisation of experiences for helping man to grow physically, mentally, socially and morally.
- *Education as the Social Process:* Dewey considered education as a process which helps in the socialization of a child. In other words education provides such an environment, in which the child learns about society's civilization and culture, he becomes capable to take part in social awareness and helps in the development of society. The existence of society is not possible without education as Dewey writes, *"What nutrition and reproduction are to the physiological life, education is to social life."* Thus the duty of education towards the society is to make social and worthy society.
- *Education as life:* Dewey emphasized that the school should be life and not preparation for life. Life is a by product of activities and education is born out of these activities. Education is a life long process. It should be such that it may give an opportunity to child to face various problem of social life. These children are to run their life in the democratic society, so it is necessary to get maximum self experiences from the point of view of life-ideals.
- *Education as the Process of Growth:* According to Dewey, every individual act and react according to his training and environment, so he grows accordingly. Education is concerned with physical, mental and emotional growth. The end of education is more growth and still more growth. But the Dewey's concept about growth is not clear, because it may be in any direction i.e. good or bad. Afterwards he defined the education in other words as, *"The process of education is a continuous of adjustment having its aim at every stage as added capacity of growth."* The words of Dewey are, 'growth, unlimited and 'illimitable' is the true objective of education.
- *Education as creator of democratic society:* Dewey believed that democracy is an ethical ideal and not just a political structure. He considered participation rather than representation as the essence of democracy. The important function of education is to create democratic society. For this

such type of opportunities should be provided, in which the differences between individual to individual should be abolished, every individual should have the opportunities to develop in a natural way, no difference in welfare of individual and society, capabilities should be developed to avail his rights and fulfill his responsibilities and a strong will to develop the society. In the words of John Dewey, *"children in school must be allowed freedom... to develop active qualities of initiative independence and resourcefulness before the abuses and failures of democracy will disappear."* Democratic life consists not only in civic and economic conduct, but more crucially in habits of problem solving, compassionate imagination, creative expression and civic self governance. The success or failure of democracy rests on education.

- *Education as the process of direction or guidance:* The function of education is to provide guidance also. The directions for the development of abilities, potentialities, capacities, interests etc should be provided in such a way that will help in the personality development in the right direction. But apart from it, we should keep in mind that proper guidance is possible only when we will provide the opportunities to remain active in social activities by directing their emotions in a proper way.
- *Education as Bi-Polar Process:* According to Dewey, education has two aspects–
  (i) *Psychological:* Psychologically, we understand the natural inclinations, interests and capabilities of the child so that we may prepare suitable curriculum for his development. Education, therefore, must begin with a psychological insight into the child's capacities, interests and habits. It must be controlled at every point by reference to these same considerations. The nature of the child is dynamic, so, education should start with the psychological nature of the child. Dewey insisted that constant experimentation be made to learn the child's nature. The child should be considered as the case of the whole educational process. The child should be put in the complete possession of all his powers, capacities, skills and judgement. The inherent powers of the child should be developed and must also be controlled through education in the interest of the society of which the child is a member. According to Dewey, the impulses of the child are of four kinds:
    – The social impulse of communication or conversation
    – The constructive impulse to make things
    – The impulse to investigate into things, and
    – The impulse of artistic or creative expression.

  Dewey believed that since child is inherently active, it is the function of education to direct him properly.

(ii) *Social Efficiency:* An individual is a part and parcel of the society. Though Dewey starts with psychological basis-child's instincts and innate powers, the sociological side was not neglected by him. The knowledge of the social condition is essential for the proper appraisal and assessment of the child's powers. All education proceeds by the participation of the individual in the social process. The society continuously shapes and modifies the individual's powers and personality. In the beginning, the activities of the child are self-centered. Therefore, he must be helped to realise the ends and purposes of the society. For this, the school should be organised as a miniature society. The child's powers are stimulated through the social medium. He lives in and for the society to which he belongs. Thus the idea of socialization given by Dewey is of the highest importance.

***Aims of Education***

John Dewey was a pragmatist. In Chapter VIII of 'Democracy and Education entitled 'Aims in Education', Dewey seems to deny the three following propositions:

- Education should serve predetermined aims.
- Education should serve aims that are external to the process of education.
- Education should serve aims that are imposed by authority.

There may be disagreement about who should have the authority to decide what aims to serve; whether they should be same for all students; and to what extent they should be subservient to overarching aims such as economic prosperity, social justice or human flourishing. Dewey objects to aims that are externally dictated ie. commended by other people. The criteria of good aims, he distinguished between aims that are 'imposed by some authority' and those that are not. The imposed ones are, typically fixed, static, rigid and limit intelligence; whereas an aim that is not imposed is flexible, experimental and hence constantly growing as it is tested in action.

According to Dewey, *"Education as such has no aim; education is an abstract idea. Only persons have aims, and the aims of persons are indefinitely varied differing with different children, and their teachers grow."* The aim of education is the development of all those capacities in the individual which will enable him to control his environment and fulfill his responsibilities. We can't decide in advance that in which direction capacities should be developed, so, the aims of education will be immediate. The aims of education can be divided in two parts: 1. Individual Aims 2. Social Aims

*Individual Aims*

From individual point of view Dewey has described the following aims:

(i) *Continuous reconstruction of experiences:* Dewey said, "Education helps in the process of reconstruction of experiences, giving it more socialised value through the medium of increased individual efficiency." Education constantly recognizes or reconstructs the human experiences. It preserve that must of experience which is valuable and re-weaves it in the light of present needs and demands.

(ii) *Adjustment to environment:* Education should develop the capacities of an individual to enable him to adjust according to the environment. The process of education is a continuous process of adjustment. The individual has always to adjust and re-adjust himself to the environment. Dewey agrees to the aim of education as preparation for life. Without adjustment to environment none can survive.

(iii) *Rich and better present life:* Dewey believed that the aim of education is preparation for life, if it refers life now and the immediate future. Pupils, he said, are not interested in the distant or remote future. Any such attempt would not stimulate them to learn. Education should ensure adequate preparation for immediate i.e. present life. This will encourage the pupil to learn. The pupil lives, grows, develops in the present world. He should realize his powers now. All educational efforts should be diverted to that goal.

(iv) *Cultivation of dynamic and adaptable mind:* Education should develop such a dynamic, flexible and adaptable mind which is always resourceful and enterprising and is able to create new values for an unknown future. Values and ideals are made on the basis of experiences.

*Social Aims*

(i) *Realisation of social efficiency:* According to Dewey, whatever a person does, he does it through participating in different activities of the society. Social efficiency is to understand the society and the skill to adjust himself in it. The aim of education is the development of social efficiency in human beings. The characteristics of a social efficient individual are as follows:

*Economic efficiency:* Social efficiency indicates the importance of industrial competency. Persons cannot live without means of subsistence; the ways in which these means are employed and consumed have a profound influence upon all the relationships of persons to one another. If an individual is not able to earn his own living and that of the children dependent upon him, he is a drag on the activities of others. He misses for himself one of the most educative experiences of life. Economic efficiency means a person should be capable to earn his livelihood.

*Negative morality*: If a person is not trained in the right use of the products of industry, there is great danger that he way deprave himself and injure others in his possession of wealth. No scheme of education can afford to neglect such basic considerations. An individual should leave those desires, which can create hindrance in the economic efficiency of others.

*Positive morality:* Positive morality means an individual should stop himself to fulfill those desires which directly or indirectly are not contributing in social progress.

(ii) *Training in democratic life:* Dewey was a firm believer in democratic values. He, therefore, insisted that education should provide suitable opportunities to the students to imbibe democratic values. According to him, an individual should have the following abilities to participate in the activities of democratic society:
- Health
- Capacity to do the activity
- Occupation
- Morality and character
- Citizenship, and
- Proper utilization of leisure time.

Thus Dewey does not believe in ultimate aim of education. He puts forward his aims of education in the light of the rapid social and economic changes in the world. To him, education is experience which is subject to constant change with the changing pattern of life. In his words, "The function of education is to help the growing, a helpless young animal into a happy, moral and efficient human being." Education should create such a capacity in the child that he is able to face social situations strongly and come out successful in the struggle. Only that education is useful that creates the will to develop continuously.

### *Curriculum*

Dewey had no faith in the traditional curriculum as it cannot fulfill the aims of education set forth by him. He did not believe in that theory of psychology which divides the mind into different compartments such as memory, imagination, perception, judgement etc. He considered mind as an organic whole. As it can't be divided in different compartments, in the same way the knowledge can't be divided in special subjects. He stresses that the curriculum should be far off from artificiality and based on real life activities of the child. Society is dynamic and it also changes according to the time and circumstances. Dewey believed that school subject should be organised not around subjects like science, history, geography, literature etc. but around the child's own activities. He has not given any fixed curriculum for any stage but gave some principles on which the curriculum should be based as:

1. *Flexible:* According to Dewey, curriculum should be flexible as to meet the requirement of the situation. It change according to the needs and interests of the child as well as of society. If the curriculum will be rigid then there will be no place for those values and experiences in it, which were created by children themselves.

2. *Interesting:* Dewey considered the child as the central front of education. The child's interests, previous experiences etc. should be kept in mind while framing the curriculum. He said, "the beginning is made with child's expressive activities in dealing with fundamental social material–food, shelter, clothing and the direct modes of social communication like speech, writing, reading, drawing, modeling, moulding etc. Thus the curriculum in the primary school should be organised according to the four-fold interests of the child in conversation, enquiry, construction and artistic expression."
3. *Child centered:* The traditional curriculum includes subjects as mere information. No attempt was made to relate them to actual needs of the child. Dewey's curriculum is based on the actual experiences, interests and impulses of the child. Thus while constructing the curriculum the child should be the central point.
4. *Correlated:* Life and knowledge are in itself a complete unit, so, in the view of Dewey, the knowledge related to it and the activities are also a complete unit. If the curriculum is bounded in different subjects and stored in a room, then the education will become only the memorization of different subject. Therefore, different subjects should be correlated and they should not be presented as distinct studies. Dewey made industrial activities—and their historical and social development—the centre of the curriculum and grouped the rest of subjects around this centre. If the children will get the education in the form of correlated subjects, the knowledge gained through this will be easy, complementary, clear, practical and permanent.
5. *Useful:* The curriculum should be based on the utility and needs of the child. The more it helps the child to adapt in his later life, the greater is the utility of his education. The aim of education is child's growth, which can be achieved through various kinds of knowledge. Thc determination of the subjects in the curriculum should not be according to the sequence of their importance but any subject which prove to be useful to make the life complete should get the place in the curriculum.
6. *Activity centered:* Dewey stressed on the principle of activity in curriculum construction. According to him those activities are to be included in the curriculum which help in development of values in the child. The child learns by active work, either in individual activity or group activity. The child will be able to learn self-experiences by self activity and will be able to develop his personality. Dewey conceived that purposeful, efficient, intelligent and orderly activities are very significant in the learning process.
7. *Integration:* Dewey has proposed an integrated curriculum and followed the principle of correlation in the organisation of the subjects. He says, if different subjects are taken from the materials of day to day life, the subject matter of each subject links the present with the past and they are taught in

such a way that their usefulness in the immediate present is emphasised. The child should be inspired to acquire knowledge of differents subjects with the help of different activities integrated into a single unit.

8. *Social experience:* Dewey view is that the development of mind and intelligence is possible in social environment. Mind, he said is essentially social. It was made what it is by society and depends for its development on social agencies. It finds its nutrients in social supplies. It is therefore essential that social experiences should form the main factor of the curriculum.
9. *Art education:* While accepting the significance of contribution of art in the development of an individual, Dewey's scheme of curriculum also included art and aesthetic education. He considered art as 'perfected expression of basic human activity.' He also writes, "arts represent not luxuries but fundamental forces of development". When the child gets creative experiences while solving the practical problems, as a result it creates realization of art skill.
10. *Moral and religious education:* Dewey wants that religious and moral education should not be taught as a subject but it should be made an integral part of the basic experiences of the child. The children should develop moral interest and insight. Morality is discipline comes through the free and purposive judgement of the individual.

Thus Dewey recommended the curriculum which has the following characteristics:

- It centres around a problem which the child is facing.
- It has its origin in the immediate life activities of the child.
- It is well integrated.
- It develops critical thinking and reasoning ability.
- It is instrumental and useful to satisfy the needs of the child.

He describes the curriculum in three phases according to the stages of development.

| *Age* | *Curriculum* |
|---|---|
| 4 to 8 | Direction of social and personal relationship-reading, writing and arithmetic as subjects of study. |
| 8 to 12 | History, Geography, experimental sciences are the subjects of study. At this stage, aim of education is to provide knowledge of social processes, securing social results and to satisfy child's curiosity to understand and participate in complex social structure. |
| Above 12 | Problems of agriculture–consumption, production, transportation, exchange, distribution etc. are subjects of study. At this stage the child has the capacity to create and solve problems. |

Thus the curriculum should be based on utility and needs of the child. The satisfaction of the needs of the child and development of social efficiency are the qualities of a successful education.

***Methods of Teaching***

Dewey was not in favour of any prefixed method of teaching. For him, all education has as its proper aim the promotion of growth and development. Growth happens through the experiences of the learner. Teaching is the ability to assist the learners in organizing, directing and maximizing the stream of developing life experiences. As he stated, *"teaching relies upon" the educational significance of social arrangement (as) means used to educate the young."*

According to him, teaching method does not mean an art of giving knowledge to the child through instructions, but it means that psychological way through which the child gets knowledge by self experiences, by innovations, by participation in various activities etc. Thus he advocated 'learning by doing' and learning by living'.

Dewey has explained his views about teaching methods in his books: 'How we Think' and 'Interest and Efforts in Education'. He suggested that method of teaching should be based on the child's own experience and that method of teaching should vary according to the interest and inclination of each individual child.

Dewey briefly recommended the following methods of teaching :

1. *Learning by doing:* He believed that the child learns by active work, either in individual activity or group activity. The teacher is to create such an environment in which the child is inspired to face the situation. The child will be able to learn by self-experience by self activities and will be able to develop his personality. These self experiences should be related to the realities and needs of life. Dewey conceived that purposeful, efficient, intelligent and orderly activities are very significant in the learning process. It is also known as activity method.
2. *Learning by integration and correlation:* The mind grasps integrated knowledge. We can't divide the knowledge in water-tight compartments. Therefore, the process of learning should be an integrated one, because it is natural for human beings to create unity in their experiences. The base of the integration can be purposeful activities. The purposive activity of one subject should be related to the purposive activity of other subject. It means that the teacher should establish the correlation between different subjects-horizontal and vertical.
3. *Learning through productive and creative activities:* Construction implies a broad field of creative and productive activities that are necessary components in self organization of learning in every learner. 'I have used the word construction'. Dewey says, to denote, "The creative mind" that

is generally productive in its operations. Every individual is unique in himself/herself. Each one experiences life from a different angle than anybody else, and consequently has something distinctive learning while turning experiences into ideas. Therefore, the child should be involved in productive and creative activities.

4. *Project Method:* Dewey recommended the project method which is based on problems, activities, experiments and interests of the learners. The pupil can learn a lot of things with the help of association and mutual cooperation. It promotes purposeful activities through a group of pupils and the pupils will work cooperatively.
5. *Problem solving:* In the famous book 'How me Think', Dewey wrote that learning is 'learning to think'. Although he recognised the existence of many ways of thinking, he insisted, 'the better way of thinking is reflective thinking'. Problem solving involved thinking. The essentials of it were described by Dewey as:
   - The pupil has a genuine situation of experience that there by continuum activity in which he is interested for its own sake.
   - A genuine problem develop with in this situation as a stimulus to thought.
   - The learner possess the information and make the observations needed to deal with it.
   - The suggested solution occur to him for which he shall be responsible for developing in an orderly way.
   - He has opportunity and occasion to test his ideas by application, to take their meaning clear and to discover himself their validity.

Thus Dewey's writings opened the door to a variety of interpretation related to problem solving as a teaching method. He believed that the key method in the process of learning is problem solving.

Thus according to Dewey, the method is always in relation with subject matter. It is not something outside of the material that needs to be studied. The method is 'The effective direction of subject matter to described results' and the effective implies processing of the content with maximum of savings in time and energy. The learning methods should be active and inquiry based and the accumulation of information and principles must be subordinated to the development of intellectual self-control. In his education theory, the issue of method is primarily an issue of development of child's powers and interests. The basic principle is that child is ever active-doing, doing and doing. While doing, he is learning, while learning he is doing.

### *Discipline*

Dewey was against the traditional concept of discipline. The teacher should encourage self discipline and group discipline. He laid stress on social discipline also.

- *Self discipline:* John Dewey defined discipline as proper use of one's energies and powers. The problem of indiscipline would not arise if education is for the solution of student's problems and satisfaction of their needs. Discipline is almost self taught through the steps one must go through when trying to create something from start to finish. He believed that one must be doing something that is for the production of results and has self meaning as shown in his statement, *"But out of occupations, out of doing things that are to produce results, and out of doing these in a social and cooperative way, there is born a discipline of its own kind and type."*

  According to Dewey, a person is disciplined, who is trained to consider his/her actions and undertake them deliberately. In addition, the person has the ability to endure distractions and difficulties.

  Discipline means power of command, mastering of the resources available for carrying through the actions undertaken. He is in favour of conceived discipline in terms of growth in ability and achievement.

  According to him, discipline has, conceived by one theory as the application of external constraints, and by another theory as an absence of restraint in the name of freedom. He claims that the first theory leads to drill and external modes of action that caused students to be disagreeable and the second theory leads to immediate expression and impulse, that fails to promote reflective thinking. He believed that discipline is positive and constructive. It provides control over the means necessary to achieve ends and the ability to value and test ends. For example a painter is disciplined to the extent that he/she can use his/her materials and can exhibit vision and imagination. Genuine freedom is intellectual; it rests in the power of thought. One is free to the extent of acting in harmony with the knowledge one possesses. Freedom implies an understanding and mastery of the situation.
- *Group Discipline/Social Discipline:* Every individual is a social individual and the society is an organic union of individuals. He viewed that school is a mode of social life. It is a place where one gains moral training. For Dewey, the school can become a miniature community. School life organizes itself on social basis. The main purpose of school discipline is the cultivation of social attitudes, interests and habits and ideals of conduct in the students, through the conjoint, activities of the school which has been organised as a community. He always stressed on the benefit of society. For social discipline he advocated group activities. It is in group activities that children become socialized and democratic ideals are fostered.

  Thus Dewey believed in self discipline and self control. Freedom and social control are important. He said that the teacher should organize different activities which exercises control over individual and imposes to maintain discipline.

***Teacher***

Dewey gave an important place to teacher. According to him, *"The teacher is always a prophet of true God. He leads to the kingdom of God."* He was of the view that the teacher should possess some qualities as:

1. *Knowledge of individual differences:* Dewey stresses the sensitivity of educationists towards learners' needs and their individual differences. For him, the teacher should realize that there is no one for all concepts of teaching and learning. Learning processes should be planned considering the aptitude, learners' former experiences and their present experiences.
2. *Good observer:* The teacher should observe the interests of the students, observe the directions they normally take and even help them in developing problem solving skills.
3. *Guide and advisor:* On the one hand the teacher must examine the child's habits and characteristics of his personality, while on the other hand he must try to discover the condition under which the child can be usefully influenced. He has to make the child to think and to act for themselves, to do rather than to know, to originate rather than to repeat. He should help the students to search knowledge for themselves and in place of giving them the ready made solutions, he should suggest them techniques to find out the solutions. In this way, he puts his students in the position of a discoverer and experimenter. According to Dewey, *"The teacher is a guide and director, he steers the boat, but the energy that propels it must come from those who are learning."*
4. *Interactive:* Dewey believed in an interdisciplinary curriculum, or a curriculum that focuses on connecting multiple aspects; where students are allowed to freely move in and out of the classrooms, as they pursue their interests and construct their own path for acquiring and applying knowledge. A teacher engaged with the learners though interaction, which is a social process. Teachers are members of the community of learning and play a major role in selecting experiences and to give a proper direction to these educative experiences.
5. *Good planner:* Dewey was specifically concerned about the rights of child as an individual, his right to exercise his decision, choices of learning and education and his participation in a democratic learning process. By nature a child is curious, social and constructive and possesses inherently the raw material to be developed by experienced guide and mentor. It is therefore the responsibility of a teacher to plan positive and constructive environment for the learners so as to create positive educative experiences for them.
   Thus the teacher's job is to keep the child alive to:
   - His purposes
   - His capacities
   - His limitations

So a teacher should be—

- The embodiment of knowledge
- Intelligent, efficient and practical
- Knowledgeable about child's interests and changing needs of the society.
- Knowledgeable about child's psychology
- Able to create a problem solving attitude in his pupils.
- Able to develop social interests, ethical habits and social attitude among the pupils.

***Teacher Education***

Dewey believed that teacher has an important place in the society as well as in individual's life of the child. The professional making will give teacher the ability to inspire and direct learning. The following specification should be taken care of:

1. *Goal:* The goal of teacher preparation should be to assist the teacher student in becoming a 'thoughtful and alert' student of education.
2. *Courses:* All teacher education courses should have a practical component and the practice in such courses should be 'intensive and typical, rather than extensive and detailed'. By intensive and typical, Dewey meant that practical work should serve a laboratory purpose. The teacher candidate should have awakening towards the meaning and vitality of educational principles. Dewey thought, that teacher candidates need to solve two main problems. First, they need to figure out how to teach subject matter to students and second, they figure out how to manage a classroom.
3. *Profound Knowledge:* Dewey expected that the teacher should have expansive and profound knowledge of subject matter. With the help of profound knowledge he/she will have the tools to identify the potential and tendency of intellectual stirring of learners. He/she will be able to provide materials and learning conditions that assist learners in developing their knowledge, skill and character. He/she will be able to assess the nature of learners' past educational experiences when contemplating directions for their future growth. In the words of Dewey, *"Only a teacher trained in the support level of intellectual method will be likely, in deed, not in mere word, to respect the mental integrity and force of children."*
4. *Practice:* Dewey's essay 'The Relation of Theory to practice in Education' is one of his few that specifically addresses the problems of preparing teachers to do the work of teaching. He proposed a 'laboratory view' of practice, where theory and practice 'grow together out of and into the teacher's personal experience' and where beginners acquire 'control of intellectual method required for personal and independent mastery of practical skills rather than at turning out at once masters of the craft.'
5. *Stages of Practice*
   (i) *Reflection*–Dewey recommended that pre-service teachers' reflection on their own past experiences be supplemented with initial observation

in school classroom, not so much to see how teachers teach, but 'to get material for psychological observation and reflection, and some conception of the educational movement of the school as a whole.' These early observations should be focused 'to see how teacher and pupils reach upon each other—how mind answers to mind—what the student needs most at this stage of growth, is ability to see what is going on in the minds of a group of persons who are in intellectual contact with one another.' After developing a richer understanding of working of the school through reflecting writing and observation, a pre-service teacher could begin to serve as assistant.

(ii) *Select and arrange subject matter*—After assisting the cooperative teacher with small tasks and putting theory and practice together through observation and reflection, pre-service teacher may begin to select and arrange subject matter.

(iii) *Co-participation in lesson planning*—The pre-service teacher should focus on one subject area across grade levels to develop the habit of viewing the entire curriculum as a continuous growth, reflecting the growth of mind itself. At this stage the prospective teacher co-participates in lesson planning by helping the cooperating teacher, find supplementary materials, creating automatic discipline-specific problems, or developing a scheme of possible alternative subjects for lessons and studies.

(iv) *Actual teaching*—Now the pre-service teacher may move to actual teaching. Here the superviser should guide the student to judge his own work critically, to find out for himself in what respects he has succeeded and in what failed, and to find the probable reasons for both failure and success.

(v) *Actual apprenticeship*—Dewey insists that apprenticeship is only useful if the programme is long enough for the beginning teachers and if the practice schools are sufficiently large to furnish the required number of children to offer all prospective teachers this opportunity.

Dewey believed that this could be accomplished best by getting things into connection with one another, so that they work easily, flexibly and fully.

### *Student*

Dewey thought that the major responsibility for education fell initially upon adults, teachers and others. He did not intend that students be held primarily responsible for their achievements or shortcomings. He considered that adults are responsible for creating learning conditions to promote educative experiences for children. He believed that the adults/teachers are matured and experienced persons of the society and the child/student is immature with his/her innate powers, capacities and capabilities. He encouraged teachers to ensure that learners come to understand their limitations and potentialities through their critiques of student performance other than feedback.

It does not mean that Dewey did not place emphasis on the learner's initiative and involvement. He clearly stated that the guidance, direction, navigation given by the teacher were impossible if the energy for learning does not come from the student. He connects both the educative process and educational theory with the student's interaction or involvement with particular societal aims, meaning and values that emerge from adult experiences. He said, "since learning is something that pupil has to do himself/herself and for himself/herself, the initiative lies with the learners". So, he expected the student to adapt to the curriculum as much as he expected the teacher to adapt material to the student.

Dewey had a confidence in the child's nature and believed that, when educators guide a student's growth, his or her natural tendencies lead to educative experiences. He identified four major instincts that educators should get hold of and direct towards something better as:

| *Instincts* | *Manifestation* |
|---|---|
| Communicative | saying, communicating |
| Constructive | making, playing, shaping |
| Investigative | finding out, inquiring |
| Artistic | creating, fashioning |

He believed that every individual is different, so, he claimed:

1. *Mind is innate*—Firstly, the importance of understanding the individual mind as a function of social life–as not capable of operating or developing by itself, but requires continuous stimulus from social agencies and finding its nutrition in social supplies.
2. *Individual as a whole person*—Secondly, he argued that the child should be understood from the perspective of emotions and endeavour as well as knowledge and intellect.
3. *Mind is not static*—Thirdly, he insisted that mind is not a static entity that comes fully developed but instead is a process and a growing affair.

Thus he argued that education is neither a drawing out' nor a 'pouring in' but a taking hold of the activities that stem from instincts of the child. He believed that the child is born with a natural desire to give out, to do, to serve, and the teachers can use it to cultivate character and good citizenship. The child should be looked upon as willful, purposeful, curious and active.

In a poem, Dewey imagined a person who is strong but not sufficiently self controlled and independent to overcome his or her burning desires and social pressures because he or she was not adequately guided earlier in life'.

*He failed, though he was strong,*
*He was not strong enough + 'await',*
*The final word of patient fate*
*He was hurried by the restless throng*

*Of feverish desires to seek*
*The promised lend of honeyed streams*
*of smooth success.*

Although children may be eager to claim a freedom or a dream, he suggested that educators should not cultivate this eagerness.

### School

Dewey considered school as the representative of society. School and society are complement to each other and both are essential. School is a live laboratory. The traditional school with its physical arrangement intended for listening, it imposed discipline by means of sugarcoating that would make the better pill more palatable. Dewey, of course did oppose the elastic thesis that school should be exclusively concerned with the development of mind and was a party to the pragmatic anti-thesis that schools should provide for the growth of the whole child.

Dewey considers the school as a miniature society when a child gets experience to act and behave according to his interests, aptitude and capacities. Different activities in play grounds, libraries, laboratories, classrooms are organised in order to develop the social qualities in the child. Thus school is not only a centre to provide education to the child but it is also a community centre where the study and investigations of ail things of community and techniques of its progress are regularly made. In this way school is a centre where the individuality of the child is developed in the right direction and social habits are also inculcated in him.

Dewey regards the school as an 'epitome' of life outside, as the 'miniature of society and the 'lengthened arm of the family'. He describes the following functions of school:

1. *Providing a simplified Environment:* The first function of the school is to select those features which are fairly fundamental and capable of being responded to by the young. The relationship of our present social life are so numerous and so interwoven that even a child placed in the most favourable position could not readily share in many of the most important of them. So, the school should provide a simplified environment so that the child can learn fruitfully.
2. *Eliminating the Unworthy Features of the Existing Environment:* Dewey explained this function as, "As a society becomes more enlightened, it realizes that it is responsible not to transmit and conserve the whole of its existing achievements but only such as make for a better future society." So, the school is the chief agency for the accomplishment of this function.
3. *Balancing the various Elements in the Social Environment:* It is the function of the school to coordinate within the disposition of each individual the diverse influences of the various social environments in to

which he enters. The school, as an institution, should simplify existing social life, should reduce it, as it were; to an embryonic form.

According to him, following are the important features of an ideal school:

- School is a provider of vocational training.
- School is a place where learning takes place through projects.
- School is a place of discipline through co-curricular activities and social environment.
- School as a miniature society.
- School as an enlarged ideal home.
- School is a place, where teacher plays the role of a friend, philosopher and guide.
- School is a place of providing rich experiences.
- School is a place of training socially useful efficient citizens,
- School is a place- of providing moral education through activities.
- School is a place where classrooms are treated as laboratories and teachers as demonstrators,
- School as a place where individual differences are properly considered.
- School as a place where teacher is responsible for securing maximum development of the pupils.

Dewey felt that the changed time demand the training of students for a complete living in the society, should be provided in the school. As a great philosopher, while designing the laboratory school in 1896, he made use of the psychological aspects. In accordance with his functional psychology and Froebel's concept of self-activity and self-creation, he regarded curiosity, action and experience as basic conditions of learning. Instead of beginning with reading, writing, arithmetic as was traditionally done, learning has to be concentrated on topics and issues pertaining to actual life and meeting basic human needs like food, clothing and shelter.

## Influence of Dewey on Contemporary Education

Dewey was known as the father of progressive education and was an advocate of social learning. He believed that school should be representative of social environment and that students learn best when in natural social settings. Today's world is the world of technology. With technology driving the social lives of students, its use in an effective way to promote student engagement, resulting in a passion for life long learning.

He has contributed greatly to the field of education as:

1. *Importance to Child:* Dewey lays emphasis on child's individuality, his needs, interests and aptitudes. Neither school, nor teacher, nor methods of teaching, nor the curriculum but it is the child who holds the central place in the education process. He condemned bookish knowledge and

formation in education and gives due place to the development of the personality of the child. Our present day education system also follows child centred education.

2. *Activity Centred:* Dewey laid stress on activity rather than ideas. The principle of learning by doing is the greatest contribution of him which have revolutioned the theory of education.
3. *Project Method:* The unique contribution is the project method in which the child indulges in creative activities results in natural progress and development. It helps not only in individual development but social development also.
4. *Democratic Outlook:* Dewey stresses on the development of democratic outlook in the child. It infuses in the child a spirit of freedom, equality and sense of responsibility. It also emphasizes on developing a sense of responsibility in relation to rights and duties of a citizen. This will help in developing social values.
5. *Infusion of Innovative Education:* Different new concepts are introduced by him in the process of education as 'New Education', 'Activity Based Education', 'Democratic Education' etc. Modernised methods of teaching as 'Programmed Instructions', 'Learning at One's own pace', 'Computerised Instruction' are based on Dewey's philosophy.
6. *Related to Life:* Dewey emphasizes that the child should be allowed to solve his own problems after placing him in problematic situation. It gives him an insight in the practical life which prepares him for future life in an effective way. It helps in gaining the experiences related to real life.
7. *Optimistic Attitude:* He emphasizes upon freedom, initiative, expression, purposeful activities and development of human values in the child. It develop the optimistic attitude and ideals. Education is growth towards progress and change so he wanted education to lead to growth which forms the basis for further growth.
8. *Balanced Approach:* Dewey advised us to have a balanced approach towards the past, present and future. The past may be glorious and rich but it must guide for living a glorious and rich life in the present. Thus too much emphasis on cultural heritage was not laid by him.
9. *Learning How to Learn:* The focus of the teaching learning process suggested by him is to enable the child how to learn. So, the child is not to memorise the facts
10. *Inflexible Methods:* According to him methods are dynamic and flexible. They are based on ability and fulfill the demands of the society. Besides project and experimental method, he emphasised learning by doing, learning by experience, learning by living, learning by activity, learning through play and motivation
11. *Correlated Methods:* He stresses that in order to make progressive methods of teaching successful and effective, there is need of correlation

of studies, integration of subjects, use of audio-visual aids, organisation of curricular activities, learning by doing and proper training of senses.

12. *Balanced approach to the Role of the Teacher and the Student:* He advocated that both the student and the teacher are important parts of the educative process. The teacher is a friend, and guide who educates the pupils in self-discipline and active participation. The student is to remain active.
13. *Social Discipline:* Dewey accords a special role to activities leading to social discipline. Today educand is trained in social control and democratic citizenship.
14. *Freeing the Over Burdened Child:* He saved the child from the burdened education which is too much centred on books.
15. *Close contact between School and Society:* The unique contribution of him is that school and society have come in close contact and the experiences of the pupil are given much importance. He regards school as a society in miniature.

Thus, Dewey has contributed tremendously and has revolutionized the whole concept of education. It is neither teacher-centred, nor curriculum-centred but it is pupil centred. It wants to develop such a dynamic, flexible and adaptable mind which is always resourceful and enterprising and is able to create new values for the development of the future. Its emphasis on child's individuality, the needs, its principles of learning by doing, its stress on integration of knowledge are all important contribution. He has given a new direction and a new purpose to all educational programmes. It has given birth to independent thinking and research. It has made education more purposive, interesting and effective. Therefore, his contribution to educational thoughts and practices cannot be overlooked.

# 15

# Mahatma Gandhi (1869-1948)

> *"Literacy is not the end of education not even the beginning. It is one of the means whereby men and women can be educated. Literacy in itself is no education."*
>
> – Mahatma Gandhi

Mahatma Gandhi, the father of nation, was born on October 2, 1869 at Porbander in the state of Kathiawar (Gujrat). He had founded the Sabarmati Ashram and Sevagram Ashram which acted as centres of most of his educational activities. He was a practical man. He wanted to establish a spiritual and harmonious society based on truth, love, non-violence, justice and equality among all men. He has secured a unique place in the galaxy of the great teachers who have brought fresh light in the field of education.

## Philosophy of Life

Gandhi Ji's view on the nature of Reality is monistic. 'I believe' he says, 'in the absolute oneness of God and therefore also of humanity.' Mahatma Gandhi, the great philosopher, educationist and experimenter expressed his views on everything. Here is given a brief description of his philosophical doctrine.

1. *Firm Faith in God:* Like all idealists, Gandhi Ji had firm faith in God. To him, God is ultimate reality and supreme ruler. God is a source of life. He is the creator, dissolver and recreater. Hence he advised to have a living and absolute God. The ultimate aim of life should be the realization of God.
2. *Truth:* To Gandhi Ji, God is truth and truth is God. Truth is the inner voice. It is the call of conscience. He wanted to realise truth himself. According to him, truth is the only way to realise God. If somebody has truth in his mind, words and deeds and uses it together with Ahimsa sincerely and constantly, he will be able to realize God someday. One should adhere even to die for truth but he should not impose his truth on any one else.
3. *Ahimsa or Non-violence:* Ahimsa or non-violence is the means to attain the goal of truth. Ahimsa includes humanity, charity, love, patience, purity of the heart and freedom from passion in thought, words or action. It inspires us to love all creatures. It purifies spirit.

4. *Satyagraha:* It is the practical application of Ahimsa. It is a method of securing a right by personal suffering and not by inflicting injury on others. Defence of peace can be constructed only through Satyagraha. This is to hold fast to death.
5. *Spiritual Nature of Individual:* Gandhi Ji believed that an individual has a divine spirit. He is a spiritual being. Therefore the aim of the individual must be spiritual and not material.
6. *Love:* Gandhi Ji had a firm faith in the love for mankind. To him *"Love is essence of morality. No morality is possible without love. Truth can be attained through love. Love takes him towards the God."*
7. *Fearlessness:* Gandhi Ji's Ahimsa had two legs to stand upon. The first is fearlessness. To him, *"Fearlessness connotes freedom from all external fear of discuses bodily injury and death or disposition of loosing one's nearest and dearest, of loosing reputation or giving offence and so on"*
8. *Spiritual Society:* Gandhi Ji was anxious to establish a spiritual society based on the principle of non-violence, truth, justice and equitable distribution of wealth. Such a society will be free from any kind of exploitation-social, political, economic and religious. This society will be free from all types of conflicts and struggles.

## Gandhi Ji as Naturalist, Idealist and Pragmatist

Mahatma Gandhiji successfully synthesized different philosophies of education and emerged as a naturalist, idealist and pragmatist. As Rousseau he criticises the environment of school and society, he gave importance to natural environment. As idealist he believes in God, as realist he believes in the education related with life and as pragmatist he correlates education with productivity. Gandhian philosophy is based on his own principles. According to Patel, *"Gandhiji's philosophy of education is naturalistic in its setting, idealistic in its aims and pragmatic in its methods and programme of work."*

Gandhi Ji's thoughts on education form the dynamic side of his genera! philosophy. His philosophy of education is based on biology, sociology, psychology and philosophy. Educational aims, curriculum, methodology, plan of organisation and financial aspect of education were directed by his philosophy of life. In the words of Dr. Patel, *"He is the starting point of modern educational theory and practice of the East."*

## Basic Principles

The following are the basic principles of Gandhiji's philosophy of education:

(i) From 7 to 14 years of age, education of each child should be free, compulsory and universal

(ii) The medium of instruction should be mother tongue.

(iii) There should be no place for English in the education of a child,

(iv) Mere literacy cannot be equated with education.
(v) Education should develop human values in the child.
(vi) Education should develop all the powers of the child according to the community of which he is an integral part.
(vii) Education should achieve the harmonious development of child's body, mind, heart and soul.
(viii) Education should employ some craft as a medium of education so that the child gains economic self reliance for his life.
(ix) All education should be imparted through some productive craft and a useful corelation should be established with that industry.
(x) Education for all subjects should be imparted through some local craft or productive work.
(xi) The industry should be such that the child is able to achieve gainful work experience through practical work.
(xii) Education should be made self-supporting.
(xiii) Education should lead to economic independence and self-reliance for livelihood.
(xiv) School should be a place of activity where the child remains busy in various experiments and gains newer and newer experiences bringing forth new researches.
(xv) Education should create useful, responsible and dynamic citizens.
(xvi) Gandhiji divided education in three phases in the theoretical development:
  (a) Formative Period—Fundamental concepts.
  (b) Experiment Period—Experiments with educational ideas and ideals.
  (c) Formulation Period—Theory and practice.

  Thus Gandhiji's education was based on:
  (i) Craft-centredness
  (ii) Chiid-centredness
  (iii) All-roundedness
  (iv) Social responsibility
  (v) Nationalism
  (vi) School as societal agency
  (vii) Religious ideals
  (viii) Creative Activity

**Meaning of Education**

"By education" says Gandhi *"I mean an all round drawing out of the best in child and man—body, mind and spirit:"* He believed that education should develop all the capacities of the child so that he becomes a complete human being. Gandhiji advocated that education should develop the child's individuality fully and harmoniously so that he will be able to realize, the ultimate aim of life which is truth or God.

## Aims and Ideals of Education

Gandhiji has recommended the following aims:

1. *Character Formation:* Like Rousseau Gandhiji also believed in paidocentric education, that is, education which centres around the child. He impressed upon people that it is through the cultural aspect that the child learns conduct and ideas and develops his character and ideals. As he puts it, *"True education is that which draws out and stimulates the spiritual, intellectual and physical faculties of the children."* For him character formation was more important than literacy. And, in character, Gandhiji addressed the importance of thought, word and deed, non-violence and truth.
2. *Complete Development:* Gandhiji viewed education from a comprehensive or broadminded standpoint. Any education that develops only one aspect of a child's personality can be called narrow and one-sided. Education must aim at developing the all round personality of the child instead of limiting itself to provide the child with bits and pieces of information. Gandhiji had made a distinction between immediate and ultimate aims of education. Getting certificate or degrees or obtaining education for livelihood should be considered as immediate aims, but the ultimate goal of education can only be self-knowledge. Realization of good is, infact, the end or the goal of all human activities and service to humanity its finest means.
3. *Livelihood or Vocational Aim:* In Gandhiji's opinion the aim of education is self-dependence. Education must enable every child to develop the ability to depend upon himself. The ability to earn one's livelihood is part of this independence or self-reliance.
4. *Democratic Ideals:* Like the contemporary Indian educationists. Gandhiji aimed at the evolution of democratic ideals through education. He aimed at an education for ideal citizenship. The school, in itself, is a democratic society in which democratic values are imparted The school works as a miniature society and the child learns the values of sympathy, service, love, brotherhood, tolerance etc. These qualities are transferred from one generation to the other generation.
5. *The Cultural Aim:* Aim of education should be to preserve, transfer and modify the culture. This aim emphasizes that knowledge should be acquired for its own sake. The knowledge which the child has to acquire in our country is the knowledge of Indian culture. This study will enable him to see things in his own correct perspectives. The soul will be pure and free and he shall have no false notion of pride and prejudice.
6. *Moral and Spiritual Development:* Gandhiji laid emphasis on the moral and spiritual development as an aim of education. Gandhiji

very much admired the Indian Gunikul system of education and the idea of Brahmacharya. Nation's greatness is not only measured by its parliamentary institutions and activities, but also by the greatness of its citizens, who should be morally and spiritually developed with the media of education.

7. *Latent Perfection:* The most important aim of education is to achieve perfection already present in the child. Elaborating his views about this aim of education, Gandhiji has said, *"By education I mean an all round drawing out the best in child and man-body, mind and spirit."* According to him all material and spiritual knowledge is already present in man covered by a curtain of ignorance. Education should tear off that cover so that knowledge shines forth as an illuminating torch to enlighten all the comers.
8. *Self Reliance:* As it has been already pointed out that Gandhiji aimed at self-reliance through education. He considered that education should be as an insurance against unemployment and i.e. why he introduced basic education.
9. *Religious Development:* God realization and self-realisation are mutually complementary. Gandhiji maintained that each individual should be able to search out and develop the religious seed embedded in him and thus find the absolute truth or reality. He advocated the training of feelings and emotions so that the whole life can be purified and sublimated.
10. *Developing Faith in One's Own-self:* Education should help in individual's development. Individual should have full confidence upon their powers. They should inculcate a spirit of self surrender, sacrifice for the welfare of other. Education should develop these qualities in an individual.

### *Harmonious Blending of Individual and Social Aim*

Gandhiji advocated both individual and social aims of education at different times. He didn't find any conflict between the two. He thought that if individuals are good, the whole society shall be good. Gandhiji always loved individual freedom but he regarded individual as a social creature. He thought that the development of personality is impossible in loneliness.

Thus, Gandhiji aimed at the development of all round personality of the child. He sought to develop physical, mental, social and spiritual powers of the child through education. He also emphasized the education of 4H's—Head, Heart, Health and Hand in addition to 4R's.

### *Curriculum*

Gandhiji's scheme of education is known as 'Basic Scheme of Education'. He advocated the inclusion of all those subjects and activities, in the curriculum, which foster material welfare with spiritual advancement.

Gandhiji's education was planned to develop a national character and national mindedness in the minds of young India. The curriculum was planned to subserve the ideals set out. The curriculum was built around the three factors i.e. physical environment, social environment and craft work, The principal idea behind the curriculum is to impart the whole education of body, mind and the soul. He suggested the teaching of following subjects in his scheme of education:

1. *Basic Craft:* Basic craft may include agriculture, spinning and weaving, card board work, wood work and metal work. These have the following educational value:
   (i) The craft is rich in educative possibilities.
   (ii) It can serve the basis of correlation with other subjects.
   (iii) It is based on the psychological principle of learning i.e. learning by doing.
   (iv) It can be economically useful as the basic craft could be utilized by the educand to earn the livelihood.
2. *Mother Tongue:* Gandhiji emphasized that the mother tongue should be medium of instruction in the school. It is the natural mode of the child's expression. It will enable the child to express his ideas and to be socially efficient.
3. *Mathematics:* Mathematics is a very useful subject for day to day life. It will develop capacity in the pupil to solve the ordinary and geometrical problems arising in connection with his home and community life speedly. In later life they will be able to solve problems related with their business life.
4. *Social Studies:* Gandhiji wanted that children should acquire knowledge of social studies including history, geography, civics etc. because it inculcates the values of cooperation in life and a proper sense of patriotism, civic responsibilities and duties and also enable the child to be a good neighbourer and develop respect for world religion.
5. *General Science:* General science including nature, biology, physiology, hygiene, chemistry, botany and astronomy should be taught for promoting intelligent and scientific outlook. Home science should be taught to the girls.
6. *Music and Drawing:* Drawing should be included because it helps in training the eye in the observation and discrimination of forms and colours, to develop the memory for forms, to appreciate the beauty i.e. to develop aesthetic sense.

Music should be included because it helps in training their emotions with right direction, to give them a knowledge of their cultural heritage.

Thus the curriculum in Gandhiji's scheme of education was activity centred. Its aim is to prepare the child for practical work, conduct experiments and do research so that he may be able to develop himself physically, mentally, socially and spiritually

### *Methods of Teaching*

Education for Gandhiji was a kind of insurance against unemployment. His educational method was chiefly craft centred. In his methods intellectual training was to be coupled with craft training. He emphasised rural crafts more than industrial trades. The educational message lies in the message of 'Charkha'. He emphasized following principles and methods:

(i) *Education through Craft:* Gandhiji emphasized that education should be given through the medium of some craft or productive work. By means of craft centred education he wanted to give manual training.

(ii) *Learning by Doing:* It was intended to satisfy the following needs of the individual's need for activity, achievement, recognition and approval etc. The activity also satisfies the urge for creativity, productivity and constructive work,

(iii) *Correlation Method:* Gandhiji advocated the method of correlation of different types as intra-subject, inter-subject, inter-environmental etc. There should be correlation with craft and with environment and coordination with subjects. The knowledge learnt in school should be correlated with that of society.

(iv) Gandhiji accepted the use of lecture method as well as questioning method.

(v) *Integration:* Gandhiji emphasized on integration of theoretical knowledge with practical experience, and scholastic life with social and physical life of the pupil.

(vi) *Imitation:* It is the tendency of every child to imitate others. So, Gandhiji believed in imitating method also. He laid emphasis that the parents and teachers should behave with the children in the same way as they are expecting from them. Besides, they should follow truthfulness, celibacy, non-stealing, fearlessness, manual labour, religious goodwill and politeness in their conduct, so, children will imitate the same thing.

(vii) *Oral method:* He believed that children are curious. Whatever teaching method the teacher may use, they should keep asking questions in between and welcome the questions asked by the students to satisfy their curiosity. Thus the children will remain active physically and mentally at all times.

(viii) *Listening, thinking and practices:* In this method, the students firstly hear the oral precepts of the teacher, think upon it and then practice it. It is a hard fact that without practice the student can't be perfect and their knowledge will not become permanent. When the students will listen to precepts, study, contemplate, discover the truth by intellect and reasoning, then they will practice the truth in practical life.

In addition to the above, he emphasized the need of co-curricular activities, socially useful productive work (SUPW), planning, realistic experiences, initiation and sense of individual responsibility to be included in methods of teaching.

### *Discipline*

Gandhiji advocated discipline through self-control. He emphasized voluntary discipline, self discipline. Self-discipline arises from fearlessness, usefulness and self sacrifice. He was strictly against corporal punishment.

His craft centred education encourages social discipline. So, in his concept of social education, he emphasized building up of ideal citizens through education. He wanted pupils to be successful and responsible future citizens of the country.

According to him, *"If boys and girls don't learn discipline in their school days, money and time spent on their education is a national loss."*

### *Teacher*

Gandhiji don't believe in teacher centred education but he thinks teacher as friend and guide of child. He believed that a teacher should be as:

(i) Comprises human qualities.
(ii) Help in increasing curiosity of the children.
(iii) Guidance in development of emotions, interests and needs.
(iv) Solve the problem.
(v) Knowledge about local conditions.
(vi) Confidence of child in him.
(vii) Efforts to fulfill his responsibilities.

He believed that a teacher should be a lover of truth and non-violence and he should possess a sound knowledge, skill, enthusiasm, patriotism, dedication, love for children and labour, respect for the dignity of individuals and special training in basic education.

Thus Gandhian philosophy is based on his own principles. He was the first Indian who advocated a scheme of education based upon the essential values of Indian culture and civilization.

## Contribution to the Theory and Practice of Contemporary Education

Gandhiji's contribution to education is unique as:

1. *All round development:* Gandhiji felt that education should aim at arousing curiosity and providing motivation to the child so that he should himself achieve his own physical, mental and spiritual development. He emphasized on the importance of acquiring manual skills, but he felt

that this training should be supplemented by knowledge of other objects also. Today's Indian education system believe in child centred education. He also felt that education should not be allowed to become mechanical but should be acquired through play. His philosophy of education is psychologically sound.

2. *Learning by doing:* Today Psychologists agree with Gandhi's theory that there should be learning by doing. Most of the educationists agree that learning through doing helps in the complete development of the child and this also enables him to earn his livelihood in the later life. The methods of teaching suggested by him have a great impact in modem time.
3. *Child centred education:* Gandhiji's philosophy of education is biologically sound. It lays stress on man's complete development. It emphasises that man should be able to fit himself in a successful existence under the conditions of a complex and changing civilization. His education is centred around the child, not around text books.
4. *Healthy citizenship:* He wanted the ideals of useful citizenship to be encouraged through education. Today there is close relationship between school and community for the development of the child as well as of society. He regards the school as a cooperative community where student can learn lessons in love, truth, justice, equality, tolerance, brotherhood, cooperation and social service ideals. All these lead to healthy citizenship.
5. *Stress on religious and moral education:* He was always an idealist. The ultimate aim of today's education is to achieve salvation. He felt that the aim of man's life is realization of God and that is why he stressed the need of moral and religious education.
6. *Development of feeling of national development in the children:* Gandhiji's education system has sociological significance also. He wanted to use education as the medium of establishing in the country a non-violent social system from which exploitation of all kinds would be absent. There is great need of national integration for the development of the nation. He stressed the importance of labour, agriculture, handicrafts, hygiene etc. and pointed out that they were most important than any curriculum. Now a days stress is to be given on environmental education and health and physical education so that pupil may be able to keep themselves fit and their environment clean.
7. *Makes children self reliant and independent through education:* From the economic stand point, Gandhiji's plan of education appears to be suitable for the economy. He suggested that the educand should himself do his own work and all work connected with the school. He should learn to respect labour and should not feel that manual work in no way worse or inferior to mental labour. India being an agricultural country, in which the villager have small pieces of land, it would be better if these people

developed various kinds of industries. With the help of this they can be self-sufficient.

8. *Impact of agricultural education for rural development:* In India a large-portion of the population live under poverty line. Most of the villagers cannot afford to pay for their children's education. On the other hand, they used assistance of their children in their own occupation. Hence, their children shall receive an education which can enable them to share their parent's burden. The existing pattern of our education prepares the young men for white-collar jobs. This type of education is not suitable for the agricultural country. Gandhiji wanted that the individual should become independent during his education, or at least that he should learn some skill which would enable him to find employment immediately after completing his education. The impact of Gandhiji's plan is that today education system is stressing more and more on professional education, so that it may help in solving the problem of unemployment. Vocationalisation of education was recommended by different education commissions time to time.
9. His plan of introducing the mother tongue as medium of instruction is implied in today's three language formula.
10. Gandhiji planned for the education of both male and female. He lays stress on population education, women education and adult education.

Thus, Gandhiji's educational philosophy is of much importance to contemporary education system. The methods and techniques advocated by him and the environment, he prescribed revolutionize the Indian thinking and way of living. His philosophy believes in individual as well as social development.

# 16

# Jean Jacques Rousseau (1712-1778)

*" God makes all things good, man meddles with them and they become evil."*
–Rousseau

Rousseau was a Genevan philosopher, writer and composer. His political philosophy influenced the progress of enlightenment throughout Europe. He was the least academic of modern philosophers and in many ways was the most influential. He propelled ethical thinking in to new channels. His reforms revolutionized taste, first in music, then in the other arts. He had a profound impact on people's way of life; he taught parents to take a new interest in their children and to educate them differently and he furthered the expression of emotion rather than polite restraint in friendship and love. He opened people's eyes to the beauties of nature, and he made liberty an object of almost universal aspiration.

## Brief Life Sketch

Rousseau was born in the independent Calvinist city-state of Geneva on June 28, 1712. His father's name was Issac Rousseau, a watchmaker and mother's name was Suzanne Bernard. His mother died 9 days after his birth, with the consequence he was brought up and educated by his father until the age of 10. At an early age he read ancient Greek and Roman literature such as the Lives of Plutarch. His father got into a quarrel with a French captain, and at the risk of imprisonment, left Geneva for the rest of his life. Rousseau stayed behind and was cared for by his uncle who sent him along with his cousin to study in the village of Bosey. He left school at the age of 12 due to the artificial environment. In 1725, he was apprenticed to an engraver and began to learn the trade. Although he did not detest the work, he thought his master to be violent and tyrannical. In 1728, he left Geneva and fled to Annecy. He was fortunate in finding the province of Savoy a benefactor, the baroness de Warens, who provided him with a refuse in her home and employed him as his steward. She also furthered his education to such a degree that the boy who had arrived at her doorstep as a stammering apprentice who had never been to school developed into a philosopher, a man of letters and a musician. Warens transformed the adventurer into a philosopher. She forced him to forfeit his Genevan citizenship (in 1754 he would make a return to Geneva and publicly convert back to Calvanism). Her morals distressed Rousseau, even then he became her lover. Thus from the age of 12 to 29 years, he remained a vagabond and during his wandering he met different types of people, learnt to sympathise with the poor.

Rousseau reached Paris when he was 30 years old and was lucky enough to meet another young man Denis Diderot from the province seeking literary fame in the capital. He worked on several articles on music for Diderot and d'Alembert's Encyclopedia. They become immensely successful as the centre of a young group of intellectuals –or philosophers—who gathered round the great French Encyclopedia, of which Diderot was appointed editor. After two years spent serving a post at the French Embassy in Venice, he returned in 1745 and met a linen-maid named Therese Levasseur, who would become his lifelong companion (they eventually married in 1768). They had five children together, all of whom were left at the Paris orphanage. At the age of 38 in 1750, he wrote his first book *Discourse on the Arts and Sciences*. This discourse is what originally made Rousseau famous as it won the Academy's prize. The work was widely read and was controversial. Music was still a major part of Rousseau's life at this point, and several years later, his opera, *Le Devin du Village* (The Village Soothsayer) was a great success and earned him even more recognition. But Rousseau attempted to live a modest life despite his fame, and after the success of his opera, he promptly gave up composing music.

The other publications of him were as follows:

- Essay on Origin of Inequality among Men (1753)
- Discourse on Political Economy (1753)
- The New Heloise-a romance (1761)
- The Social Contract (1762)
- Emile (1762)

In the remaining years of his life he produced primarily autobiographical writings, mostly intended to justify himself against the accusations of his adversaries. The most important was his 'Confessions'. He also wrote 'Rousseau, Judge of Jean Jacques' and the *'Reveries of the Solitary Walker'* to reply to specific charges by his enemies.

Rousseau revolted against the cannons of society and advocated the doctrine of 'Back to Nature'. He wrote 'Man is born free but everywhere he is in chains'. His ideas were opposed by the establishment. His books were burnt. He had to live in exile for many years. He was so much disgusted and disappointed that on July 2, 1778 following his usual early morning walk he died of apoplexy (a hemorrhage-some of his former friends claimed he committed suicide). However, his greatness was recognised later and his views had tremendous influence on the outbreak of the French Revolution in 1789.

## Rousseau's Philosophy

Rousseau was developed as a revolutionary philosopher. He was influenced mainly by three aspects-circumstances, life experiences, and free and emotional nature. His philosophy was originated as a reaction to the protest to prevailing social and political conditions. He was against the prevailing social conditions and was in favour of the view 'back to Nature'. His philosophy is known as 'Naturalism'. The major aspects of his philosophy were 'natural state', 'natural man', and establishment of 'natural civilization'. By 'natural state' he meant a state in which no evils, no corruption and lack of social division exist. He saw a fundamental division between society and human nature. He believed that man was good when he was in the state of nature but has been corrupted by the artificiality of society and growth of social interdependence. For Rousseau, society's negative influence on man centres on its transformation of a positive self-love which he saw as the instinctive human desire for self- preservation, combined with the human power of reason into a kind of artificial pride which forces man to compare himself to others, thus creating unwarranted fear and allowing man to take pleasure in pain or weaknesses of others. It means that society makes the man self -centred human being. He claimed that 'state of nature' was a primitive and brutish condition without law or morality, which man deliberately left for the benefits and necessity of cooperation. He believed, 'Man is born free, and everywhere he is in chains, one man thinks himself the master of others, but remains more of a slave than they'.

His 'natural man' is such a truthful man who being uncivilized remain free from social traditions and develop according to the nature. By 'natural civilization' he meant that civilization which is free from the artificial environment and rigid restrictions that pollute the piousness of the nature. So, education of the child should be in the natural environment and according to the nature of the child. According to Rousseau feelings of child should be the basis of all his activities. The naturalism propounded by him only means that development of child should be according to his natural tendencies and inner feelings. Rousseau's important words were-'Naturalism', which is free, developmental, and interesting and activity based. These are the only words which are life and soul of modern and progressive education.

His philosophy can be summarised in the following way:

- Material world is the real world.
- Mind is subordinate to nature.
- Nature gives importance to unsocial education.
- Nature means natural tendencies.
- Cities are the mosques of human race.
- Nothing beyond nature.
- Priority should be given to individuality.

- Man creates society to fulfil his needs.
- All real values are present in nature.
- Nature is the source of complete knowledge.
- Nature is pure in complete form.
- The senses of man are the gateways of knowledge.

Thus Rousseau advocated the concepts of liberty, equality and fraternity.

***Three Fold Meaning of Nature***

Rousseau has taken the wider meaning of nature in the following way:

1. *Isolation from society:* Rousseau believed that when a thing comes from nature, it is good, but as he reaches in the hands of man, it becomes evil. As a consequence, the child should be kept safe from the evil effects of society. By keeping the child isolated from the society, the opportunities should be provided to develop him in the beauty of nature. Nature and society are opposite to each other. It is commonly called natural education which is not founded upon meaningless traditions and formalities of society.
2. *Innate tendencies of the child:* Innate tendencies of a child means his/her inner interests. Rousseau believed that a child can learn much more if the opportunities are given for spontaneous development of his innate tendencies in a free environment. He writes, 'Education is no longer a procedure, artificial, harsh, dull, unsympathetic and repressive of all natural inclinations. It is on the other hand, an organic growth; it is a development from within.' So, the education of the child should begin with the development of his innate tendencies.
3. *Contact with natural environment:* Rousseau himself was a lover of nature. He indoctrinate the view that the child's relation should be with hills, trees, plants, birds, animals, wood, stories, and physical forces. He believed that one who is nourished and taught in natural environment automatically becomes a natural man. Thus the child should be brought up in natural environment. As a result of it he will automatically become a rational being and act according to the voice of his conscience.

**Educational Philosophy of Rousseau**

Rousseau believed that the child should never be ignored. His 'Emile' awared the children of Europe. He wanted to keep the child away from family, society and artificial environment of school. He was against the prevailing system of education and wanted to make the human nature of child as the basis of education. He was very much disgusted from the old traditions of society and wanted to keep the child away from its artificiality. As a votary of naturalistic education, he sounded a death knell to the pattern of education aimed at imparting information or doses of knowledge artificially. He writes in 'Emile', "The internal development of our organs and faculties is the education of nature, the use we are taught to make of that development is the education given us by men, and the acquisition made by our own experiences on the objects that surrounds us consists our education from things."

Thus according to him there are three sources of education:

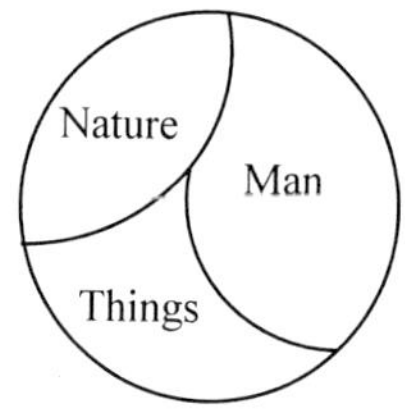


**Fig. 16.1: Sources of Education**

A. *Education from nature:* Education from nature means development of the child according to his/her tendencies and capacities. It consists in the spontaneous development of one's endowment and faculties i.e. of child's natural tendencies and interests. He gave it the top priority. Thus education from nature means when the development of child takes place according to his/her natural capabilities and achievements.

B. *Education from men:* While living in the society we can't ignore it. Therefore education from men means importance should be given to society also. It consists in influencing our social contracts and various groups. Rousseau did not favour it at least in initial stage but when the child becomes mature then he should know how to utilise that learning in the society.

C. *Education from things or circumstances:* The objects around us also play important role in providing experiences to us. It consists in the acquisition of knowledge and information through contacts with physical surrounding and our experiences of dealing with the things.

For Rousseau, education does not mean merely imparting information or storing knowledge in different compartments. It is the development of the child with the above said factors. His conviction was that education should be considered as, 'the process of development in to an enjoyable, rational, harmoniously balanced, useful, and hence natural life'. The principles of his educational philosophy can be summarised as follows:

- Emphasis on physical environment.
- Emphasis on present life of the child as the basis of education.
- Important place to freedom in child's education.
- Education is dynamic aspect of philosophy.
- Secondary place to bookish knowledge.
- Education should be according to the nature of the child.
- Important place to innate tendencies and interests of the child.

### *Kinds/Types of Education*

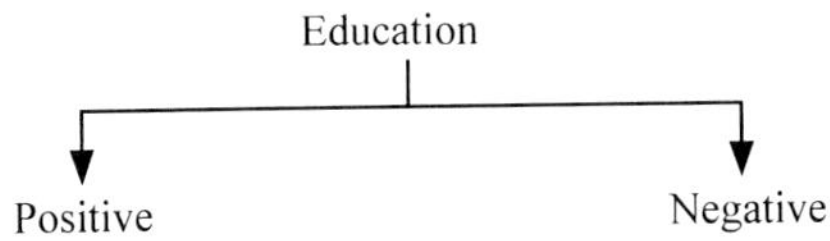


According to Rousseau education is of two types:

1. *Positive Education:* Rousseau writes, *"I call positive education one that tends to form the mind prematurely and to instruct the child in the duties that belong to man."* He was against the positive education and revolted against it because he termed it as unnatural and inhuman. The characteristics of positive education are:
   - Stress on verbalism.
   - Stress on strict discipline.
   - Emphasis on duty, morality and religion.
   - Importance to social education.
   - Emphasis on formation of habits.

   It was due to revolt against positive education that he advocated negative education.
2. *Negative Education:* Negative education is that education which make the means of education strong. Rousseau believed that everything is good as it comes from nature and it generates in the hands of men, so he advocated that the education of the child should be negative. The child should not be taught the principle of truth and virtue but guarded against evil. He held the opinion, *"I call negative education that which tends to perfect the organs that are the instruments of the knowledge, and endeavours to process the way for reasons, by the proper exercise of the senses."* It does not inculcate truth. It does not give virtues, it protects from vice. It projects from errors. It lays emphasis on learning by experiences instead of booking knowledge. Following are the characteristics of negative education.
   (i) *No place for formal lessons:* Rousseau did not believe in the efficiency of verbal lessons. He stated, *"get rid of the lesson and one get rid of the chief cause of their (children) sorrow."* He also remarked, *"Give me a child of five who know nothing and at the fifteen, I shall return him to you knowing as much as those who have under instructions since infancy with difference that your pupil only knows things by heart while mine know how to use his knowledge."* He believed that verbal lesson only increases the burden on the minds of children and from education point of view it is wastage of time. The child should learn through his own experiences.
   (ii) *No bookish learning:* Rousseau said 'Reading is the curse of childhood.' He hated books, as they are of no value. He considered

them to be the cause of child's misery and suggest a remedy for its removal by saying, *"By relieving school children of their courses and books, we can take away the cause of their misery."* Instead of making the child stick to his books, we should keep him busy in the workshop. The work done by his hands will work to the profit of his mind.

(iii) *No direct moral education:* Rousseau is not in favour of teaching of morals. Let the child to left free to act and learn what is right and wrong by the consequences of his own actions. For imparting moral education example is better than precept.

(iv) *Lose time wisely:* Rousseau said, *"Do not save the time but lose it."* Let the child during childhood run, jump and play all day long. In all these activities he will have a continuous reconstruction of experiences which is nothing but education, pure and simple. Childhood is not the time for intellectual pursuits.

(v) *No habit formation:* Rousseau said, *"The only habit a child is to form is not to form any habit at all."* He was not in favour of any habit formation. Young children should not be made slaves of rigid habits. They should be left free in all their activities. Although he was in favour of forming natural habits i.e. why he believed that if any habit is to be formed in childhood, let them form natural habits.

(vi) *No social education:* Rousseau believed that the education of child should not be in the society. He held the view that society is corrupt and it degenerates him. So he should be protected from its evil influences.

(vii) *No formal discipline:* Rousseau believed in discipline according to natural consequences. If the child climbs a tree, let him fall and learn not to attempt it again. The human beings should not influence to protect or punish the child. It shows that Rousseau was in favour of self-discipline.

(viii) *No sticking to old customary procedure of education:* Rousseau was greatly disgusted with the prevailing social, political, economical, religious and educational conditions in his country. So he said, *"Follow the reverse of the current practices and you will almost do right."* Once he remarked, *"man was once happy, now he is miserable. Undo what had been done and he will be happy again."*

Thus Rousseau's education system believed in negative education and specifically any type of formal education should not be provided till the age of 12 years. According to him the real education is that which helps in natural development of the child and in which the instructions given by any individual or society is minimum.

### *Aims of Education*

In 18th century, man was considered bad by nature and he was not trusted. So an effort was made to change the nature of man through religious education or any other education as social education, vocational education etc. and the ideals accepted by the society were to be implanted on the human mind. But Rousseau had full belief in human nature and he wanted to change the prevailing education system. According to him the aim of education should be the development of an individual in natural way, so that his life will become balanced, fruitful, enjoyable and the nature will become natural. The real aim of education is to bring the child in that direction which makes him great.

He stated *"To live is not merely to breath. It is to act, to make use of our organs, senses, our faculties and of all those parts of ourselves, which give us the feeling of our existence."* He believed that education is a life long process, which starts from the birth and go on till death. It is the development of innate tendencies not an imposition from outside. For him education in itself is life and not the preparation for future. The following are aims of education:

1. *To acquire present happiness:* According to Rousseau the aim of education is to develop the innate tendencies and interests in such a way that they may acquire present happiness. He believed that such type of education is wastage which sacrifies present happiness for happiness in future life. The aim of education should be to make our life happy in the present times.
2. *To acquire freedom:* Rousseau had love for freedom. The definition of freedom is obeying the laws that you make for yourself. The aim of primary education is to provide proper freedom to the child to learn. Rousseau believed that the aim of education should be to help the child to remain free from the outer customs, traditions, rituals, laws etc. so that his individuality may be developed in the right direction.
3. *To develop child's inner faculties:* Rousseau says that the important aim of education is to develop the child's inner facilities and powers. The child gets pleasure in moving his organs, using his senses and applying his strength. So the aim of education is not to keep the child engaged in reading and writing but to develop his various powers by helping him in his natural activities.
4. *Aim of education at different stages:* Rousseau has divided the whole life of a child in four stages and there are different aims for every stage:

| *Stage* | *Aims of Education* |
|---|---|
| Infancy (birth - 5 years) | Physical development |
| Childhood (5 - 12 years) | Development of sense organs |
| Boyhood (12 - 15 years) | Development of power of understanding |
| Adolescence (15 - 20 years) | Development of emotional, moral and religious feelings |
| Adulthood (20 years onwards) | Development of abilities to lead a good family life. |

(i) *Development of well regulated freedom through physical development:* Rousseau was of the view that it is necessary to give education to a child as a child and not as an adult. It is not at all necessary that a thing useful for an adult should also be useful for the child. In the infancy period the child's body is not fully developed, so at this stage the aim of education should be to do physical development of the child. *"A feeble body makes a feeble mind. All wickedness comes from weakness. Give his body constant exercise to make it strong and healthy"*. To fulfill this aim a well regulated freedom according to child's capacities should be provided.

(ii) *Sense training:* According to Rousseau at the childhood stage i.e. 5 to 10 years, the aim of education is to train the sense organs of the child, so that their sense organs may be developed in a proper way. His advice for this is "exercise the body, the organ, the senses and powers and keep the soul lying fellow, as long as you can. Rousseau believed that hands, legs are the first teacher of a child.

(iii) *Intellectual development:* At the boyhood stage i.e. from 12 to 15 years, the aim of education is to develop the intellect. Education should help in the acquisition of knowledge which may enable him to the practical needs of life.

(iv) *Development of heart:* During the adolescence period i.e. from 15 to 20 years, the individual should learn to live for others and to live together in social relationship. His emotions should be sublimated. It will be proper to arouse moral, religious and social feelings in him. Rousseau has rightly said, "We have formed his body, his senses and his intelligence, it remain to give him a heart."

(v) *Household education:* During the adulthood period i.e. from 20 years onwards, the household education should be provided to an adult. A person should go to the society and should imagine the vices pervading the society by visiting hospitals, orphanages and prisons. It will develop the feeling of comparison. As the individual enters in the adulthood stage, he/she is to lead the family life. Rousseau believed that women education is also essential to lead a complete life.

### *Curriculum*

The fundamental base of Rousseau's education is matter, so, he wanted to make the child dependent on things in place of other men. He wanted to establish harmony in 'nature', 'man' and 'object'. All the three sources have a strong relationship with the subjects taught to the children. Physical science and geography are related with nature; and psychology, history, political science, economics, social science, literature, language etc. are related to man. Even in framing the curriculum, Rousseau paid attention to stages of development of child. It can be explained as shown below:

| *State* | *Curriculum* |
|---|---|
| 1. Infancy | The activities helpful in making the child physically strong as playing, jumping, wandering here and there etc. |
| 2. Childhood | The activities for the development of sense organs: Playing, counting, observation, dance, music, objects etc. No place for bookish knowledge and moral education. Learning by activities and experiences. |
| 3. Boyhood | To make practical life successful and for intellectual development curriculum is to include different subjects and activities. Art, geography, handwork, Natural science, mathematics, languages, activities in workshop, training regarding industrial exchange, banking and transportation. |
| 4. Adolescence | Study of science, society, politics, economics, history and religion to understand complex social relationship. Training for moral qualities as benevolence, kindness, service and sympathy. Travel to other countries, sex education and an explanation of mysteries of creation in the world of plant, animals and men in a dispassionate manner. |
| 5. Adulthood | For successful family life the individual should have the knowledge about future life through the subjects: Physical education, home science, painting, music, art, dance, stitching, knitting, human psychology, moral education etc. |

Thus the curriculum should be framed according to the maturity of the child in different stages of life. More stress should be on activities, and less on bookish knowledge. The child should learn maximum through activities and experiences.

### *Methods of Teaching*

Rousseau believed that the child must be free from society imprisoning institution of which the school was one of the most coercive. He was emphatic in saying that education is a process of development into an enjoyable, rational, harmoniously balanced, useful and hence natural life. Simple and direct methods were created by him. He laid emphasis on following method :

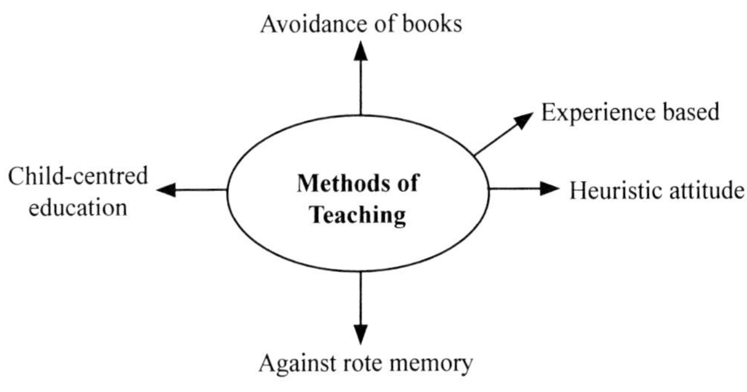


**Fig. 16.2: Methods of Teaching**

(i) *Direct experience:* While favouring direct method Rousseau said, "Experience before expression, words should subordinate aim." He said, "Give your scholar no verbal lesson, he should be taught by experience alone." The knowledge gained through experiences remains permanent, so, perceptual knowledge or real knowledge is more useful and that knowledge is real which is accumulated through one's own experiences.

(ii) *Learning by doing:* Rousseau said, "Teach by doing whenever you can, and only for fall back upon words when doing is out of question." He also said, "I hate books, they only teach us to talk about things that we know nothing about." So, the child should take part in various activities and learn in natural way. It will help him in satisfaction of creative abilities.

(iii) *Education through senses:* Rousseau believed that senses are the gateway of knowledge. He said that, first we are to develop the sense organs of the child, his/her mental development will be automatically done. While teaching we should lay stress on the utilization of sense organs.

(iv) *Self-thinking:* Rousseau believed that the child should be encouraged to know the result of his own thinking through his/her experiences. This is the reason he wanted to give Emile the education of natural science in such a way that it can develop awareness, curiosity, eagerness and discovery tendencies. On this basis the self knowledge method or scientific method was originated. The child is to be given an opportunity to make experiments with the apparatus that he made himself as inventor or discoverer.

(v) *Teaching through concrete objects:* Laying special emphasis on objects teaching Rousseau remarked, "Let the sense always be the guide, let there be no book but the world and no other instructions then facts." His advice was that, "In general, never, substitute the sign for the thing itself, save when it is impossible to show the thing, because the sign absorb the attention of the child and make him forget the thing represented." The education given by the use of concrete objects will be permanent.

(vi) *Play way method:* Rousseau favours play way method. He asserts that for the child playing and working both are the same things. The knowledge gained through playing will be enjoyable and permanent.

(vii) *Learning through example:* For moral education, Rousseau stated, "Example is better than percept "The teacher should practice morality. He should provide opportunities to practice virtue. Lecture on morality will not be useful.

(viii) *Individualised instruction:* Rousseau asserted that every individual child has his own interest, capabilities and abilities. The teacher should recognise the individuality of the child and provide individualised instructions accordingly.

(ix) *Social participation:* During the adolescence stage, the individual is to understated and develop social relations. It can be possible only through visiting places and establishing contacts with the members of the community practically. The teacher should include co curricular activities also.

All the above explained percepts of Rousseau are being increasingly recognised in modern education. He advocated that playing is the best method to make children learning. Knowing childhood was his first concept. Ignorance of child nature is the root of educational errors. The teacher should study the nature of his pupil. Each mind has a form of its own; but the traits of child's mind can be learnt only by observation as they develop.

### *Teacher*

Rousseau did not assign high place to the teacher. He asserted that the teachers have a special tendency for lecturing and they want to pour and impose their knowledge on children. The teacher speaks so much that the children are not able to understand him. The teacher should always remember that the children get tired of lengthy lectures of talks and do not take any interest. Children are interested in activities and they do not like to sit idle. The teacher is not called an instructor but only a guide. His main responsibility is to motivate the child to learn. The teacher should see that education of the pupil is the free development of their interest and motives. He should provide suitable opportunities. He should protect the child from repression, mental conflicts and mental disorders of all kinds.

The teacher should be:

- Guide
- Friend
- Helper
- Not an authority
- Sympathetic
- Exemplar
- Not punishment giver
- Developer of innate tendencies of the child

### *Discipline*

At the times of Rousseau, repressionistic discipline was followed. The teacher believed in spare the road and spoil the child. At that time education was confined with in the rigid rules of discipline. Rousseau asserted, *"A child born, lives and dies in a state of slavery. At the time of birth he is stitched in swaddling clothes and at the time of death he is nailed in a coffin. And as long as he preserve the human form he is fettered by our institutions. Man was born free everywhere he is in shackles."* He advocated maximum freedom for the child and further stressed in freeing the child from the tyranny of rigidity, interference and strict discipline. The freedom of the child disciplines him and he is naturally controlled by his own learning and experience. The stress is given to discipline by natural consequences.

Rousseau asserted that all discipline should derive from natural elements of the situation. The situation will provide a form of innate discipline. To illustrate, a child learns to avoid hot objects because he has experienced the discomfort and pain which follow his touching them. The pupil learn to cooperate with other pupils when he finds himself ostracized by his classmates.

In fact, let the child suffer the consequences for which he is responsible himself for going against nature. When a child begins to expect such consequences as certain to follow if he does not measure up to what is expected of him, he will act so as to enjoy the benefits which follow from appropriate conducts. The way of discipline proposed in theory of Rousseau can be summarized as follows:

- Discipline by natural consequences
- Emancipationist discipline
- No punishment

### *Women Education*

Jean-Jacques Rousseau is considered one of the key enlightenment philosophers, and his writings reveal that he was concerned with, equality among men but he certainly did not make women's equality his focus. According to him, women needed to rely on men for their wellbeing because they were less rational then men. In 'Emile' he writes about the difference between what he believes women and men need in education. Since the main purpose in life, to Rousseau, is for a woman to be a wife and mother, she doesn't need to be educated to the extent that men traditionally have. In his words, "what is most wanted in woman is gentleness, bound to obey a creature so imperfect as a man, should learn to submit to injustice and to suffer the wrongs inficted own sake not his."

Sophie, the imagination of Rousseau, the young woman, Emile is destined to marry as his representative of ideal womanhood, is educated to be governed by her husband while Emile, as his representative of the ideal man, is educated to be self governing. This is not an accidental feature of Rousseau's philosophy. It is essential to his account of the distinction between private, personal relations and the public world of political relations. Rousseau anticipated the modern idea of the bourgeole nuclear family with the mother at home taking responsibility for the household and for child care and early education.

In the earlier writings Rousseau gave women a higher place than men. He remarked that women were born to govern the men. They were the chaste guardians of our morals and the sweet security for our peace. They were the makers of men. Before 'Emile; he listed the numerous woman heroes who'd impacted society: He discusses Zenobia Dido, Joan of Arc, Fulvia, Elizabeth and so many. He said that if given the opportunity to shape society as men had, women could very well change the world. Whatever biological differences between men and women existed, the so-called weaker sex had shown repeatedly that they were capable of greatness.

But Rousseau own bitter experiences with women changed his view and he misconceived women nature. According to him, the ideal nature of woman is modest, guide, tolerant, submissive, amicable and charitable to her thoughts and words. Regarding women and her education, Rousseau's views were as follows:

- *Aim:* He believed that woman should be educated to become a suitable companion of man. The aim of educating woman is to make her a perfect housewife. She should be capable of bringing up the men in his childhood, tend him in his youth and provide him a counsel and consolation throughout his life. She must be soft and sweet.
- *Curriculum:* Rousseau believed that a woman can please a man only when she will be healthy and beautiful. So, she should be given physical education, education of domestic work, morality and religion. It is an accepted experience that if mother is healthy, children will naturally be healthy. A healthy mind lives in a healthy body and provides peace and pleasure to the domestic life. The curriculum for physical education should include physical activities, some games etc. Rousseau believed that she should be proficient in home science also. So, the curriculum should include stitching, embroidery, lace work, dancing, singing, child rearing knowledge, art of making delicious food etc. Knowledge of philosophy and science may not be of any use to her.

  In the words of Rousseau, *"When you teach religion to little girls, never make it gloomy or tire some, never make it a task or duty and therefore, never give them anything to learn by heart not even their prayers. It does not matter that a girl should learn it thourghly and still more she should learn to love it."*

  He asserted that women should learn about ethics and religion as they have to look after the family. He said, *"Every daughter should have the religion of her mother and every wife of that of her husband."*
- *Methods:* The women should learn to be obedient towards her parents as well as husband. They should be taught to be busy and that is the ideal method of their education. Activity method should be used and some instructions should be provided to them.

- *Discipline:* Rousseau suggested smart discipline for women. He does not believe in giving freedom. He says that obedience and gentleness are the best qualities of a women.

  We can conclude women education in the words of Rousseau, "Once it is demonstrated that man and woman are not, and should not be constituted the same, either in character or in temperament, it follows that they should not have the same education. In following the directions of nature they must act together but they should not do the same thing; their duties have a common end, but the duties themselves are different and consequently also the tastes that direct them. After having tried to form the natural man, let us also see, in order not to leave our work complete, how the woman is to be formed who suits this man."

  Although Rousseau advocated very specific roles as kind hearted, submissive, disciplined etc., but it would be a mistake to take the view that he regards men as simply superior to women. Women have particular talents that men do not. Rousseau said that women are cleverer than men and that they excel more in matters of practical reasons.

### Influence of Rousseau in Contemporary Education

It has rightly been said that due to his influence on the educationists of 19th and 20th century Rousseau is known as the originator of present theories of education and its practical shape. In the western philosophy his name comes after Plato and Comenius. He wanted reforms and revolution in the field of education. In the field of education an important place is given to him in the whole world because he introduced a new way for the coming generation. In the words of R.H. Quick, *"Rousseau did in the world of ideas what French Revolutionists afterwards did in the world of politics. He made a clean sweep and endeavoured to start afresh."* He lighted a path on which the future educators of the universe were to travel. His influence in the field of education can be seen as follows:

1. *Development of Psychological tendencies:* Rousseau is the forerunner of modern psychology because whatever thoughts he presented related to education, are based on the innate tendencies and powers of the child. According to him, "Children should be considered as children before they are adults." He recognised individual differences among children. Every child has certain values, interests and tendencies. Educator should try to find out these interests and tendencies and encourage their development. In this way he advocated child centered education and started a new age or psychological age in the field of education. In the present scenario also we believe that education is for the child not the child is for the education.
2. *New concept of education:* Rousseau discarded the old concept of education aiming at providing factual knowledge to the child. He gave a new concept of education. He believed that education is a natural activity, which should help in the natural development of the child and in which the

interference and instructions given by the individuals and society should be very less. In the words of Rousseau, "Education is an organic growth, it is a development from with in, it comes through the working of natural instincts and not through responses to external force." It plans for the development of inner capacities of the child. It starts from infancy and continues till death.

3. *Development of scientific tendency:* Rousseau exphasized scientific approach. He asserted observation of nature and advocated that the child should be given opportunity to observe various facts of nature. He gave an important place to natural science in the curriculum, as a result in the present age the study of physical science, zoology, life science is considered important. The knowledge gained through scientific approach becomes a part and parcel of child's life. On the basis of scientific thinking of Rousseau, Spencer and Huxley also developed scientific tendencies in education. Thus when we give importance to scientific tendency in education in the modern age, the credit goes to Rousseau.
4. *Provide sociological emphasis to education:* Rousseau also laid the foundation for sociological tendency in modern education. He emphasised that education should be based on individual differences but importance was also given to development of sociological tendencies. He clearly talked about cooperation, sympathy, working together and benevolence. He laid emphasis on vocational education, physical activities, physical and emotional science, and training of senses. The emphasis in present day education system on moral education, social and vocational education find their root in Emile.
5. *Modern teaching methods:* Before Rousseau, the children were learning about those subjects which were practised by adults. The child was understood as a reflection of an adult. Rousseau said that child is a child, not a small adult and his powers, interests and tendencies are different from adult. As a result, he always criticized the traditional, uninterested and rigid methods of teaching and opted play way method and activity method.

   His first slogan was 'back to nature' and as a result he was against the lecture method. His second slogan was 'learning by doing and self experience', as a result he was in favour of heuristic method. He advocated simple and direct methods of instructions and urged, "Experience before expression' and 'objects before words'. He said, "Give your scholar no verbal lesson. He should be taught by experience alone. Teach by doing whenever you can and only fall back upon words when doing is out of question."

   His third slogan was 'education through senses', so he laid emphasis on child's senses and activities to solve the problems. His fourth slogan was 'give complete freedom to the child while learning', so his education should be according to his innate powers, interests, aptitude and needs. In the present age all the educationists agree with the views of Rousseau but they don't agree on the point i.e. the child should get opportunities to learn in the lap of nature aloof from the society. But many methods of teaching based on the psychology of the child were propounded by Rousseau as—observation method, experiment method, heuristic method, Dalton method, problem solving method, project method etc. Thus Rousseau is known as the first originator of modern methods of teaching.

6. *Broad curriculum:* According is Rousseau the fundamental aim of education is not the rote memorization of the information, but it was the development of intelligence and wisdom which is based on the experiences gained through objects. He said that no such subject should be included in the curriculum which will not provide direct experiences to the child. He emphasized on the inclusion of physical science, social relations and vocations in the curriculum. In the present age, we agree that the curriculum should be constructed based on child's interests, physical and mental capabilities and needs, but many educationists don't agree regarding the fixed aims and curriculum at different age levels.
7. *Free and positive discipline:* Rousseau gave two principles regarding discipline first complete freedom and second is natural consequences. "Free and positive discipline originated when he said," The child should be free in the lap of nature, he will learn everything on the basis of his experiences, so that he will be able to involve in the daily life activities in a natural way." He did not believe in 'spare the rod and spoil the child.' In the present age also we believe in democratic or self discipline but complete freedom is not correct.

Thus the contribution of Rousseau in the present era is great. Robert Rusk described his work as, "Rousseau nevertheless stands to modern education as Plato to ancient education."

In the words of Munroe, Rousseau lighted a path on which the future educators of the universe were to travel.

## Limitations of Rousseau's Educational Thoughts

1. *Unsocial view:* Rousseau does not favour society. In reality every society is not bad. Society also plays an important role in the education and development of a child. Social development of the child is possible only while living in the society. The child needs both individual development and social development. In the words of Munroe, "Rousseau's conception, however based upon a wholly misanthropic view of the life of man in society, was not quite so genial" Complete isolation from society is neither possible, nor desirable.
2. *Place of women:* Rousseau's view that literary education will not suit women and a woman of culture is the plague to all, are reactionary and do not suit the modern world. In the present era equal opportunities are being provided to men and women.

3. *Full freedom is dangerous:* Rousseau's theory of discipline through natural consequences is very dangerous. He did not opine that the natural consequences may be harmful for the whole life of the child. They may effect his entire personality. If the child is left to his own judgement and wisdom as a result of complete freedom, he might receive a blow. So some control of the adults are required.
4. *Natural discipline is immoral and useless:* We can't hope that natural discipline will help in the development of character of the child. It will not be useful for his life because nature is blind. There is no place of morality or immorality. In nature Rousseau's theory of discipline through natural consequences is very dangerous. His thought that the nature will punish the child for his wrong deeds and as a result he will not do it again is not correct.
5. *School organisation:* Rousseau's view was that the school should provide such facilities which will help in the child to grow in a natural way. If there is no time table, no fixed functioning, the teacher will not know what and when he is to do something then no system is possible in the school and the development of the child will not be in the right direction in a right way.

On the basis of above discussion, we can say that Rousseau's contribution to education has been profound. The great educationists as Pestalozzi, Froebel, Herbert, Gandhi Ji etc. gave practical base to education on the basis of principles given by Rousseau. Munroe rightly remarked, "Out of Rousseau's teachings came new education of nineteenth century based on interest. It gave clear formulation of direct impetus of psychological, sociological and scientific conception of education." The keynote of, Rousseau's philosophy is to have a 'state of nature', 'Natural man' and 'Natural civilization.' The great contribution of Rousseau to the present age is child centred education.

# 17

# Paulo Freire (1921-1977)

*"Learning is a process where knowledge is presented to us, then shaped through understanding, discussion and reflection".* –Paulo Freire

Paulo Reglus Neves Freire was a Brazilian educationalist and philosopher who has made a thoughtful impact not only in the field of education, but also in the entire struggle for national development, in the third World countries. For a while, the methodology he developed was considered such a threat to the established order that he was jailed for some time and forced to leave Brazil for about twenty years.

Paulo Freire is neither an idealist, nor a realist or a mechanist. He denies the thought that man is abstract, isolated, independent and uncommitted to the universe. His location is close to the existentialists who give much emphasis on existential man equipped with strong will power who can transform the universe with his own feats. In short, the use of 'human being as a subject in the world and with the world'.

Freire's work mainly concerned literacy and the desire to assist humans and women overcome their sense of powerlessness by acting on their own behalf. The oppressed, as he called them, could transform their situation in life by thinking critically about reality and taking action. He thought that the education system plays a key part in maintaining oppression and therefore it had to be regenerated in order for things to change for the oppressed.

Knowledge is not an isolated phenomenon. It comprehends both action and reflection. In his words the act of knowing involves the dialectical movement which moves from action to reflection and from reflection upon action to new activity.

## Biography and Life Sketch

Paulo Reglus Neves was born on September 19, 1921 to a middle class family in Recife in the state of Pernambuco in the northeast of Brazil. He had learned to read and write at an early age, the outdoors serving as his classroom, but hunger took its toll on his performance at school. His results were improved with the better circumstances of his family. The 'Economic Depression of the 1930s, hit Freire's middle class family, and his studies got disturbed and he fell behind in school. He was so stirred up that he got a vow at the age of eleven that he would give his life to the struggle against hunger so that other kids would not bear to confront the torment he was then receiving. He suffered bouts of depression, later linking these to the death of his father in 1934. His initial studies were in law but his time in the field of law was short lived and he went on to a position with Social Service of Industry (SESI). It helped him in sharpening his understanding of class differences. In 1944, he was appointed Director of Department of Education and Culture of Social Service in the state of Pernambuce.

He got his Ph.D. In 1959 from the University of Recife. In 1961, he was appointed as Director of Department of Cultural Extension of Recife University and in 1962 he got the first opportunity for significant application of his theories, when 300 sugarcane workers were taught to read and write in just 45 days. In response to this experiment, Brazilian Govt. approved the creation of thousands of cultural circles around the country. In 1964, a military camp put an end to his efforts. He was imprisoned as a traitor for 70 days. After a brief exile in Bolivia, he worked in Chile for 5 years for the Christian Democratic Agrarian Reform Movement and Food and Agriculture Organisation of the United Nations.

He acted as a Consultant at Harvard University's School of Education and worked in close connection with a number of groups engaged in new educational experiments in rural and urban regions. He worked as Secretary of Education in Sao Paul city Brazil and Professor at the Pontifical Catholic University of Sao Paulo, PUC/ SP. He served as special consultant to the Office of Education of the World Council of Churches in Geneva. As member of UNESCO's International Jury, he received honorary degrees from twenty-nine universities in Europe, North and South America.

He was the 20th century Brazilian educator and philosopher, a leading advocate of critical pedagogy. He studied law, philosophy specifically phenomenology and the psychology of language. In 1967, he published his first book 'Education as the Practice of Freedom'. Some Important publications of Freire are:

- Cultural Action of Freedom,
- A Pedagogy of Liberation,
- Critical Literacy,
- Education for Critical Consciousness,
- Pedagogy of the Heart,
- Learning to Question,
- Education as the Exercise of Freedom,
- Theory and Practice of Liberation,
- Pedagogy of the Oppressed,
- Teachers as Cultural Workers,
- Pedagogy of the Freedom, &
- A Revealing of the Pedagogy of the Oppressed.

Some of Freire's books have been translated into over eighteen languages. One of his books Pedagogy of the Oppressed, written in 1970 became so popular that within three decades of its publication, over 5,00,000 copies had been sold worldwide. He was an influential philosopher and politician. His ideas on empowering and democratizing were very far reaching. He died of heart failure on May 2,1997 in Sao Paulo.

## Philosophy of Education

Freire's philosophy of education is not a simple method but rather an organic political consciousness. The domination of some by others must be overcome, in his view, so that the humanization of all can take place. Authoritarian forms of education, in serving to reinforce the oppressors' view of the world, and their material privilege in it, constitute an obstacle to the liberation of human beings. The means of this liberation is a praxis, or process of action and reflection, which simultaneously names reality and acts to change it. Freire criticized views that emphasized either the objective or subjective aspect of social transformation, and insisted that revolutionary change takes place precisely through the consistency of a critical commitment in both word and deed. This dialectical unity is expressed in his formulation, 'To speak a true word is to transform the world' Freire was influenced by three major philosophical traditions in education.

They are:

- Anarchist tradition
- Marxist-Socialist tradition
- Freudian Left

| | *Philosophical Traditions* |
|---|---|
| Anarchist tradition | The Anarchist opposed national systems of education because of their conviction that education in the hands of the state would serve the political interests of those in control. They advocated the promotion of personal freedom and autonomy of the learner by removing education from state control. |
| Marxist-Socialist tradition | The Marxist-Socialist tradition in education advocated a revolutionary change from a capitalistic political economy to a socialist form of government and economy in order to produce a free and autonomous person. |
| Freudian Left | The Freudian Leftists addressed the problem inherent in the Marxist-Socialist assumption that once people become aware of what they view as evil structures; they will be able to bring about the necessary changes. The persons are prevented from acting in their own self-interests because of man's development. They, therefore, advocated sexual freedom, changes in family organization, and libertarian methods of child-rearing and education as the solutions to this structure of authoritarianism. |

Freire's educational project was conceived in solidarity with anti-capitalist and anti-imperialist movements throughout the world. It calls upon the more privileged educational and revolutionary leaders to commit "class suicide" and to struggle in partnership with the oppressed. Though this appeal is firmly grounded in a Marxist political analysis, which calls for the reconfiguring of systems of production and distribution, Freire rejected elitist and sectarian versions of socialism in favor of a vision of revolution from "below" based on the work of autonomous popular organizations. Not only does Freire's project involve a material reorganization of society, but a cultural reorganization as well. Given the history of European imperialism, an emancipatory education of the oppressed involves a dismantling of colonial structures and ideologies. The literacy projects he undertook in former Portuguese colonies in Africa included an emphasis on the reaffirmation of the people's indigenous cultures against their negation by the legacy of the metropolitan invaders.

Freire's work constitutes a rejection of voluntarism and idealism as well as determinism and objectivism. The originality of Freire's thought consists in his synthesis of a number of philosophical and political traditions and his application of them to the pedagogical encounter. Thus, the Hegelian dialectic of master and slave informs his vision of liberation from authoritarian forms of education; the existentialism of Jean Paul Sartre and Martin Buber makes possible his description of the self-transformation of the oppressed into a space of radical inter subjectivity; the historical materialism of Karl Marx influences his conception of the historicity of social relations; his emphasis on love as a necessary precondition of authentic education has an affinity with radical Christian liberation theology; and the anti-imperialist revolutionism of Ernesto Che Guevara and Frantz Fanon under gird his notion of the "oppressor housed within" as well as his commitment to a praxis of militant anticolonialism.

### *Meaning of Education*

Freire believed that "education makes sense because women and men learn that through learning they can make and remake themselves, because women and men are able to take responsibility for themselves as beings capable of knowing—of knowing that they know and knowing that they don't."

According to Freire, education is "an act of knowing and not memorizing". "It is a learning situation in which the cognizable objects intermediate the cognitive actors-teacher on the one hand and student on the other". It is a "culture action for freedom and a practice from freedom". He was against idealistic, realistic and mechanistic theory of education. He believed in the existentialist's philosophy, which emphasized the ability of man to transform the world with his own effort. He believed that education is not the transfer, or transmission of knowledge or culture, nor it is the extension of technical knowledge. It is not the act of depositing reports or facts in the educatee. It is not an attempt to adapt the educatee to the surroundings.

"I see education as the practice of freedom above all as a truly neurological situation. In the educational process of liberation, educator-educate and educator are both cognitive subjects before knowable objects which mediate them. Placed face to face before themselves they investigate and question themselves. The more they ask questions the more they feel that their curiosity about the object of their knowledge is not decreasing. It only dismisses if it is isolated from human beings and the world."

### 1. *Aims of Education*

Education should raise the awareness of the students so that they become subjects, rather than objects, of the world. This is done by teaching students to think democratically and to continually question and make meaning from (critically view) everything they learn.

He upheld that education should lead to the development of critical consciousness. It can be achieved through his pedagogy of literacy education. It involves not only reading the word, but also the world. The formation of the critical consciousness allows people, as subject to question the nature of their historical and social situation -to read their world. The awaking of critical consciousness precisely leads the way to the expression of social discontents precisely because these discontents are real components of an apprentice situation. The function of education is to humanize individuals through conscious actions for the purpose of transforming the world.

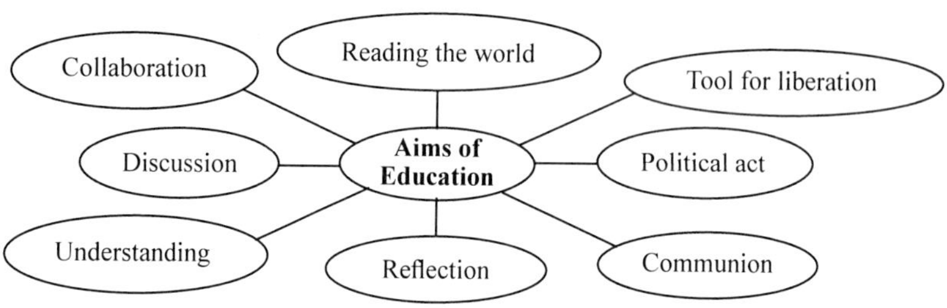


**Fig. 17.1: Aims of Education**

- *To make the learner creator:* Education is a cultural tool for liberation from oppression. It must provide learner the tools to be creator of their own reality.
- *To make the learner an instrument:* Education is always a political act. It can't be politically neutral. It can either be an instrument of domination or liberation.
- *To make the learner able to exchange thoughts with dialogue:* Education is a communion (the state of exchanging thoughts and beliefs) between participants in a dialogue characterised by a reflexive, reciprocal and socially relevant exchange, rather than the unilateral action of one individual agent for the benefit of the other.

- *To construct knowledge:* Knowledge is not a set commodity of the other that is passed from the teacher to the learners. They must construct knowledge from knowledge they already possess.
- *To make the learner active:* Learning begins with action. It is a process where knowledge is presented to learners, then shaped through understanding, discussion and reflection.
- *To view individual differences:* Students should not be viewed as an empty account to be filled in by the teacher. They should know that students have life experiences and their own knowledge is the key in shaping their education and learning.
- *To act in collaboration:* Education is a phenomenon in which educator and educatee educate each other through the act of education.
- *To make the learners subjects:* Education is critical understanding of reality. Reading the 'word' cannot be separated from reading the 'world'. Education should raise the awareness of the students so that they become subjects, rather than objects, of the world.

***Critical Pedagogy***

It is an educational approach to develop critical awareness or critical consciousness in the educatee. Critical consciousness is the ability to perceive critically the causes of social, political and economic oppression and to take action against the oppressive element of the society. It enables educatee to question and challenge domination, the beliefs and practices that dominate.

It is an educational methodology that seeks to increase educatee's awareness of the hidden curriculum's inequalities and multiple forms of oppression that exist in the society and encourage them to take steps towards creating a more democratic and equitable society. It focuses on how and in whose interests knowledge is to be produced and 'passed on' and view the ideal aim of education as emancipator. It considers how education can provide individuals with the tools to better themselves and strengthen democracy to create a more egalitarian and just society and this to deploy education as a process of progressive social change.

Important features of critical pedagogy are:

- It is based on the assumption that all education is pedagogy.
- It is a cultural instrument for release from oppression. It must give learners the tools to be creators of their own reality.
- Educational practice is not considered as 'extending' but as 'communicative'. Extension is negative in nature and communication, positive in nature.
- Learning begins with action. It is a process where knowledge is presented to learn, then shaped through understanding, discussion and thoughtfulness.
- It is the state of exchanging ideas and feelings between participants in a dialogue characterized by a reflective, reciprocal, and socially relevant exchange, rather than the unilateral activity of individual agent of the benefit of the other.

- Cognition is not a set of commodity that passed from the instructors to the pupils. Learners must construct knowledge from the knowledge they already have.
- Its approach is problem based.
- It transforms the learner from object to subject.
- Its aim is to create a just and egalitarian society.
- It argues for an approach to education that is rooted in the experience of marginalised people.
- It needs to create a new form of knowledge through its emphasis on breaking down disciplinary boundaries and creating new spaces where knowledge can be produced.

***Education for Liberation***

Freire wanted to empower illiterates, to raise their consciousness of their own fatalism, to motivate them to take charge of their lives to a greater extent. Through a critical analysis of education (societal and formal), he created a philosophically principled plan for liberation, organic and indigenous, not an imposed regimen formatted to liberate.

He is considered as a representative of the reaction of a creative mind and sensitive conscience to the enormous misery and suffering of the oppressed. He argues that the ignorance and lethargy of the poor are the direct result of the total state of affairs created by the economic, societal and political control of a few. By being held in such a position, the disadvantaged are kept 'submerged.'

He called those people marginalized, impoverished, dejected, and cheated of social justices, the 'oppressed.' Those in power or powerful class, who have wealth and legal protection, are the "oppressors." While not all oppressors have direct contact in the mistreatment and dehumanization of the oppressed, they are gears within the social, economic, and governmental machine, which structures and perpetuates a system of domination and abuse. Societies based on poverty, cheap exploited labour, discrimination, unequal education, and unequal health care rely on some people (men and women) being treated as partly human and, thus, are oppressive. It is this oppression that Freire hoped to change. He provided an equally eloquent solution from the opposite end of the earth. He proposed that both the oppressors and the oppressed should join in the effort to perform their "historical and ontological vocation" of becoming more fully human. He was convinced that in some countries, the oppressors use the scheme of education to preserve the culture of silence', i.e., Illiteracy and ignorance, while in others the advancement of technology has adversely affected many people. He pleaded that through the right sort of education, avoiding authoritarian teacher-pupil models and based on factual experience of pupils and on continual shared investigation, every human being, no matter how impoverished or illiterate, can build up a new consciousness of ego which will release him to be more than passive objects responding to uncontrollable change.

The parent-child relationship in the home usually reflects the cultural status of the surrounding social structure. The authoritarian cultural conditions penetrate the house as comfortable as the school. The authoritarian, rigid and oppressive cultural environment determines relations between parents and children. The children increasingly view parents and teachers authoritarianism as unfavorable to their own freedom. The surroundings of the home are prolonged in the schoolhouse.

According to Freire, "A humanizing education is the path through which men and women can become conscious about their presence in the world."

Freire was convinced that every human being, no matter how 'ignorant' or 'submerged' in the 'culture of silence' he or she may be, is capable of looking critically at the universe in a 'dialogical encounter' with others. The individual provided with the proper tools for such an encounter can gradually perceive personal and social reality as well as the contradictions in it. He/she, with this, can become conscious of his or her own perception of that reality and deal critically with it. A peasant can facilitate this operation for a neighbourer more effectively than a 'teacher' brought from 'outside'. He believed that "people educate each other through the mediation of the world."

Freire's view was that the process of liberation must not involve propaganda, management, and manipulation described as arms of domination which cannot be the instruments of dehumanization. It must be done dialogically through education that is provided by true generosity with the intent of freedom. Thus, dialogue is never an end in itself but a means to develop a better comprehension about the object of knowledge. Education should be the practice of freedom, the means by which men and women deal critically and creatively with reality and discover how to participate in the transformation of their world.

Paulo Freire's Pedagogy of the Oppressed recognizes that the oppressor cannot be the champion of liberation. Since liberation requires power, and the oppressed lack power, how is their liberation possible? Systematic Education requires political power to implement educational reform. Educational project does not require political power for implementation of education reform. Liberation achieved by individuals at the expense of others is an act of oppression. Personal freedom and the development of individuals can only occur in mutuality with others. Social power he held that is geared through education for liberation of the oppressed. Shared power in learning is exercised in control over the curriculum, its contents and methods, and over the coordination of all learning activities.

Education for liberation provides a forum open to the imagination and free exercise of control by learners, teachers, and the community, while also providing for the development of those skills and competencies without which the exercise of power would be impossible. Empowerment is both the means and the outcome of this pedagogy which some have come to call 'liberatory education'.

### *Foundation Principles*

- Man's ontological vocation is to be a Subject who acts upon and transforms his world, and in so doing, moves toward ever-new possibilities of fuller and richer life individually and collectively.
- Every human being is capable of looking critically at the world in a dialogical encounter with others. The individual can gradually perceive personal and social reality as well as the contradictions in it. He/she becomes conscious of his or her own perception of that reality, and deal critically with it.
- Reality is divided into two distinct complementary components:
  (i) the Objective reality—objects, structures, roles that are external to people.
  (ii) Subjective reality—ideas, thoughts, values that are internal to people.
- These two realities interact in a dialectical process. Friere's theoretical framework includes that knowledge is not neutral but it is the expression of historical moments where some groups exercise dominant power over others. Oppressed group of individuals often experience life as "objects" being acted upon rather than "subjects" of their own lives. "Objects" often lack certain critical skills essential for influencing the institutions that have control over their lives. "Subjects" not only have skills for influencing institutions, but also have the opportunity to exercise these skills.
- The learners are the subjects in the learning process and not the objects as they have to be subjects of their destiny. The learners and educators are equal participants in the learning process. The objective of the learning process is to liberate the participants from their external and internal oppression; to facilitate learners becoming capable of changing their lives and the society they live in.
- The pedagogy is based on a critically affirmative language. The educators must work constantly on both their own and the experiences of learners. It requires that we democratize language teaching and break down the elitist mould or paternalistic barriers to the development of the communicative competence and ensure equality of all learners

Thus in the liberating classroom, suggested by Freire's ideas, teachers pose problems derived from student life, social life, and academic subjects, in a mutually created dialogue.

### 2. *Curriculum Planning*

Freire said that the curriculum should not be fixed by the authorities at any level. From his perspective, curriculum planning is a fully people-oriented process in which starting point is people, their expectations and wants. He believed that curriculum planning is an ongoing process which can be done through mutual participation of teachers and students. On this basis curriculum planning is not upward-down process and all of the people who are involved in the education and learning process should play their role in educational plan in the best manner. In his curriculum planning perspective, teaching is an instrument for increasing people's critical consciousness that their mental progress is prevented because of political and social conditions of the society.

According to him, the following principles for curriculum planning should be kept in mind to achieve the consciousness:

- *Importance to traditional and indigenous context of society:* Freire (1984) indicated that it is necessary to concentrate on rural reality in order to adapt education with realities of country. It was observed in many cases that educational plan is regulated based on the needs and wants of higher classes of society. It was the main effective factor on developing gap between social classes. This was the reason that Freire (1989) believed in common educational plans, which are not based on local conditions, cannot result in deep condition.
- *Mutual participation of students and authorities:* Freire believed that elites and senior managers are not the only officers of educational plan development, but curriculum planning is a participative process in which all educational officers and managers are involved in it. Since Freire's curriculum plan derived from learners' experiences and their life realities, so, it should be developed based on the views of professors, experts, parents, teachers, local groups; as well as needs and realities of social life. In this regard, Freire focused on the role of parents and students' councils in school's decisions and to develop a democratic climate in educational system.
- *Consider political position of education:* He believed that education is a political activity and its mission is to analyze the social relations. In other words, actual education develops people's political consciousness. The questions 'what', 'why', 'how', 'for whom', and 'for what purpose' have critical role in any educational effort.
- *Cultural segments:* Cultural segments play important role in teaching-learning process. In cultural segments, students change educational method and curriculum contents radically.
- *Relationship with economic production process:* Based on Freire curriculum planning, process of knowledge expansion and development is done with practical participation in work and economic effort simultaneously. Primary school, high school, and university should not be separated from factory, workshop, etc. The curriculum planning should include more practical efforts in place of theory, so that the learners may be able to help in the economic development of the society.
- *Inclusion of adult education:* Freire indicated that if the poor people cannot be emancipated from silence culture, there will not be any path to emancipate them from social and political slavery. In this regard, he

focused on adult education seriously and introduced many comprehensive literacy plans for informing this class which has a considerable effect on development of adults' public consciousness in developing countries. Literacy is not valuable unless it results in critical perception in social areas. Such an education is a favorable form of education for authorities. In adult education it is very important that learners should understand and make their understanding more deeper in critical analysis.

- *Oppressed people education:* According to Freire it is necessary to attempt to educate oppressed people. He believed that oppressed people don't have any critical thinking power because of different reasons. This is why on the one hand he attempted to encourage them toward critical thinking through different methods, and on the other hand, maintenance of existing conditions by dominated system implies that any effort to emancipation should be eliminated. Freire suggested different measures for society in which silence culture is dominated and oppressed people are prevented from their rights. Knowledge of these measures is necessary for curriculum planning. These include: Critical consciousness of massification and Education based on problem and narrative education.

On the basis of above discussion we can say that Freire's curriculum planning is a horizontal process in which all as the participants (such teachers, students, and even parents) are involved in curriculum planning. The main purpose of Freire is emancipative, as his curriculum planning has correspondence with traditional and cultural context. Based on his perspective to curriculum planning, school cannot be separated from economy and productive institutes.

### 3. ***Methodology of Teaching***

The methodology of teaching suggested by Freire comprises 3 interrelated stages as follows:

*Stage I: Find the Problems (Generating Themes)*

The teacher poses a problem derived from students' own context and encourages them to put forward their ideas freely. It will be a continuous stage of listening. New ideas will emerge during the discussion. Every participant will get equal opportunities to generate topics and themes but they should be relevant and meaningful. At this stage the teacher's role is to encourage all the participants to keep the discussion relevant. Thus the teacher will be helpful in enhancing the confidence and cooperative skills of the students.

*Stage II Produce the Codes (Codification)*

At this stage the issues emerged in stage I are modified. These codification represent familiar local situations and presented as challenges to be decided by the participatory group. On the basis of their previous knowledge and experiences, the students are encouraged to reflect critically on these codes.

They enrich the discussion with the help of their previous knowledge and it works as an instrument for acquiring new knowledge. Thus a relationship will be established between the prior knowledge and experiences with the new knowledge and experiences. When the stage of codification revealed the issues of discussion, more discussion follows about their implications.

*3 Steps Inductive Questioning Process*

1. To see (the situation lived by the participants)
2. To analyse the situation (Analysing the root causes)
3. To act (To change this situation, following the precepts of social justice)

Theory and practice are inseparable: Theory is a moment of practice; from the practice born the theory, and the theory goes back to practice to be changed and reformulated.

(i) To see the situation as participants experienced
- describe the situation shown in the CODE
- define the problems in the situation
- make the link between participant and problem

(ii) To analyse the situation (the Problem Tree)
- Why did this happen?
- How is this perpetuated and/or sustained?
- what are the immediate effects and root.

(iii) To act to change the situation
- short term action (next 3 days, 3 weeks, 3 months affecting one of the Problem Tree's leaves)
- long term action (next 3 months, 3 years affecting one of the Problem tree's source roots)

  Action + Reflection = Praxis

*Stage III De-codification*

In this stage the students can discover the dangers existing in their context in collaboration with the teacher. Then, all the possibilities of how these problems can be addressed will be put forward and the debate will be done by the students. The solutions proposed lead to more discussion and more criticism is encouraged.

A fourth stage has been added to the method which Freire himself had called **"post literacy"** or **"political literacy."** This is concerned with the development of critical consciousness among those who are already literate. Rather than generative words, generative themes now form the basis of education. Pedagogy of the Oppressed shows how this form of education may be the preparatory stage of revolutionary action. Such themes as 'oppression,' 'domination,' 'imperialism,' 'welfarism' would serve as the basis for discussion and action.

As the students participate in all the stages (listening, codifying & reflect critically, acting decodifying) of addressing their problems, they feel empowered and thus become more responsible.

4. ***Banking Education***

Freire had introduced the new terminology of 'banking' concept in education. He criticized the prevailing forms of education as reducing students to the status of passive objects to be acted upon by the teacher. He excused this by saying that the recital of the teacher turns students into 'containers', into 'receptacles' to be 'filled'. Education thus becomes an act of depositing, in which the students are the sources and the instructor is the investor. Instead of communicating, the teacher issues communiques and makes deposits which the students patiently receive, memorize and repeat. This is the 'banking concept' of education, in which the scope of education allow the students to extend only as far as receiving, filling and storing the deposits that is the ideology of the oppressed. Banking education means manipulating learners through forcing them to confirm to the objectives of the dominant elite who do not wish to love their powers.

The banking concept of education means knowledge becomes a gift bestowed by those who regard themselves knowledgeable upon those whom they consider to know nothing. Friere says, "The more students work at storing the deposits entrusted to them, the less they develop the critical consciousness which would result from their intervention in the world as transformers of that world". This projection of an absolute ignorance on others by the knowledgeable is a characteristic of the ideology of oppression. It negates education and knowledge as processes of inquiry. The students accept their ignorance like a slave. Freire here made an interesting point by saying "but unlike the slave, they never learn that they educate 'the teacher."

Banking education, which emphasizes the teacher's role as the active one and student's role as passive and the teacher student relationship as an anti-dialogical approach, is worthless and anti -democratic. It serves the oppressor by denying the learner an active role in the learning. It does not engage students in critical thinking-which is compulsory in a democratic society-instead, it requires the students to be passive and to adapt thereby serving the purposes of oppression. It inhibits creativity, it resists dialogue and it is laid-back in nature. As banking education is a way of dehumanization, Freire advocated for a more authentic education, which aims 'Conscientization'. According to him, this 'authentic' approach to education must allow people to be aware of their incompleteness and strive to be more fully human. The attempt to use education as a means of consciously shaping the person and the society is called conscientization. Libertarian, progressive education needs to 'begin with the solution of the teacher-student contradiction, by reconciling the poles of the contradiction so that both are simultaneously teachers and students'. True education is that which is progressive, democratic and denies the banking method.

Following are the chief characteristics of the banking education which lead to several contradictions in the system:

- The teacher teaches and the students are instructed.
- The teacher knows everything and the students know nothing.
- The teacher thinks and the students think about.
- The instructor talks and the students listen modestly.
- The teacher disciplines and the pupils are disciplined.
- The teacher picks out and he enforces his choice, and the students comply.
- The teacher acts and the students sustain the illusion of acting through the activity of the teacher.
- The instructor takes the program content and the students (who is not consulted) adopt it.
- The teacher confuses the authority of knowledge with his own professional authority which he sets in opposition to the freedom of the students.
- The teacher is the subject of the learning process, while the pupils are mere objects.

The banking system reduces the creative ability of the students. This is in the involvement of the oppressors. The oppressors, through their welfare schemes what they call 'humanitarianism' preserve their superiority. The oppressed are termed as` marginal', incompetent' and 'lazy'. The banking approach 'dehumanizes the students and adults in place of humanizing' them.

5. ***Problem-posing Education***

Against banking system of education, Freire proposed a dialogical problem-posing method of teaching. He believed that classroom is a place where knowledge is sought not transmitted. He argued for an education approach which enables pupils to discuss and intervene courageously the problem of their context. Problem posing education is based on the principle that a student learns better when he creates knowledge and deposits it in the mind. The basic assumptions are:

1. No one can teach anyone else

2. No one can learn alone

3. People learn together acting in and on their world

This method starts from the life situation and reality of learners. Their life situation is made into a problem posing offers all subjects matter as historical products to be questioned rather than as a central bank wisdom to be accepted. It encourages student to become active in thinking about and acting upon their world. Students and teacher become co-investigator of knowledge and the world. The content of this education cannot be determined in advance, through the expertise of the educator, but must instead arise from the lived experiences of the students or learners. It is not the task of the teacher to provide solution of the problem, but to help students to achieve a form of critical thinking, that will make possible an awareness of society as mutable and potentially open to transformation. As a result students may be able to think about new reality. It stimulates students' creativity and triggers their curiosity which could be triggered by an approach of questions not of answers.

### *Features of Problem Posing Education*

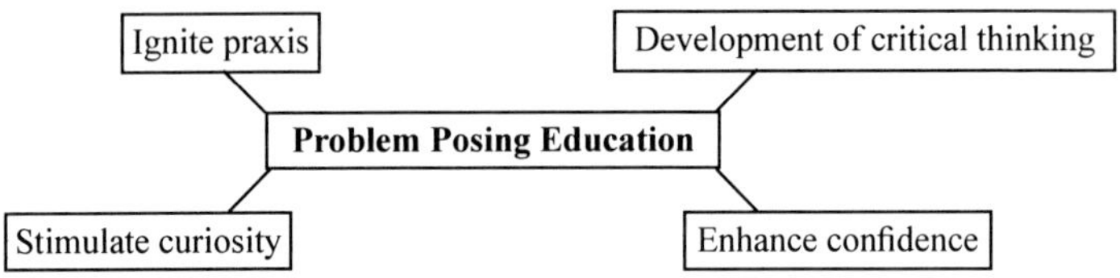


- It encourages learners to think actively.
- It encourages the students to think critically.
- Problem posing ignites praxis and leads to action.
- Teachers and students learn together.
- The content is not pre-determined.
- It starts from the life situations and reality of learners.
- It stimulates curiosity of the students.
- It enhances students' confidence.

### *Difference between Banking Education and Problem Posing Education*

| *Banking Education* | *Problem Posing Education* |
|---|---|
| • It considers education as a process of transferring knowledge. | • It is an act of cognition taking place through dialogue. |
| • Teacher owns knowledge and the student is to get the knowledge. | • No one owns knowledge and everyone teach each other. |
| • Teacher Centered curriculum. | • Students' life related problems are the part and parcel of the curriculum |
| • It involves transference of availabilities. | • There is co-construction of knowledge. |
| • Facts learned in isolation. | • Facts, beliefs and questions connected. |
| • Emphasis on memorisation and regurgitation. | • Emphasis on exploration and application. |
| • Considers student as passive and insect individual learner. | • Considers student as interactive social learner. |
| • Learners are involved in the mission of knowledge registering. | • Students are involved in the mission of knowledge creation. |
| • It anesthetizes and inhibits creative powers. | • It involves a constant unveiling of reality. |
| • It is oppressing in nature. | • It is liberating in nature. |
| • Its scope is limited. | • Its scope is vast. |

| *Banking Education* | *Problem Posing Education* |
|---|---|
| • It is characterised by vertical teacher pupil relationship. | • It is characterised by horizontal relationship. |
| • It attempts to maintain submersion of consciousness. | • It strives for the emersion of consciousness and critical powers. |
| • It consists mainstream, canonical texts. | • It consists diverse, multicultural contexts. |
| • Banking education treats students as objects of assistance. | • Problem-posing education makes them critical thinkers. |
| • The banking method emphasizes permanence and becomes reactionary. | • Problem-posing education-which accepts neither a 'well-behaved' present nor a predetermined future-roots itself in the dynamic present and becomes revolutionary. |

Thus Freire was in favour of problem posing education system because the whole learning is driven by a problem that pop up from the life situation of the learner. It is student centric methodology.

6. ***Dialogic Method***

The 'teacher-of-the students' and the 'students-of- the-teacher' leads to a situation wherein the teacher is no longer merely the-one-who-teaches, but one who is himself taught in dialogue with the students, who in turn while being taught also teach. They become jointly responsible for a process in which all grow. In the dialogical relations, arguments based on authority are no longer valid. Authority is on the 'side' of freedom, not 'against' it. In this relation, no one teaches another, nor is anyone self-taught. People teach each other. In this system, the students are no longer passive listeners, now they are co-investigators in dialogue with the instructor. In Dialogical system, knowledge does not remain at the opinion level, but reaches the level of the 'Logos' (reason). Dialogue cannot be reduced to the act of one person depositing ideas in another, nor can it become a simple exchange of ideas to be 'consumed' by the 'discussants'. It must be meaningful to all. It cannot exist without humility. Faith is 'a priori' requirement for dialogue.

Dialogue has unique capacity to ensure freedom, enjoy liberalism in education, develop critical thinking and reflective interaction in learning and protect cultural synthesis. Dialogue requires mutual respect and cooperation not only to develop understanding, but also to change the world. Friere says "Dialogue cannot exist unless the dialoguers engage in critical thinking. Without dialogue there is no communication, and without communication there can be no true education". He warned that the limits imposed upon both the oppressor and the oppressed dehumanize everyone involved, thereby removing the ability for dialogue to occur, inevitably barring the possibility of transformation. He proposes 'dialogic' as an instrument to free the oppressed, through the use of cooperation, unity and organization and cultural synthesis. Dialogue is the way to overcome problems in society to liberate human beings. The dialogical cultural action leads to praxis and it is the step to critical consciousness through critical reflection and action.

Freire suggested the following method:

(a) Active, 'dialogical', critical and criticism-stimulating method.
(b) Change in the 'programme' and 'content' of education.
(c) Use of 'techniques' like thematic "breakdown" and "codification"

The method based on dialogue is a horizontal relationship between persons.

← DIALOGUE
A with B = Communication
→ Intercommunication

The relation of "empathy" between two "poles" who is engaged in joint research.

MATRIX: Loving, humble, hopeful, trusting, vital

Acquitted of a critical matrix, dialogue creates a critical position, it is nurtured by love, humility hope, religious belief, and confidence. When the two "poles" of the dialogue are thus united by love, hope and mutual confidence, they can unite in a critical search for something. Only dialogue truly communicates.

ANTI-DIALOGUE

A Over B = Communique

The relation of "Empathy" is broken

MATRIX: Loveless, arrogant, hopeless, mistrustful, a critical.

Teaching cannot be managed from the top down, but only from the inside out, by the illiterate himself with the collaboration of the pedagogue.

The program has the following phases:

| | |
|---|---|
| Phase 1 | Investigation by the educational team and volunteers from the area into the 'present, existential, concrete situation' to discover the people's thematic universe; in other words, the main issues of their situation. This phase also involves linguistic research to find significant word, typical sayings, and expressing linked to the existential situation of the people. |
| Phase 2 | Certain key words and themes are selected for discussion and analysis. The words are chosen based on the richness of the phonemes, degree of phonetic difficulty and degree of practical content. Words which have a concrete reference to economic, social and political problems of the area are chosen. e.g. Domination, underdevelopment and so on. |
| Phase 3 | This phase is a codification stage. Codifications are made of the generative themes or words. Codification could be drawings, posters, and slides, i.e. visual representations of the existential situation. These would pose the issues for discussion. Discussions will lead to a more critical consciousness and simultaneously the learners learn to read and write. Though the codifications represent local situations, they are sufficient to open perspectives for the analysis of regional and national problems. |
| Phase 4 | In this phase agendas are developed as guidelines for the coordinators. The coordinators are guided through a training programme in which new attitudes are created, especially with regard to a dialogical approach. |

Phase 5 Here, various kinds of educational materials are produced. For literacy, this includes cards for each generative word with the breakdown of its phonemic families. One important factor here is that the materials in Freirean method are not illustrations or just pictures; rather they are codes of a complex and relevant social reality.

Phase 6 Once the above steps are taken the codified situation is taken to the cultural circle for "decoding". The participants are invited to express their opinion, objectify their problems, reflect on them and in reflecting on the problems, recognize themselves as subjects. There is no teacher-student relationship rather a subject's relationship.

- Once the generative word is introduced the semantic link between the word and the object is established.
- Then the word is broken into syllables and once these are recognized, the card presenting the phonemic families is shown. Using these cards, the learners form new words combining syllables.
- The group would decide which combination is meaningful and which are not.
- Combinations, which do not mean anything, are called, "words of thinking."

The best way to maintain reflective and meaningful communication inside the classroom is problemizing knowledge. Problemization is a dialectic process characterised by true and equal engagement of all participants. The essential condition to make the communication act successful are-mutual respect and understanding, confidence, willingness to take risks, and cooperation.

7. ***Praxis***

Once students have become critical thinkers they will be able to begin a process that could lead to their humanization. Freire referred to this process as praxis. It is a synthesis of reflection and action (theory and practice) in the learning process. Freire considered it (informed action) as the goal of problem posing education. It is a complex activity by which individual create culture and society, and become critically conscious human being. However, Freire believed that this process cannot be carried out in authoritarian form of education such as banking education which inhibits the liberation and freedom of the oppressed. He argued that change could come through a process of dialogue and reflection leading to change through action or intervention. Freire believed that Praxis is at the heart of transforming the world and thus becoming 'fully human'. Education as a praxis of freedom opposing domination is actually necessary aspect of being fully human. Without this kind of praxis, human beings cease to be makers of their way and they become simply what history makes of them. It challenges teachers and students to empower themselves for social change, to advance democracy and equality as they advance their literacy and knowledge.

8. ***Teacher***

It seems inconceivable to think of education without teachers. This is because teachers play fundamental role in enabling people to speak, read, write, think critically, and lead an ethical life. The teacher aims to make students autonomous learners. He/she does not provide information but he works as co-communicator actor with the students in the dialogue process. The teacher and the students share the responsibility of managing and directing the learning process. He/she is not to impose his/her ideas on the students but he/she should employ his/her authority to encourage students' participation, criticism and thinking. He should help students to achieve their critical consciousness by engaging them in problem posing dialogue. However, he should be aware that only those dialogues are permitted that require critical thinking and capable of generating critical thinking.

In the traditional education system the teacher as a mature person teaches to the students. In this process, education consists in extending 'knowledge' to passive educatees preventing them from going through the development of the active, participatory conditions, characteristic of someone who knows. This false conception of education is a basic obstacle to transformation. Education systems based on this conception surround themselves with a 'barricade' which inhibits creativity.

The teacher in Freire's conception, is not neutral, but intervenes in the educational situations in order to help the students to overcome those aspects of his or her social constraints that are paralyzing to learn and to think critically. Conscientization is a basic dimension of reflective action which should continue whenever and wherever the transformed reality assumes a new face. They should be aware that the dialogue is not to invade, or to manipulate, but to exchange thoughts with students on equal rights of accepting, criticizing or rejecting all or some of these ideas.

The task of the teachers is to have a great deal to do with shaping of the minds and hearts of pupil. Teachers are not task masters; instead, they are the animators of human creativity, the facilitators of human spirit, and the instructors in the art and science of humanizing. Therefore teachers should cultivate a love for human creativity, coupled with critical attitude of the past, dynamically creative response to the present, and an optimistic outlook on the future. There is respect for students' interior life and for ultimate questions. At the very least, a holistic learning environment offers periods of time or physical spaces of respite from the competitive materialism, constant noise, distraction, and titillation of modern civilization. Students are encouraged to wonder about deeper questions, about the meaning of life; their existential concerns are taken seriously. This open-ended, student-centered plus teacher-centered approach encourages a diversity of personal paths and need not involve the explicit teaching of religion or religious values.

Freire urged both students and teachers to unlearn their race, class and gender privileges and to engage in a dialogue with those whose experiences are very different from their own. He did not uncritically affirm student or teacher experiences but provided the conceptual tools to critically interrogate them so as to minimize their politically domesticating influence.

Freire believed that the teachers also need to be aware of the characteristics of critically transition consciousness as:

- Depth in the interpretation of problem.
- Testing of one's findings by openness to revision.
- Refusing to transfer responsibilities.
- Soundness of argumentation.
- Practicing dialogues rather than polemics.
- Rejecting passive positions.
- Accepting what is valid in both old and new.
- Avoiding distortion when perceived problems and pre-conceived notions when analysing them.
- The receptivity to the new for reason beyond mere novelty and by the good sense, not to reject the old only because it is old.
- A problem-poser who asks thought-stimulating questions and advances pupils to take their doubts.
- Filled with a profound trust in the creative power of his students.
- Cannot think 'without' the pupils, nor 'for' the pupils, but only 'with' the pupils.

Freire rejected 'assistencialism' as an approach for teaching learning because it does not lead to produce critical learners. Some teachers believe that by implementing banking education they assist students through offering them a packed content of knowledge to repeat and memorize. It is false belief. This assistance will definitely lead to disempowering students and increasing their passivity. He believed that by adapting this approach, teachers lead to student to adapt what they want them to adapt, but never encourage them to think or criticize. Assistencialism is both an effect and a cause of massification. It offers no responsibility, no opportunity for making decisions, but only gesture attitudes which encourage passivity. It never leads to democratic destination.

The characteristics of a teacher can be summarised as:

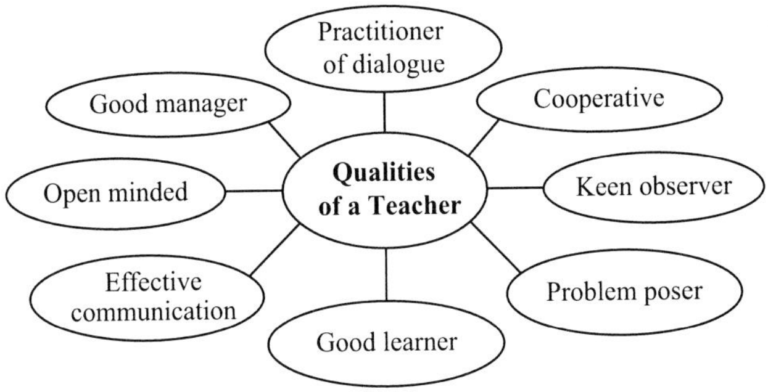


**Fig. 17.2: Qualities of a Good Teacher**

The role of the teacher is to create together with the students the conditions under which true knowledge can be attained. The teacher should consider himself/ herself as students among students giving rise to a new term that is teacher-student with students-teachers that is a teacher who learns and learner who teaches. The basic assumptions are that 'no one can teach anyone else', 'no one can learn alone' and that 'people learn together, acting in and on their world'.

### Contribution of Freire in Educational Practices

Paulo Freire is acknowledged as one of the most powerful voices in education theory and practice. His revolutionary pedagogical theory influenced educational and social movements throughout the world. His philosophical writings influenced academic disciplines that include theology, sociology, anthropology, applied linguistics, pedagogy and cultural studies. His specific contributions are as:

i. Freire's pedagogy starts from the deep love for, the humility before, poor and oppressed people and a respect of their common sense. This humility helped to bring the teacher and learner at the same platform where knowledge is generated and shared for the benefit of the society.
ii. He is widely regarded as the father of the critical pedagogical perspective of education. His critical pedagogy demobilized people from the oppressive yoke of the banking system. His work influenced all over the world educators in the context of emerging traditions of critical pedagogy, issues –centered learning and social constructivism.
iii. Freire's problem posing education, is the basis of present day problem based learning which invites the learner to explore their social reality as a problem to be transformed.
iv. He provides the conceptual tool for student and teacher with which they critically interrogate them so to minimize their domesticating influences.
v. He proposed dialogue and horizontal relationship between teachers and students, and encouraged active learning.
vi. Freire's pedagogy allowed intellectuals to make a useful contribution to the most marginalized people's struggle for social change.
vii. Freire viewed education as a deep political project oriented towards the transformation of society.
viii. His impact upon peace education, adult education, non-formal education and critical literacy has been incalculable.
ix. It has given momentum to the movement aimed to build a more just and egalitarian society.
x. Activity-based learning over theory-based learning, promising an increase in capacity for employment, adoption of advanced pedagogies

mainly by Indian Certificate of Secondary Education (ICSE) and Central Board of Secondary Education (CBSE) boards and approval to the participation of students in co-curricular activities.

xi. Relevance of Freire to Indian education depends on necessity to frame syllabus with high-quality comments and output in teaching-learning process, initiative in acceptance of critical pedagogy, aliveness in pursuing critical pedagogy along with progression, enhancement of self-commitment and work satisfaction among teachers, exposure to latest worldly experiences, disapproval to theoretical knowledge, conduct economical and practical new classroom experiments and learning activities, approach of teacher toward students be fair, diligent and supportive and conviction upon fruits of success arise from roots of active learning.

xii. Encouragement of Freirean critical ideologies and pedagogies in schools by government, expansion of activity-based courses, correlation of co-curricular activities with academics, universal practice of constructivism, orientation to transform mentality of elite parents, mass awareness campaigns, creation of miniature society in classroom, imparting of knowledge of the world in minutiae, guidance to parents and students for acceptance of modern pedagogies, more focus on scholastics of poor students, practice of teaching-learning activities to be done in every school and time be given for acceptance of Freirean ideology in India.

Freire's ideas are particularly relevant to the teachers and educatees in the developing nations. His work constitutes a rejection of voluntarism and idealism as well as determination and objectivism. The originality of his thoughts consist in his synthesis of a number of philosophical and political traditions and his application of them in the pedagogical encounter.

This is especially true in case of adult, non-formal and extension education programs. Though the values of his philosophy and techniques cannot be ruled out for the education of the young age groups as well. Paulo Freire's critique of traditional education that suppress the oppressed and helps to keep the oppressed in subjugation need to be applied to the Indian educational system. In Indian system too much emphasis is on narration and rote memorization, not on the development of creative and critical thinking. This methodology needs to be changed completely. Although, Freire has opened a frontier of liberating education but it has to be reinvent according to one's own situations and in one's own words. Besides educational impacts, in India there are vast majority of people who are oppressed. Many are not aware of their rights. His contribution to the empowerment of marginalised section has been substantial. The method followed was one of dialogue and confrontation. Freire's thinking brought some advances and theoretical support for alternative educational methodology. Action researchers, in-service-learning, cognitive apprenticeship, adult literacy have seen new avenues of influencing and pushing social change. In addition, other aspects of education and sociology have been enriched by his contributions, for example health promotion and occupational safety.

Freire is often described as a humanist, militant educator who believed that solutions in education are always found in concrete context. Students should be asked what they want to learn. It is very important to note that Freire's work continues to be reinvented and, reclarified according to the changing political and intellectual thought and social movements. As long as the struggle for more humane educational practices, for deeper insights into constructions of power and oppression, and the impulse for people to invent their own identities and realities exist - Freirean praxis will challenge every person toward personal and social liberation, both in thought and deed.

# Bibliography


Aggarwal, J.C. (2020), *Basic Ideas in Education,* 10th Ed., Shipra Publications, Delhi.

Aggrawal, J.C. (2017), *Basic Ideas in Educational Psychology,* 7th Ed., Shipra Publications, Delhi.

Alston, Phillip, and Frederic Margret, (2014). *The United Nations and Human Rights: A Critical Appraisal* (Ed). Second Edition. Oxford University Press.

Ananth, T.S. (1999). *A Gandhian Approach to Technological Wonders for the 21st Century,* Gandhi Peace Foundation, Bangalore.

Apple Michael (2004). *Ideology and Curriculum,* Routledge, New York.

Arora, G.L. (2002), *Teacher and their Teaching – Need for New Perspectives,* Ravi Books, New Delhi.

Arora, Pankaj & Gandhi, Haneet (2021), *National Education Policy 2020: Paving ways for Transformational Reforms,* Ed., Shipra Publications, Delhi.

Bond, D. Keogh, R. Walker, D. (1985). *Reflection: Turning Experience into Learning.* London: Kogan page.

Constitution of India, Government of India, New Delhi.

Darling John (1994). *Child-Centred Education and its Critics.* Paul Chapman, London.

Delors Jacques (1996), *Learning the Treasure within,* UNESCO Publishing, Paris.

Dent, N.J.H. (1989). *Rousseau: An Introduction to his Psychological, Social and Political Theory.*

Dewey J. (1933). *How we think. A restatement of the reflection of reflective thinking to the education process* (Revised Ed.), Boston: D.C. Health.

Dube, S.C. (1996). *Indian Society,* National Book Trust, New Delhi.

Govinde, & Diwan Rashmi (2003). *Community Participation and Empowerment in Primary Education,* Sage Publications, New Delhi.

Harris, M. (1974), *Cows, pigs, wars and witches: The riddles of culture;* New York, MY: Vintage Banks.

Kelley, A.V. (1995). *Education and Democracy: Principles and Practices,* Paul Chapman, London.

Kothari D.S. (1966). Report of the Education Commission 1964-66, Government of India, New Delhi.

Kumar Rusen, Singh Rana (2020). *India's National Education Policy 2020: An Overview.*

Maciver, R. M. and Page, C.H. (1996). *Society: An Introductory Analysis,* Macmillan India, Madras.

Meenai Zubain (2008). *Participatory Community Work,* Concept Publishing Company, New Delhi.

Mehrotra Dheeraj (2021). NEP 2020 — At a Glance for Educators: Towards Excellence.

MHRD (1986). National Policy on Education 1986, Government of India, New Delhi.

MHRD (1992). National Policy on Education 1986: Programme of Action. Government of India, New Delhi.

MHRD (2009) The Right of Children to Free and Compulsory Education Act 2009, Government of India, New Delhi.

Mohanty P.C. (1992). *Mass Media and Education,* Ashish Publishing House, New Delhi.

Mohanty, Jagannath (2011), *Dynamics of Educational Thoughts and Practices,* Shipra Publications, Delhi.

Morgan K. William: John Dewey in the 21st Century. *Journal of Inquiry and Action in Education* 9(1), 2017.

Murji Karim, Sarah Neal, John Solomos (2021), *An Introduction to Sociology,* Sage Publishing, New Delhi.

Musgrave. P.W. (ed.) (1970): *Sociology: History and Education,* Mathuen & Co. Ltd. London.

Paul Freire (1970). *Pedagogy of Oppressed,* (Translated in 1982). Seabury Press, New York.

Public Report on Basic Education in India (1999): Oxford University Press, New Delhi.

Rajput, J. S. (2016), *Indian Education in Times of Global Change,* Shipra Publications, Delhi.

Rao, D.B. (2004). *The School and Community Relations,* Discovery Publishing House Pvt. Ltd. New Delhi.

Report of the Secondary Education Commission 1952. Government of India, New Delhi.

Report of the University Education Commission. 1948-49. Government of India, New Delhi

Ryan Alex (1995). John Dewey and the High Tide of American Liberalism. W.W. Norton, London.

Safaya, R.N. (1983), *Current Problems in Indian Education, Delhi,* Dhanpat Rai and Sons.

Schneider L. ab Silver man, A (2010), *Global Sociology: Introducing five contemporary societies* (5th ed.) New York, McGraw-Hill.

Sinha, K. (1995), *Education Comparative Study of Gandhi and Freire,* Commonwealth Publisher, New Delhi.

Sivarajan, K. (2008), *Education in the Emerging Indian Society,* Calicut University Publishers.

Snook, I.A. (1972). *Indoctrination and Education,* Routledge and K. Paul, London.

World Education forum: NGO Declaration on Education for all, Dakar 25 April 2000.